Graphing Calculator Instruction Guide

to accompany

Calculus Concepts:
An Informal Approach to the Mathematics of Change

LaTorre/Kenelly/Fetta/Harris/Carpenter

Iris Brann Fetta

Preliminary Edition

Address editorial correspondence to:
D. C. Heath and Company
125 Spring Street
Lexington, MA 02173

Published simultaneously in Canada.

Printed in the United States of America.

International Standard Book Number: 0-669-39869-1

10   9   8   7   6   5   4   3

Preface

The use of technology is an integral part of your study of calculus using the text *Calculus Concepts: An Informal Approach to the Mathematics of Change*. This *Guide* provides instruction for using the techniques illustrated in the text for the TI-82, TI-85, and HP 48G/GX. Materials for the HP 38, Sharp EL-9200/9300C, Casio fx-9700G, and Casio CFX-9800G graphing calculators are available upon request. This *Guide* is broken into parts, where each part contains all the instruction for a particular calculator model. Within each part, the discussions are ordered to match the organization of the text chapters, and you should refer to these materials for explanations of how to use your calculator with *Calculus Concepts* as you cover each section of the text.

Throughout this *Guide*, the following notation conventions will be used to help you recognize various commands and keystrokes:

- Main keyboard keys are enclosed in rectangular boxes (for example, ENTER) except for certain numeric keys, English alphabet letters, and the decimal point.

- The second-function of a key is listed in parentheses after the main keyboard keystrokes used to activate the second-function (for example, 2nd LN (e^x)).

- The alpha-function of a key is listed in parentheses after the main keyboard keystrokes used to activate the alpha function (for example, ALPHA SIN (E)).

- For all calculators except HP models, function keys and menu items are indicated by the main keyboard key followed by the keystroke sequence necessary to access the item and the name of the item (for example, STAT 1 (Edit)). Menu keys for HP calculators are indicated in outline type (for example, ZOOM).

Programs referenced in these materials are listed in a separate *Appendix* for each calculator.

This *Guide* does not replace your calculator's instruction manual. You should refer to that manual to learn about the basic operation of your calculator and any additional capabilities it may have.

The author team of *Calculus Concepts* gives special thanks to the calculator manufacturers: Texas Instruments, Sharp, Hewlett-Packard, and Casio, for their helpfulness during the preparation and field-testing of the text manuscript and *Guide*.

Graphing Calculator Instruction Guide

for

Calculus Concepts:
An Informal Approach to the Mathematics of Change

Contents

		PAGE
Part A	Texas Instruments TI-82 Graphics Calculator	A-1
Part B	Texas Instruments TI-85 Advanced Scientific Calculator	B-1
Part C	Hewlett Packard 48G Series Calculators	C-1

Detailed contents begin on page v.

iv

Use the following table to locate the part in which your calculator model is discussed:

Part	Calculator Model
A	Texas Instruments TI-82
B	Texas Instruments TI-85
C	Hewlett Packard HP 48G/GX

The section references of the form *x.y.z* in the detailed table of contents below should be read as follows:

> *x* refers to the chapter of your *Calculus Concepts* text.
> *y* refers to the section of your *Calculus Concepts* text.
> *z* is the *Guide* section.

For example, the detailed table of contents below indicates that there are 4 different sections in the Guide (1.2.1 through 1.2.4) pertaining to the mathematics in Section 1.2 of your text. The discussion in 1.2.3 refers to the material on finding intercepts in Section 1.2 of your text.

Suppose you wanted to determine what page of the *Guide* you should turn to in order to review this discussion on intercepts. If you were using a TI-82 calculator, you would confine your search to the first column of page numbers (that is, the column for Part *A*) and find where it intersects the row for 1.2.3. You would find that you should turn to page A-10 in the *Guide*.

When there is no reference to a certain section in the text, either there is no new procedure to learn or techniques have been covered in an earlier section of this *Guide*.

		PART		
CHAPTER		A	B	C
1: THE INGREDIENTS OF CHANGE: FUNCTIONS AND LINEAR MODELS				
	Setup **Page**	A-1	B-1	C-1
1.1.1	Calculating	A-1	B-1	C-2
1.1.2	Using the ANS Memory	A-2	B-2	---
1.1.3	Answer Display	A-2	B-2	C-3
1.1.4	Storing Values	A-2	B-2	C-4
1.1.5	Error Messages	A-3	B-3	C-4
1.1.6	Entering an Equation in the Graphing List	A-3	B-3	C-4
1.1.7	Drawing a Graph	A-3	B-3	C-5
1.1.8	Changing the View of the Graph	A-4	B-4	C-6
1.1.9	Tracing	A-4	B-4	C-6
1.1.10	Estimating Outputs	A-5	B-5	C-6
1.1.11	Evaluating Outputs	A-6	B-6	C-7
1.2.1	Evaluating Functions	A-7	B-7	C-8
1.2.2	Solving for Input Values	A-8	B-8	C-8

1.2.3	Graphically Finding Intercepts	A-10	B-10	C-10
1.2.4	Combining Functions	A-11	B-10	C-11
1.3.1	Entering Data	A-12	B-12	C-12
1.3.2	Editing Data	A-12	B-12	C-14
1.3.3	Deleting Old Data	A-12	B-13	C-14
1.3.4	Aligning Data	A-13	B-13	C-14
1.3.5	Plotting Data	A-13	B-13	C-14
1.3.6	Finding First Differences	A-14	B-14	C-15
1.3.7	Finding a Linear Model	A-15	B-15	C-16
1.3.8	Pasting a Model into the Function List	A-15	B-15	C-17
1.3.9	Graphing a Model	A-15	B-16	C-17
1.3.10	Predictions Using a Model	A-16	B-16	C-17
1.3.11	Copying Graphs to Paper	A-16	B-16	C-18
1.3.12	What is "Best Fit"?	A-17	B-17	C-18
1.3.13	Finding SSE for a Line	A-18	B-18	C-19

2: THE INGREDIENTS OF CHANGE: NON-LINEAR MODELS

2.1.1	Finding Percentage Change	A-19	B-19	C-21
2.1.2	Finding an Exponential Model	A-19	B-19	C-21
2.1.3	Finding a Logistics Model	A-20	B-20	C-22
2.1.4	Random Numbers	A-22	B-22	C-25
2.2.1	Replay of Previous Entries to Find Formula Outputs	A-23	B-23	C-25
2.2.2	Finding Present Value	A-24	B-24	C-27
2.3.1	Finding Second Differences	A-24	B-24	C-27
2.3.2	Finding a Quadratic Model	A-25	B-25	C-28
2.3.3	Finding a Cubic Model	A-26	B-26	C-28

3: DESCRIBING CHANGE: RATES

3.1.1	Finding Average Rates of Change	A-27	B-27	C-31
3.4.1	Magnifying a Portion of a Graph	A-28	B-28	C-31
3.5.1	Percentage Change and Percentage Rates of Change	A-29	B-29	C-32

4: DETERMINING CHANGE: DERIVATIVES

4.1.1	Numerically Investigating Slopes	A-31	B-31	C-35
4.3.1	Discovering Slope Formulas	A-33	B-32	C-36
4.4.1	Numerically Checking Slope Formulas	A-34	B-34	C-38
4.4.2	Graphically Checking Slope Formulas	A-35	B-34	C-39

5: ANALYZING CHANGE: EXTREMA AND POINTS OF INFLECTION

5.1.1	Finding Local Maxima and/or Minima	A-37	B-37	C-41
5.1.2	Finding x-Intercepts of Slope Graphs	A-38	B-38	C-42
5.2.1	Finding Inflection Points	A-40	B-39	C-43

6: ACCUMULATING CHANGE: LIMITS OF SUMS

6.1.1	Using a Model to Determine Change	A-43	B-43	C-45
6.1.2	Using Count Data to Determine Change	A-44	B-44	C-47
6.2.1	Left-Rectangle Approximation	A-45	B-45	C-48
6.2.2	Right-Rectangle Approximation	A-46	B-46	C-49
6.2.3	Trapezoid Approximation	A-46	B-46	C-49
6.2.4	Midpoint-Rectangle Approximation	A-47	B-47	C-50
6.2.5	Simpson's Rule	A-48	B-48	C-51
6.3.1	Simplifying Area Calculations	A-49	B-49	C-52
6.3.2	Limits of Sums	A-51	B-51	C-54
6.4.1	Finding Integral Formulas	A-51	B-51	C-55
6.5.1	The Fundamental Theorem of Calculus	A-54	B-54	C-57

7: MEASURING THE EFFECTS OF CHANGE: THE DEFINITE INTEGRAL

7.2.1	Antiderivatives	A-55	B-55	C-59
7.2.2	Evaluating a Definite Integral on the Home Screen	A-55	B-55	C-60
7.2.3	Rates Into Amounts	A-56	B-56	C-60
7.2.4	Integrals and Area	A-57	B-57	C-62
7.2.5	Evaluating a Definite Integral from the Graphics Screen	A-58	B-58	C-63
7.3.1	Average Value of a Function	A-59	B-59	C-64
7.4.1	Future and Present Value of an Income Stream	A-60	B-60	C-65
7.4.2	Present Value in Perpetuity	A-61	B-61	C-65
7.5.1	Consumers' and Producers' Surplus	A-62	B-62	C-66

Appendix		A-63	B-63	C-69

Part A   Texas Instruments TI-82 Graphics Calculator

CHAPTER 1.   THE INGREDIENTS OF CHANGE: FUNCTIONS AND LINEAR MODELS

Setup: Before you begin, check the TI-82's basic setup by pressing [MODE]. Choose the settings shown in Figure 1. Check the statistical setup by pressing [STAT] [▶] (CALC) [3] (SetUp). Choose the settings shown in Figure 2. Check the window format by pressing [WINDOW] [▶] (FORMAT), and choose the settings shown in Figure 3.

- If you do not have the darkened choices shown in each of the figures below, use the arrow keys to move the blinking cursor over the setting you want to choose and press [ENTER].

- Press [2nd] [MODE] (QUIT) to return to the home screen.

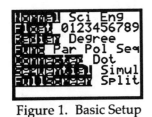

Figure 1. Basic Setup

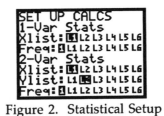

Figure 2. Statistical Setup

Figure 3. Window Setup

SECTION 1.1 FUNDAMENTALS OF MODELING

1.1.1 Calculating: You can type in lengthy expressions; just make sure that you use parentheses when you are not sure of the calculator's order of operations. As a general rule, numerators and denominators of fractions and powers consisting of more than one term should be enclosed in parentheses.

Evaluate $\dfrac{1}{4*15+\frac{895}{7}}$.
 	
 Evaluate $\dfrac{(-3)^4-5}{8+1.456}$. (Use [(-)] for the negative symbol and [−] for the subtraction sign.)
	```1/(4*15+895/7)```
	`                .0053231939`
	`((-3)^4-5)/(8+1.`
	`456)`
	`              8.037225042`

Evaluate $e^3*0.027$ and $e^{3*0.027}$.
 	
 The calculator will assume you mean the first expression unless you use parentheses around the two values in the exponent. (It is not necessary to type in the 0 *before* the decimal point.)
	```e^3*.027```
	`                .5423094969`
	`e^(3*.027)`
	`              1.084370897`

1.1.2 Using the ANS Memory: Instead of again typing an expression that was evaluated immediately prior, use the answer memory by pressing $\boxed{\text{2nd}}$ $\boxed{\text{(-)}}$ (ANS).

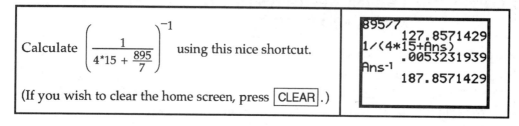

Calculate $\left(\dfrac{1}{4*15 + \dfrac{895}{7}}\right)^{-1}$ using this nice shortcut.
 	
(If you wish to clear the home screen, press $\boxed{\text{CLEAR}}$.)
	895/7
	          127.8571429
	1/(4*15+Ans)
	          .0053231939
	Ans⁻¹
	          187.8571429

1.1.3 Answer Display: When the denominator of a fraction has no more than three digits, the TI-82 can provide the calculated answer as a fraction. When an answer is very large or very small, the calculator displays the result in scientific notation.

The "to a fraction" key is obtained by pressing $\boxed{\text{MATH}}$ $\boxed{1}$ (▸Frac).	2/5+1/3
	          .7333333333
	Ans▸Frac
	               11/15
	.3875▸Frac
	               31/80

The calculator's symbol for "times 10^{12}" is **E**12.
Thus, 7.945**E**12 means 7,945,000,000,000.
 	
The result 1.4675**E**⁻6 means $1.4675*10^{-6}$, the scientific notation expression for 0.0000014675.
	5600000000000+23
	45000000000
	               7.945ᴇ12
	.00025*.00587
	               1.4675ᴇ-6

1.1.4 Storing Values: Sometimes it is beneficial to store numbers or expressions for later recall. To store a number, type the number on the display and press $\boxed{\text{STO▸}}$ $\boxed{\text{ALPHA}}$, type the letter in which you wish to store the value, and then press $\boxed{\text{ENTER}}$. To join several short commands together, use $\boxed{\text{2nd}}$ $\boxed{\text{.}}$ (:).

Store 5 in A and 3 in B.
 	
Calculate $4A - 2B$.
 	
To recall a value stored in a variable, use $\boxed{\text{ALPHA}}$ to type the letter in which the expression or value is stored and then press $\boxed{\text{ENTER}}$. The value remains stored until you change it.
	5→A:3→B
	                    3
	4A-2B
	                   14
	A
	                    5

1.1.5 Error Messages: When your input is incorrect, an error message is displayed.

If you have more than one command on a line without the commands separated by a colon (:), an error message results when you press ENTER.	`2→AX+2→B`▪

Choose 1 (Goto) to position the cursor to the place the error occurred so that you can correct the mistake or choose 2 (Quit) to begin a new line on the home screen.	`ERR:SYNTAX`
	`1▪Goto`
	`2:Quit`

1.1.6 Entering an Equation in the Graphing List: Press Y= to access the graphing list. The graphing list contains space for 10 equations, and the output variables are called by the names Y1, Y2, ..., and Y0. When you intend to graph an equation you enter in the list, you must use X as the input variable.

If there are any previously entered equations that you will no longer use, clear them out of the graphing list.	Position the cursor on the line with the equation and press CLEAR.

Enter $A = 1000(1 + 0.05t)$ in the graphing list.
 	
For convenience, we use the first, or Y1 , location in the list. We intend graph this equation, so enter the right hand side as 1000(1 + 0.05X).
(Type X by pressing X-T-θ, not the times sign X .)
	`Y1▪1000(1+.05X)`
	`Y2=`
	`Y3=`
	`Y4=`
	`Y5=`
	`Y6=`
	`Y7=`
	`Y8=`

1.1.7 Drawing a Graph: Follow the basic procedures shown next to draw a graph with your calculator. Always begin by entering the equation in the Y= list using X as the input variable. Let us draw the graph of Y1 = 1000(1 + 0.05X).

Press ZOOM 4 (ZDecimal).
 	
Notice that the graphics screen is blank.
	`ZOOM MEMORY`
	`1:ZBox`
	`2:Zoom In`
	`3:Zoom Out`
	`4▪ZDecimal`
	`5:ZSquare`
	`6:ZStandard`
	`7↓ZTrig`

Press WINDOW to see the view set by ZDecimal.	`WINDOW FORMAT`
	`Xmin=-4.7`
	`Xmax=4.7`
	`Xscl=1`
	`Ymin=-3.1`
	`Ymax=3.1`
	`Yscl=1`

- Xmin and Xmax are the settings of the left and right edges of the viewing screen, and Ymin and Ymax are the settings for the lower and upper edges of the viewing screen. Xscl and Yscl set the spacing between the tick marks on the x- and y-axes.

1.1.8 Changing the View of the Graph:
If your view of the graph is not good or if you do not see the graph, change the view with one of the ZOOM options or manually set the WINDOW. (We later discuss the ZOOM options.)

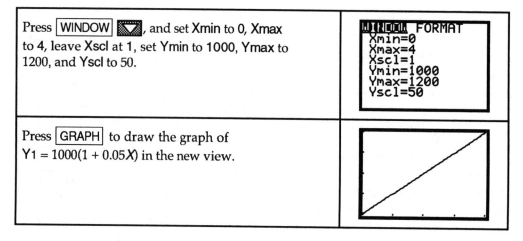

Press WINDOW ▼, and set Xmin to 0, Xmax to 4, leave Xscl at 1, set Ymin to 1000, Ymax to 1200, and Yscl to 50.	`WINDOW FORMAT`
	`Xmin=0`
	`Xmax=4`
	`Xscl=1`
	`Ymin=1000`
	`Ymax=1200`
	`Yscl=50`

Press GRAPH to draw the graph of $Y_1 = 1000(1 + 0.05X)$ in the new view.	

1.1.9 Tracing:
You can display the coordinates of certain points on the graph by *tracing* the graph. The x-values shown when you trace are dependent on the horizontal view that is set for the graph, and the y-values are calculated by substituting the x-values into the equation that is being graphed.

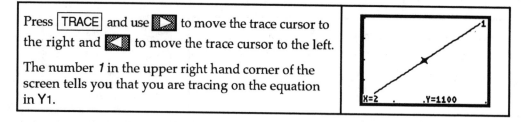

Press TRACE and use ▶ to move the trace cursor to the right and ◀ to move the trace cursor to the left. The number *1* in the upper right hand corner of the screen tells you that you are tracing on the equation in Y1.	`X=2        .Y=1100`

Trace past the edge of the screen and notice that even though you cannot see the trace cursor, x and y values of points on the line are still displayed at the bottom of the screen. Also notice that the graph scrolls to the left or right as you move the cursor past the edge of the current viewing screen.	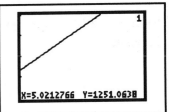 X=5.0212766 Y=1251.0638

1.1.10 Estimating Outputs: You can estimate outputs from the graph using TRACE. It is important to realize that such outputs are *never* exact values unless the displayed x-value is *identically* the same as the value of the input variable.

Estimate the value of A where $A = 1000(1 + 0.05X)$ when X = 5, X = 7, and X = 10. Press WINDOW . If you do not have the settings shown to the right, reset those values.	WINDOW FORMAT Xmin=0 Xmax=4 Xscl=1 Ymin=1000 Ymax=1200 Yscl=50
Press GRAPH ZOOM 3 (Zoom Out) ENTER . After the graph finishes being drawn, again press ENTER to enlarge your view of the graph. (Press WINDOW and observe the values now defining the graphics screen.)	X=2 . . . . . .Y=1100 . . . .
Press TRACE and use ▶ to move as close as you can to X = 5. (Your displayed coordinates may not be exactly the same as the ones shown on the right.) An *estimate* for A when X = 5 is 1253.19. Continue pressing ▶ to obtain an *estimate* for A when X = 7 to be approximately 1346.81.	X=5.0638298 .Y=1253.1915 .

- If your WINDOW has Xmax = 10, you should obtain from tracing the *exact* value $A = 1500$ when X = 10 because 10, not a value "close to" 10, is shown when tracing.

- If you want "nice, friendly" values displayed for x when tracing, set Xmin and Xmax so that Xmax–Xmin is a multiple of 9.4, the width of the ZDecimal viewing screen. For instance, if you set Xmin = 0 and Xmax = 18.8 in the example above, the *exact* values when X = 5, X = 7, and X = 10 are displayed when you trace since 18.8 equals 2(9.4). Try it!

1.1.11 Evaluating Outputs: Begin by entering the equation whose output you want to evaluate in the Y= list. Even though you can use any of the ten locations, let us say for this illustration you have Y1 = 1000(1 + 0.05X).

First, return to the home screen.	Press 2nd MODE (QUIT) as many times as necessary.
Go to the Y-VARS menu by pressing 2nd VARS (Y-VARS).	Y-VARS 1:Function... 2:Parametric... 3:Polar... 4:Sequence... 5:On/Off...
Choose 1: Function by pressing 1 or ENTER, and choose 1: Y1 by pressing 1 or ENTER. (To choose another Y= location, simply press the number corresponding to that function.)	FUNCTION 1:Y1 2:Y2 3:Y3 4:Y4 5:Y5 6:Y6 7↓Y7
Y1 shows on your screen. Type the x-value at which you want to evaluate the equation, and press ENTER. Evaluate Y1 at $x = 5$. (Note: You can, but do not have to, type in the *closing* parentheses on the right.)	Y1(5 1250

Evaluate Y1 at $x = 7$ by recalling the previous entry with 2nd ENTER (ENTRY), edit the 5 to 7 by pressing ◄ and typing over the 5, and press ENTER.	Y1(5
	                1250
	Y1(7)
	                1350

Evaluate Y1 at $x = 10$ by recalling the previous entry with 2nd ENTER (ENTRY), edit the 7 to 10 by pressing ◄ and typing over the 7, and press ENTER.	Y1(5
	                1250
	Y1(7)
	                1350
	Y1(10)
	                1500

• The values obtained by this evaluation process are *actual* output values of the equation, not estimated values such as those generally obtained by tracing.

SECTION 1.2 FUNCTIONS AND GRAPHS

1.2.1 Evaluating Functions: Function outputs can be determined by evaluating on the home screen, as discussed in 1.1.11. You can also evaluate functions using the TI-82 TABLE. The calculator can generate a list of input values beginning with TblMin and differing by ΔTbl or you can ask for specific values of the input.

Let us use the TABLE to evaluate the function $A = 1000(1 + 0.05x)$. Press $\boxed{Y=}$, clear the function locations, and enter 1000(1 + 0.05X) in location Y1 of the Y= list.

Choose the TABLE SETUP menu.	Press $\boxed{2nd}$ $\boxed{WINDOW}$ (TblSet).
To generate a list of values beginning with an input of 5 with the table input values differing by 1, enter 5 in the TblMin location, 1 in the ΔTbl location, and choose AUTO in the Indpnt: and Depend: locations. Remember that you "choose" a particular setting by positioning the blinking cursor over that setting and pressing $\boxed{ENTER}$.	TABLE SETUP TblMin=5 ΔTbl=1 Indpnt: **Auto** Ask Depend: **Auto** Ask
Observe the list of input and output values by pressing $\boxed{2nd}$ $\boxed{GRAPH}$ (TABLE). Notice that you can scroll through the table with ▼, ▶, ▲, and/or ◀.	X ∣ Y1 5 ∣ 1250 6 ∣ 1300 7 ∣ 1350 8 ∣ 1400 9 ∣ 1450 10 ∣ 1500 11 ∣ 1550 X=5
Return to the TABLE SETUP menu with $\boxed{2nd}$ $\boxed{WINDOW}$ (TblSet). To compute specific outputs rather than a list of values, choose ASK in the Indpnt: location. (When using ASK, the settings for TblMin and ΔTbl do not matter.)	TABLE SETUP TblMin=5 ΔTbl=1 Indpnt: Auto **Ask** Depend: **Auto** Ask
Press $\boxed{2nd}$ $\boxed{GRAPH}$ (TABLE), type in the x-value(s) at which the function is to be evaluated, and press $\boxed{ENTER}$. You can scroll through the table with ▼, ▶, ▲, and/or ◀. Unwanted input entries can be cleared with $\boxed{DEL}$.	X ∣ Y1 5 ∣ 1250 7 ∣ 1350 10 ∣ 1500 X=

1.2.2 Solving for Input Values: Your calculator solves for input values of any equation that you have put in the form *"expression = 0"*. The expression can, but does not have to, use X as the input variable. However, you must specify the variable you are using. The form is *Solve(expression, variable, initial guess)*.

Press [2nd] [MODE] (QUIT) to return to the home screen. Access the MATH menu with [MATH]. Use ▼ to locate 0: solve(.	**MATH** NUM HYP PRB 4↑³√ 5:ˣ√ 6:fMin(7:fMax(8:nDeriv(9:fnInt(0⊟solve(
Press [ENTER] or [0] to copy the instruction to the home screen.	solve(
Suppose we want to solve $A = 1000(1 + 0.05t)$ for t when $A = 1500$. Since the equation you enter is "expression = 0", subtract 1500 from both sides of the equation $1500 = 1000(1 + 0.05t)$, tell the calculator the variable with [ALPHA] [4] (T), provide a guess, and press [ENTER].	solve(1000(1+.05 T)-1500,T,8) 10

Note that your *guess* can be obtained by drawing a graph of the equation and tracing.
 	
Your guess is not extremely important unless the equation has more than one solution. In that case, the calculator will return the answer that is closest to your guess. (See below.)
	solve(1000(1+.05
	T)-1500,T,8)
	         10
	solve(1000(1+.05
	T)-1500,T,25)
	         10

Suppose you want to solve the equation $-2x^3 + 8x^2 + 4x - 4 = (x + 3)^2 - 8$.

Enter the two sides of this equation in the Y= list. (Remember that if the input variable in the equation is not x, you must rewrite the equation in terms of x to graph using the Y= list.)	Y1⊟-2X^3+8X²+4X- 4 Y2⊟(X+3)²-8 Y3= Y4= Y5= Y6= Y7=

To better obtain a guess as to where these two functions are equal (intersect), graph the equations.

If you are not told where you want to view the graph, begin by pressing ZOOM 4 (ZDecimal) or ZOOM 6 (ZStandard).

You want to see a "good" graph, that is, one that shows all the important features. In this case, the important features are where Y1 and Y2 intersect.

Neither graph on the right is a good graph.

To improve the view, press WINDOW and change the settings to Xmin = ‾3, Xmax = 5, Ymin = ‾15, and Ymax = 30.

Draw the graph with GRAPH.

Press TRACE and use ▶ and/or ◀ to move along the graph of the equation in Y1.

Press ▼ to jump from the graph of Y1 to the graph of Y2. Tracing reveals that guesses for the input values where these two graph intersect could be X = ‾0.6, X = 1.3, and X = 2.8.

X=1.3404255   Y=10.839294

Return to the home screen with 2nd MODE (QUIT).

Enter the expression on the right with the keystrokes MATH 0 (solve() 2nd VARS (Y-VARS) 1 (Function) 1 (Y₁) − 2nd VARS (Y-VARS) 1 (Function) 2 (Y2) , X-T-θ , (-) .6 ENTER.

solve(Y₁−Y₂,X,‾.6)
        -.6640156447

Recall the last expression you typed with 2nd ENTER (ENTRY). Use ◀ to edit the ‾.6 to the guess for the second intersection point, 1.3. Press ENTER to solve. Once again recall the last expression and solve for the third intersection point with the guess 2.8.

The three solutions to the equation, recorded to five decimal places, are x = ‾0.66402, 2.83685, 1.327167.

        -.6640156447
solve(Y₁−Y₂,X,1.3)
        1.327166753
solve(Y₁−Y₂,X,2.8)
        2.836848891

1.2.3 Graphically Finding Intercepts:
To find the y-intercept of a function $y = f(x)$, set $x=0$ and solve the resulting equation. To find the x-intercept of a function $y = f(x)$, set $y=0$ and solve the resulting equation. The solving process can be done graphically as well as by the methods indicated in 1.2.2 of this *Guide*.

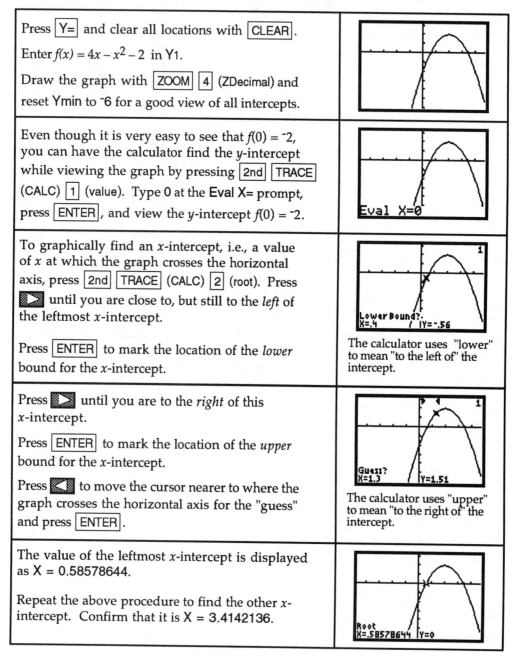

Press $\boxed{\text{Y=}}$ and clear all locations with $\boxed{\text{CLEAR}}$. Enter $f(x) = 4x - x^2 - 2$ in Y1. Draw the graph with $\boxed{\text{ZOOM}}$ $\boxed{4}$ (ZDecimal) and reset Ymin to ⁻6 for a good view of all intercepts.	
Even though it is very easy to see that $f(0) = $ ⁻2, you can have the calculator find the y-intercept while viewing the graph by pressing $\boxed{\text{2nd}}$ $\boxed{\text{TRACE}}$ (CALC) $\boxed{1}$ (value). Type 0 at the **Eval X=** prompt, press $\boxed{\text{ENTER}}$, and view the y-intercept $f(0) = $ ⁻2.	Eval X=0
To graphically find an x-intercept, i.e., a value of x at which the graph crosses the horizontal axis, press $\boxed{\text{2nd}}$ $\boxed{\text{TRACE}}$ (CALC) $\boxed{2}$ (root). Press $\boxed{\blacktriangleright}$ until you are close to, but still to the *left* of the leftmost x-intercept. Press $\boxed{\text{ENTER}}$ to mark the location of the *lower* bound for the x-intercept.	Lower Bound? X=.4 Y=⁻.56 The calculator uses "lower" to mean "to the left of" the intercept.
Press $\boxed{\blacktriangleright}$ until you are to the *right* of this x-intercept. Press $\boxed{\text{ENTER}}$ to mark the location of the *upper* bound for the x-intercept. Press $\boxed{\blacktriangleleft}$ to move the cursor nearer to where the graph crosses the horizontal axis for the "guess" and press $\boxed{\text{ENTER}}$.	Guess? X=1.3 Y=1.51 The calculator uses "upper" to mean "to the right of" the intercept.
The value of the leftmost x-intercept is displayed as X = 0.58578644. Repeat the above procedure to find the other x-intercept. Confirm that it is X = 3.4142136.	Root X=.58578644 Y=0

1.2.4 Combining Functions: The TI-82 can easily draw the graph of the sum, difference, product, quotient, and composition of two functions. You can use the home screen or the TABLE to determine outputs for function combinations.

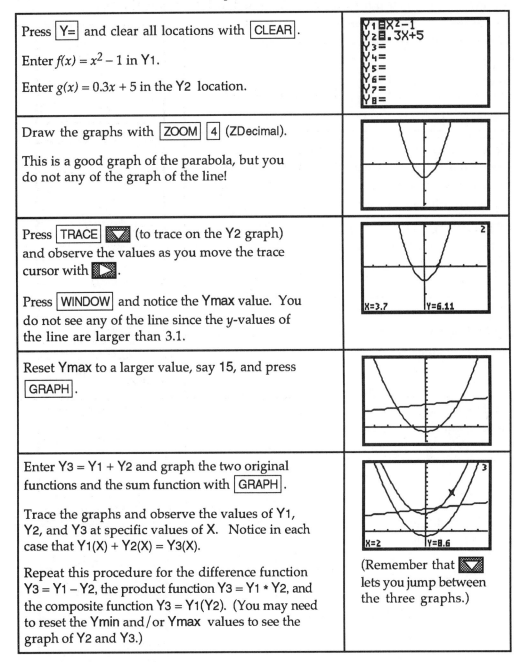

Press Y= and clear all locations with CLEAR. Enter $f(x) = x^2 - 1$ in Y1. Enter $g(x) = 0.3x + 5$ in the Y2 location.	Y1∎X²−1 Y2∎.3X+5 Y3= Y4= Y5= Y6= Y7= Y8=
Draw the graphs with ZOOM 4 (ZDecimal). This is a good graph of the parabola, but you do not any of the graph of the line!	
Press TRACE ▼ (to trace on the Y2 graph) and observe the values as you move the trace cursor with ▶. Press WINDOW and notice the Ymax value. You do not see any of the line since the y-values of the line are larger than 3.1.	X=3.7 Y=6.11
Reset Ymax to a larger value, say 15, and press GRAPH.	
Enter Y3 = Y1 + Y2 and graph the two original functions and the sum function with GRAPH. Trace the graphs and observe the values of Y1, Y2, and Y3 at specific values of X. Notice in each case that Y1(X) + Y2(X) = Y3(X). Repeat this procedure for the difference function Y3 = Y1 − Y2, the product function Y3 = Y1 * Y2, and the composite function Y3 = Y1(Y2). (You may need to reset the Ymin and/or Ymax values to see the graph of Y2 and Y3.)	X=2 Y=8.6 (Remember that ▼ lets you jump between the three graphs.)

SECTION 1.3   LINEAR FUNCTIONS AND MODELS

1.3.1 Entering Data: Press $\boxed{\text{STAT}}$ $\boxed{1}$ (EDIT) to access the six lists that hold data. You only see the first three lists, L1, L2, and L3, but you can access the other three, L4, L5, and L6, with $\boxed{\blacktriangleright}$. (In this text, we usually use list L1 for the input data and list L2 for the output data.)   If there are any data values in your lists, see 1.3.3 of this *Guide* and first delete the "old" data.

Enter the following data:

x	1984	1985	1987	1990	1992
y	37	35	29	20	14

Position the cursor in the first location in list L1. Enter the *x*-data into list L1 by typing the entries from top to bottom in the L1 column, pressing $\boxed{\text{ENTER}}$ after each entry.	![L1/L2/L3 list screen showing 1984,1985,1987,1990,1992 in L1 and 37,35,29,20,14 in L2, with L2(6)=]
After typing the L1(5) value, 1992, use $\boxed{\blacktriangleright}$ to go to the top of list L2. Enter the *y*-data into list L2 by typing the entries from top to bottom in the L2 column, pressing $\boxed{\text{ENTER}}$ after each entry.	

1.3.2 Editing Data: If you incorrectly type a data value, use the cursor keys to darken the value you wish to correct and type the correct value. Press $\boxed{\text{ENTER}}$.

To *insert* a data value, put the cursor over the value that will be directly below the one you will insert, and press $\boxed{\text{2nd}}$ $\boxed{\text{DEL}}$ (INS). The values in the list below the insertion point move down one location and a 0 is filled in at the insertion point. Type the data value to be inserted and press $\boxed{\text{ENTER}}$. The 0 is replaced with the new value.

To *delete* a single data value, move the cursor over the value you wish to delete, and press $\boxed{\text{DEL}}$. The values in the list below the deleted value move up one location.

1.3.3 Deleting Old Data: Whenever you enter new data in your calculator, you should first delete any previously-entered data. There are several ways to do this, and the most convenient method is illustrated below.

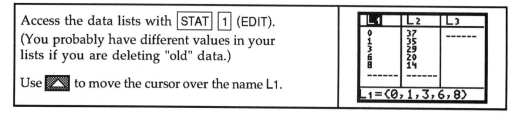

Access the data lists with $\boxed{\text{STAT}}$ $\boxed{1}$ (EDIT). (You probably have different values in your lists if you are deleting "old" data.) Use $\boxed{\blacktriangle}$ to move the cursor over the name L1.	

Press [CLEAR] [ENTER].	(L1 L2 L3 screen with L2 values 37, 35, 29, 20, 14 and prompt L₁(1)=)
Use [▶] [▲] to move the cursor over the name L2. Press [CLEAR] [ENTER]. Repeat this procedure to clear data from any of the other lists you want to use.	(L1 L2 L3 screen, all columns cleared, with prompt L₂=)

1.3.4 Aligning Data:

Suppose you want L1 to contain the number of years since a certain year (here, 1984) instead of actual years. That is, you want to *align* the x-data.

Position the cursor over the L1 at the top of the first column. Replace the L1 values with L1 − 1984 values by pressing [2nd] [1] (L1) [−] 1984 [ENTER].	(L1 L2 L3 screen with L1 values 0, 1, 3, 6, 8 and L2 values 37, 35, 29, 20, 14; prompt L₁=L₁−1984)

1.3.5 Plotting Data:

Any functions you have in the Y= list will graph when you plot data. Therefore, you should clear or turn them off before drawing a scatterplot.

Access the Y= graphing list. If any entered function is no longer needed, clear it with [CLEAR]. If you want the function to remain but do not want it to graph, position the cursor over the "=" and press [ENTER] . A function does not graph when the equals sign is not darkened.	$Y_1=X^2-1$ $Y_2=$ $Y_3=$ $Y_4=$ $Y_5=$ $Y_6=$ $Y_7=$ $Y_8=$ A "turned off" function.

Press [2nd] [Y=] (STAT PLOT) to display the STAT PLOTS screen.
 	
Note: When drawing a graph from the Y= list, you may get an error message or see a scatterplot of "old" data. If so, turn off the STAT PLOTS with option 4: PlotsOff.
	STAT PLOTS
	1:Plot1...
	   Off ⌐⋰ L1 L2 ▫
	2:Plot2...
	   Off ⌐⋰ L1 L2 ▫
	3:Plot3...
	   Off ⌐⋰ L1 L2 ▫
	4↓PlotsOff

Press ENTER to display the Plot1 screen, press ENTER to turn Plot1 "On", and select the options shown on the right. (You can choose any of the three "marks".)	Plot1 On Off Type: ▦ ⬈ ⬚ ⬛ Xlist: **L1** L2 L3 L4 L5 L6 Ylist: L1 **L2** L3 L4 L5 L6 Mark: □ + ·
Press ZOOM 9 (ZoomStat) to have the calculator set an autoscaled view of the data and draw the scatterplot. (ZoomStat does not reset the x and y-axis tick marks. You should do this manually if you wish different spacing between the marks.)	(scatterplot)

1.3.6 Finding First Differences:
When the input values are evenly spaced, use program DIFF to compute first differences in the output values. If the data is perfectly linear (i.e., every data point falls on the linear model), the first differences in the output values are constant. If the first differences are "close" to constant, this is an indication that a linear model *may* be appropriate.

Program DIFF is given in the TI-82 Appendix. To run the program, press PRGM followed by the number of the location of the program and press ENTER. The message on the right appears on your screen.	HAVE X IN L1 HAVE Y IN L2—SEE 1ST DIFF IN L3, 2ND DIFF IN L4, PERCENT CHANGE IN L5 Done
Press STAT 1 (EDIT) to view the first differences in list L1. Notice the results of program DIFF are **not valid** for the data shown on the right because the x-values are *not* evenly spaced. First differences give no information about a possible linear fit to these data.	L1 | L2 | L3 0 37 -2 1 35 -6 3 29 -9 6 20 -6 8 14 L1(1)=0

• Don't be concerned with the results in L4 and L5 -- they are used in later sections.

1.3.7 Finding a Linear Model: Use your calculator to obtain the linear model that best fits the data. The TI-82 can find two forms of the linear model: $y = ax + b$ or $y = a + bx$. For convenience, we always choose the model $y = ax + b$.

Press STAT ▶ (CALC) 5 (LinReg(ax+b)) ENTER.	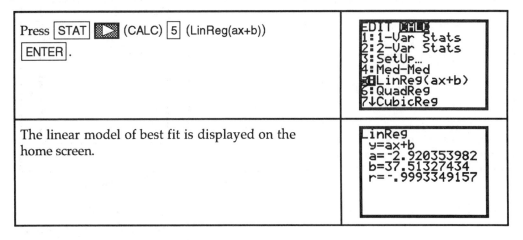
The linear model of best fit is displayed on the home screen.	LinReg y=ax+b a= -2.920353982 b=37.51327434 r= -.9993349157

1.3.8 Pasting a Model into the Function List: To overdraw the model on the scatterplot of the data, copy the model into the Y= list. The values found by the calculator should *not* be rounded. This is not a problem because the calculator will paste the entire model into the function list!

Press Y= and clear any function in the Y1 location. With the cursor in the blank Y1 location, press VARS 5 (STATISTICS) ▶ ▶ (EQ) 7 (RegEQ). Remember "VARS 5 ▶ ▶ 7 ". You will use it many times!	Y1 -2.9203539823 009X+37.51327433 6284 Y2= Y3= Y4= Y5= Y6=

1.3.9 Graphing a Model: You should always overdraw the model on the scatterplot to check the fit to the data.

Press GRAPH to overdraw the model on the scatterplot.	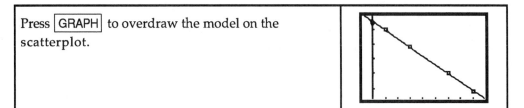

1.3.10 Predictions Using a Model: Use one of the methods described in 1.1.11 or 1.2.1 of this *Guide* to evaluate the linear model at the desired input value. Remember, if you have aligned your data, the input value at which you evaluate the model may not be the value given in the question you are asked.

Predict the value of $y(x) = ^-2.92036x + 37.513274$ in 1988 from the home screen. (Remember that you should always use the full model, i.e., the function in Y1, for all computations.) Note that 1988 is four years since 1984, so $x = 4$.	``` Y1(4) 25.83185841 ```

Predict the value of y in 1991 using the **TABLE**.
 	
Note that 1991 is seven years since 1984, so $x = 7$.
 	
(You can type over x-values already in the table when using Indpnt: **ASK**, or you can press DEL to delete previously-entered values.)
	``
	 X │ Y1 │
	 7 │ 17.0859│
	    │ │
	    │ │
	Y1=17.0707964602
	``

1.3.11 Copying Graphs to Paper: Your instructor may ask you to copy what is on your graphics screen to paper. If so, use the following to more accurately perform this task.

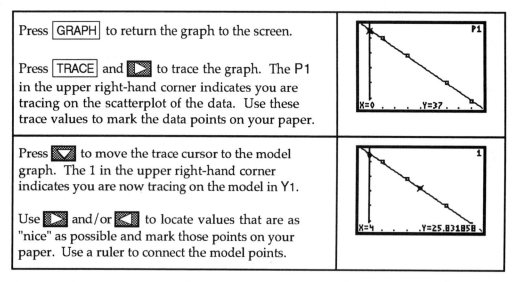

Press GRAPH to return the graph to the screen. Press TRACE and ▶ to trace the graph. The P1 in the upper right-hand corner indicates you are tracing on the scatterplot of the data. Use these trace values to mark the data points on your paper.	
Press ▼ to move the trace cursor to the model graph. The 1 in the upper right-hand corner indicates you are now tracing on the model in Y1. Use ▶ and/or ◀ to locate values that are as "nice" as possible and mark those points on your paper. Use a ruler to connect the model points.	

1.3.12 What Is "Best Fit"? Even though the TI-82 easily computes the values a and b for the best fitting linear model $y = ax + b$, it is important to understand the method of least-squares and the conditions necessary for its application if you intend to use this model. You can explore the process of finding the line of best fit with program **LSLINE**. (Program **LSLINE** is given in the TI-82 Appendix.) For your investigations of the least-squares process with this program, it is better to use data that is not perfectly linear and data for which you do *not* know the best-fitting line.

Before using program **LSLINE**, clear the Y= list and enter your data in lists L1 and L2. Next, draw a scatterplot. Press WINDOW and reset Xscl and Yscl so that you can use the tick marks to help identify points on the graphics screen. Press GRAPH to view the scatterplot.

To activate program **LSLINE**, press PRGM followed by the number of the location of the program, and press ENTER. The program first displays the scatterplot you constructed and pauses for you to view the screen.

- While the program is calculating, there is a small vertical line in the upper-right hand corner of the graphics screen that is dashed and "moving". The program pauses several times during execution. Whenever this happens, the small vertical line is "still". You should press ENTER to resume execution.

The program next asks you to find the y-intercept and slope of *some* line you estimate will go "through" the data. (You should not expect to guess the best fit line on your first try!) After you enter a guess for the y-intercept and slope, your line is drawn and the errors are shown as vertical line segments on the graph. (You may have to wait just a moment to see the vertical line segments before again pressing ENTER.)

Next, the sum of squares of errors, **SSE**, is displayed for your line. Choose the "TRY AGAIN" option by pressing 1 ENTER. Decide whether you want to move the y-intercept of the line or change its slope to improve the fit to the data. After you enter another guess for the y-intercept and/or slope, the process of viewing your line, the errors, and display of SSE is repeated. If the new value of SSE is smaller than the SSE for your first guess, you have improved the fit.

When it is felt that an SSE value close to the minimum value is found, you should choose 2 at the "TRY AGAIN" prompt. The program then overdraws the line of best fit on the graph for comparison with your last attempt and shows the errors for the line of best fit. The coefficients a and b of the best-fitting linear model $y = ax + b$ are then displayed along with the minimum SSE. Use program **LSLINE** to explore finding the line of best fit.

1.3.13 Finding SSE for a Line: The TI-82 lists are useful when finding the deviation (error) of *each* data point from a line entered in the Y= list and then computing SSE.

Clear any old data in your lists, and enter the data shown on the right in lists L1 and L2.	L1 L2 L3 0 37 1 35 3 29 6 20 8 14 ------- L2(6)=
Clear the Y= list. Use $\boxed{\text{STAT}}$ $\boxed{\blacktriangleright}$ (CALC) $\boxed{5}$ (LinReg(ax+b)) to find the best fitting linear model, and paste it in Y1.	Y1=37.5132743362 84+-2.9203539823 009X Y2= Y3= Y4= Y5= Y6=
Return to the lists and enter in list L3 the y-values calculated from the model.	L1 L2 L3 0 37 37.513 1 35 34.593 3 29 28.752 6 20 19.991 8 14 14.15 ------- L3=Y1(L1)
Press $\boxed{\blacktriangleright}$ and enter in L4 $\text{deviation} = \text{error} = y_{data} - y_{line}.$	L2 L3 L4 37 37.513 -.5133 35 34.593 .40708 29 28.752 .24779 20 19.991 .00885 14 14.15 -.1504 ------- L4=L2-L3
Press $\boxed{\blacktriangleright}$ and enter the squares of each of the errors in list L5.	L3 L4 L5 37.513 -.5133 .26345 34.593 .40708 .16571 28.752 .24779 .0614 19.991 .00885 7.8E-5 14.15 -.1504 .02263 ------- L5=L4²
Return to the home screen and compute SSE, the sum of the squared errors, as sum L5 by pressing $\boxed{\text{2nd}}$ $\boxed{\text{STAT}}$ (LIST) $\boxed{\blacktriangleright}$ (MATH) 5 (SUM) $\boxed{\text{2nd}}$ $\boxed{5}$ (L5) $\boxed{\text{ENTER}}$.	sum L5 .5132743363

CHAPTER 2. THE INGREDIENTS OF CHANGE: NON-LINEAR MODELS

SECTION 2.1: EXPONENTIAL FUNCTIONS AND MODELS

2.1.1 Finding Percentage Change: When the input values are evenly spaced, use program DIFF to compute percentage change in the output values. If the data is perfectly exponential (i.e., every data point falls on the model of best fit), the percentage change in the output values is constant. If the percentage change is "close" to constant, this is an indication that an exponential model *may* be appropriate.

Clear any old data, and enter the following in lists L1 and L2:

x	0	1	2	3	4	5	6	7
y	23	38.4	64	107	179	299	499	833

Run program DIFF and observe the percentage change in list L5. The percentage change is very close to constant, so an exponential model may be a good fit. Construct a scatterplot of the data. An exponential model certainly seems appropriate!	``` L3 L4 L5 15.4 10.2 ▓▓▓▓▓ 25.6 17.4 66.667 43 29 67.188 72 48 67.29 120 80 67.039 200 134 66.89 334 ----- 66.934 L5(1)=66.956521... ```

2.1.2 Finding an Exponential Model: Use your calculator to obtain the exponential model that best fits the data. The TI-82's exponential model is of the form $y = ab^x$.

Press STAT ▶ (CALC) ALPHA A (ExpReg) ENTER.	``` EDIT CALC 5↑LinReg(ax+b) 6:QuadReg 7:CubicReg 8:QuartReg 9:LinReg(a+bx) 0:LnReg A:ExpReg ```
The best fitting exponential model is displayed on the home screen. Copy the model to the Y= list, overdraw the graph on the scatterplot, and see that it gives a very good fit to the data.	``` ExpReg y=a*b^x a=22.98235364 b=1.670230098 r=.9999997223 ```

2.1.3 Finding a Logistics Model: Use your calculator to obtain the logistics model with limiting value L that best fits the data. Use program LOGISTIC to fit the logistic model $y = \dfrac{L}{1 + Ae^{-Bx}}$. (Program LOGISTIC is given in the TI-82 Appendix.)

Clear any old data, and enter the following in lists L1 and L2:

x	0	1	2	3	4	5
y	1	2	4	6	8	9

Construct a scatterplot of the data. A logistics model seems appropriate. Run program LOGISTIC by pressing PRGM followed by the number of the location of the program and press ENTER.	
The program gives you some information.	DATA IN L₁,L₂ PROGRAM CLEARS L₃,L₄ AND LEAVES EQ IN Y₀ ENTER CONTINUES
After again showing a scatterplot of the data, ENTER draws a graph of a *possible* logistics model fit to the data. This may or may not be the best-fitting logistics model. (Usually, it will *not* be the best fit.)	

Press ENTER and observe the values of the quantities shown on the right.
 	
SSY is the *total variation* of the output variable. SSY gives the maximum value for SSE, the sum of squared errors. SSE changes with different limiting values L, but SSY remains constant for a particular data set.
	SSY=
	              52
	L=
	    9.775280899
	SSE=
	    .0539914561

Press ENTER and choose option 1: CHANGE L by pressing 1 or ENTER. At the L=? prompt, type 11 and press ENTER.	SELECT ONE 1:CHANGE L 2:NEW L, GRAPH 3:QUIT ON GRAPH 4:QUIT ON MODEL

The SSE for L=11 along with the previous value for SSE are displayed. The fit is not as good as when using L = 9.77528089888 because the SSE value is higher.	```
	L=
	        9.775280899
	SSE=
	          .0539914561
	L=?11
	SSE=
	          .2431007793
	``

Press ENTER and choose option 1: CHANGE L by pressing 1 ENTER. At the L=? prompt, type 10 and press ENTER.
 	
The SSE value and the context of the problem confirm that a limiting value of 10 seems best in this situation.
	``
	          .0539914561
	L=?11
	SSE=
	          .2431007793
	L=?10
	SSE=
	          .0332408123
	``
	
	You should try different limiting values L until the lowest SSE is determined.

To visually verify the fit, press ENTER and choose option 2: NEW L, GRAPH. At the L=? prompt, type 10 and press ENTER. (If you want to view the graph each time you change L, always choose option 2 instead of option 1.)	

Press ENTER twice, and choose option 4: QUIT ON MODEL by pressing 4 ENTER.	```
	Y=L/(1+Ae^(-BX))
	  L= 10
	
	  A= 9.221114127
	
	  B= .8885983473
	
	SSE= .0332408123
	``

If you now want to *view* the graph of this model or trace it, press Y=, move the cursor to the Y0 location, press ◄ to position the cursor over the = and press ENTER to turn on Y0. Press GRAPH.	``` Y4= Y5= Y6= Y7= Y8= Y9= Y0■L/(1+Ae^(-BX)) ```
If you choose option 3: QUIT ON GRAPH instead of option 4, the graph is automatically displayed and selected and the last instruction above is not necessary. (Note that any other functions you have entered in the Y= list will also "turn on" at this point and graph with the logistics curve.)	``` SELECT ONE 1:CHANGE L 2:NEW L, GRAPH 3▪QUIT ON GRAPH 4:QUIT ON MODEL ```

| If you need to recall the values of A and B for the logistics model, return to the home screen and type ALPHA MATH (A) ENTER and then ALPHA MATRIX (B) ENTER. | A
B   9.221114127
   .8885983473 |

- Program DIFF might be helpful when you are trying to determine if a logistics model is appropriate for certain data. If the first differences (in list L3 after running program DIFF) *begin small*, *peak in the middle*, and *end small*, this is an indication that a logistics model may provide a good fit to the data. (For this particular example, there is not enough data for DIFF to be helpful.)

2.1.4 Random Numbers: Imagine all the real numbers between 0 and 1, including the 0 but not the 1, written on identical slips of paper and placed in a hat. Close your eyes and draw one slip of paper from the hat. You have just chosen a number "at random". Your calculator doesn't offer you a choice of all real numbers between 0 and 1, but it allows you to choose, *with an equal chance of obtaining each one*, any of 10^{14} different numbers between 0 and 1 with its random number generator called rand.

First, "seed" the random number generator. (This is like mixing up all the slips of paper in the hat.) Pick some number, <u>not</u> the one shown on the right, and store it as the "seed". (Everyone needs to have a different seed, or the choice will not be random.) The random number generator is accessed with MATH ◄ (PRB) 1 (rand).	658→rand 658

Enter rand again, and press ENTER several times. Your list of random numbers should be different from the one on the right if you entered a different seed.	rand
	  .5789882558
	  .1825542239
	   .286871645
	  .7527620949
	  .8421450981
	  .8800382855

If you want to choose, at random, a whole number between 1 and N, enter int(N rand + 1) by pressing MATH ► 4 (int) (N MATH ◄ (PRB) 1 (rand) + 1) ENTER for a specific value of N.
 	
Repeatedly press ENTER to choose more random numbers. For instance, the screen to the right shows several values that were chosen with N = 10.
	int (10rand+1)
	         4
	         2
	         4
	         7
	         7
	         1

SECTION 2.2 EXPONENTIAL MODELS IN FINANCE

2.2.1 Replay of Previous Entries to Find Formula Outputs: You can recall expressions previously typed by repeatedly using the calculator's last entry feature.

On the home screen, type the amount formula $\left(1+\frac{1}{n}\right)^n$ and press ENTER. The output amount depends on the value of n.
 	
You probably obtained a different output value because you have a different value stored in N.
 	
Store 1 in N.
	(1+1/N)^N
	            2.691588029
	1→N
	                        1

Press 2nd ENTER (ENTRY) twice (or as many times as it takes to again display the amount formula on the screen), and then press ENTER. The formula is now evaluated at N = 1.
 	
Store 2 in N and repeat the procedure.
	(1+1/N)^N 1
	2→N 2
	                    2
	(1+1/N)^N
	                 2.25

- Since this formula contains only one input variable, you could enter it in the Y= list, using X as the input variable, and find the outputs using the TABLE.

Enter Y1 = (1 + 1/X)^X. Refer to 1.2.1 of this *Guide* for evaluating outputs using the TABLE.	X Y1 1 2 2 2.25 X=

- When the formula contains more than one input variable, it is easier to recall the last entry on the home screen than to try to use the TABLE. To illustrate, consider the simple interest formula -- one that contains several input variables.

Type in the formula for the amount in an account paying $r\%$ simple interest on an initial deposit of P over a period of t years: $A = P(1 + rt)$. The value obtained depends on the values stored in P, R, and T.
 	
Store 100 in P, 0.05 in R, and 1 in T.
	P(1+RT)
	              .525
	100→P
	              100
	.05→R: 1→T
	                1

Press 2nd ENTER (ENTRY) three times (or as many times as it takes to again display the formula on the screen) and then press ENTER. The formula is now evaluated at the stored values of the variables.	`100→P` `.525`
	
	              `100`
	`.05→R: 1→T`
	                  `1`
	`P(1+RT)`
	                `105`

Determine the accumulated amount if $500 is invested at 5% interest for 3 years by repeating the procedure described above. (Note that since the value of R has not changed, it is not necessary to again store 0.05 to R.)	`          105`
	`500→P`
	          `500`
	`3→T`
	              `3`
	`P(1+RT)`
	          `575`

• Use the last entry feature as described above to find future value.

2.2.2 Finding Present Value:

The present value of an investment is easily found with the calculator's **solve** routine. For instance, suppose you want to solve the equation

$$9438.40 = P\left(1 + \frac{0.075}{12}\right)^{60}$$ for the present value P.

Refer to 1.2.2 of this *Guide* for instructions on using the TI-82's solve routine and enter the expression on the right. Remember that a *guess*, here entered as 7000, can be obtained from viewing a graph of Y1 = 9438.4 − X(1+.075/12)^60 and tracing to the approximate location where that graph crosses the horizontal axis.	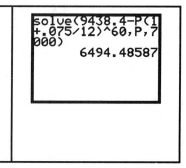

• If you prefer, you could find the x-intercept of Y1 = 9438.4 − X(1+.075/12)^60 to find the present value. Refer to 1.2.3 of this *Guide* for more detailed instructions.

SECTION 2.3 POLYNOMIAL FUNCTIONS AND MODELS

2.3.1 Finding Second Differences:

When the input values are evenly spaced, use program DIFF to compute second differences in the output values. If the data is perfectly quadratic (i.e., every data point falls on the quadratic model), the second differences in the output values are constant. If the second differences are "close" to constant, this is an indication that a quadratic model *may* be appropriate.

Clear any old data, and enter the following in lists L1 and L2:

x	0	1	2	3	4	5
y	12	14	22	35	54	80

| Run program DIFF and observe the second differences in list L4.<br><br>The second differences are close to constant, so a quadratic model may be a good fit.<br><br>Construct a scatterplot of the data. An quadratic model seems appropriate! | ```
L2    L3    L4
12    2     6
14    8     5
22    13    6
35    19    7
54    26    -----
80    -----
-----
L4(1)=6
``` |

2.3.2 Finding a Quadratic Model:
Use your calculator to obtain the quadratic model that best fits the data. The TI-82's quadratic model is of the form $y = ax^2 + bx + c$.

| Press $\boxed{\text{STAT}}$ $\boxed{\blacktriangleright}$ (CALC) $\boxed{6}$ (QuadReg) $\boxed{\text{ENTER}}$. | ```
EDIT CALC
1:1-Var Stats
2:2-Var Stats
3:SetUp...
4:Med-Med
5:LinReg(ax+b)
6:QuadReg
7↓CubicReg
``` |
| The best fitting quadratic model is displayed on the home screen. | ```
QuadReg
y=ax²+bx+c
a=2.928571429
b=-1.128571429
c=12.14285714
``` |
| Copy the model to the Y= list, overdraw the graph on the scatterplot, and see that it gives a good fit to the data. | 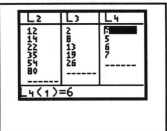 |
```

2.3.3 Finding a Cubic Model: Whenever a scatterplot of the data shows a single change in concavity, a cubic or logistic model is appropriate. If a limiting value is apparent, use the logistic model. Otherwise, a cubic model should be considered. When appropriate, use your calculator to obtain the cubic model that best fits data. The TI-82's cubic model is of the form $y = ax^3 + bx^2 + cx + d$.

Clear any old data, and enter the following in lists L1 and L2:

Year	'80	'81	'82	'83	'84	'85	'86	'87	'88	'89	'90
Price	3.68	4.29	5.17	6.06	6.12	6.12	5.83	5.54	5.47	5.64	5.77

First, clear your lists, and then align the data so that x represents the number of years since 1980.	
Draw a scatterplot of these data. Notice that a concavity change is evident, but there do not appear to be any limiting values. Thus, a cubic model may fit the data.	
Press STAT ▶ (CALC) 7 (CubicReg) ENTER .	
The best fitting cubic model is displayed on the home screen. Copy the model to the Y= list, overdraw the graph on the scatterplot, and see that it gives a good fit to the data.	
Copy the model to the Y= list, and overdraw the graph on the scatterplot.	

CHAPTER 3.   DESCRIBING CHANGE: RATES

SECTION 3.1: AVERAGE RATES OF CHANGE

3.1.1 Finding Average Rates of Change:
Finding the average rate of change using a model is just a matter of evaluating the model at two different values of the input variable and dividing by the difference in those input values. Let us consider the example where the April temperature is given by *temperature* = $-0.8t^2 + 2t + 79$ °F where $t = 0$ at noon and we wish to calculate the average rate of change between 11 a.m. and 6 p.m.

Enter the model in the Y1 location of the Y= graphing list. (Remember that you must use x as the input variable in the graphing list.)	```Y1⊟-.8X²+2X+79 Y2= Y3= Y4= Y5= Y6= Y7= Y8=```

Return to the home screen with 2nd MODE (QUIT).
 	
Evaluate the model at ⁻1 (11 a.m.).
 	
Store this result, for easy recall, in some variable, say A.
	``Y1(-1)
	               76.2
	Ans→A
	               76.2```

Evaluate the model at 6 (6 p.m.).
 	
Store this result, for easy recall, in another variable, say B.
	`` 76.2
	Ans→A
	               76.2
	Y1(6)
	               62.2
	Ans→B
	               62.2```

Evaluate the average rate of change $\dfrac{B-A}{6-{}^-1}$. Remember that you must enclose the numerator and denominator of a fraction in parentheses when either consists of more than one term.	```(B-A)/(6--1) -2```
You could type the expression directly without using the above the storing process, but be careful that you correctly use parentheses.	```(Y1(6)-Y1(-1))/(6--1) -2```

SECTION 3.4: DERIVATIVES

3.4.1 Magnifying a Portion of a Graph: The ZOOM menu of the TI-82 allows you to magnify any portion of the graph of a function. Suppose we are investigating the graph of $y = ^-x^2 + 40x + 50$ and the tangent line, $y = 20x + 150$, to the graph of this function at $x = 10$.

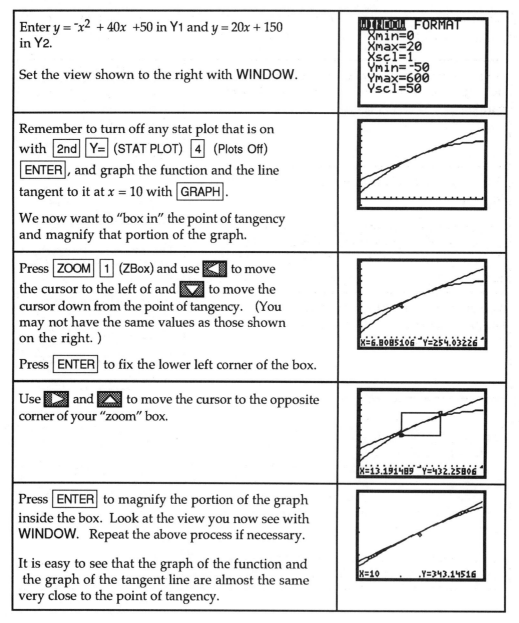

Enter $y = ^-x^2 + 40x + 50$ in Y1 and $y = 20x + 150$ in Y2. Set the view shown to the right with **WINDOW**.	WINDOW FORMAT Xmin=0 Xmax=20 Xscl=1 Ymin=-50 Ymax=600 Yscl=50
Remember to turn off any stat plot that is on with 2nd Y= (STAT PLOT) 4 (Plots Off) ENTER, and graph the function and the line tangent to it at $x = 10$ with GRAPH. We now want to "box in" the point of tangency and magnify that portion of the graph.	
Press ZOOM 1 (ZBox) and use ◀ to move the cursor to the left of and ▼ to move the cursor down from the point of tangency. (You may not have the same values as those shown on the right.) Press ENTER to fix the lower left corner of the box.	X=6.8085106 Y=254.03226
Use ▶ and ▲ to move the cursor to the opposite corner of your "zoom" box.	X=13.191489 Y=432.25806
Press ENTER to magnify the portion of the graph inside the box. Look at the view you now see with WINDOW. Repeat the above process if necessary. It is easy to see that the graph of the function and the graph of the tangent line are almost the same very close to the point of tangency.	X=10 .Y=343.14516

SECTION 3.5: PERCENTAGE CHANGE AND PERCENTAGE RATES OF CHANGE

3.5.1 Percentage Change and Percentage Rates of Change: Recall that
program DIFF stores percentage change in data in list L5. Consider the following data
giving quarterly earnings for a business:

Quarter ending	Mar '93	June '93	Sept '93	Dec '93	Mar '94	June '94
Earnings (in millions)	27.3	28.9	24.6	32.1	29.4	27.7

Align the input data so that x is the number of quarters since March, 1993, and input x in L1 and earnings (in millions) in L2.	L1 L2 L3 ... L2(7)=
Run program DIFF and view the percentage change in list L5. Notice that the percentage change from the end of Sept '93 through Dec '93 is approximately 30.5%. Also, from the end of March '94 through June '94, the percentage change is approximately ⁻5.8%.	L3 L4 L5 ... L5=(5.860805860...
You may find it easier to calculate these using the percentage change formula than have the program do it for you.	(32.1-24.6)/24.6*100 30.48780488 (27.7-29.4)/29.4*100 -5.782312925

To evaluate percentage rate of change at a point, suppose you are told or otherwise find
that the rate of change at the end of the June, 1993 is 1.8 million dollars per quarter.

Divide the rate of change at the end of June, 1993 by the earnings, in millions, at the end of June, 1993 and multiply by 100 to obtain the percentage rate of change at that point. The percentage rate of change in earnings at the end of June, 1993 is approximately 6.2% per quarter.	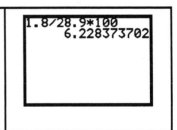

CHAPTER 4.   DETERMINING CHANGE: DERIVATIVES

SECTION 4.1: NUMERICALLY FINDING SLOPES

4.1.1 Numerically Investigating Slopes:
Finding slopes of secant lines joining the point at which the tangent line is drawn to increasingly "close" points on a function to the left and right of the point of tangency is easily done using your calculator. Suppose we want to find the slope of the tangent line at $t = 8$ to the graph of the function $y = \dfrac{44000}{1 + 484e^{-0.7698\,t}}$.

Enter the equation in the Y1 location of the Y= graphing list. (Carefully check the entry of your equation.)
 	
We now evaluate the slopes joining nearby points to the *left* of $x = 8$:
	`Y1=44000/(1+484e`
	`^(-.7698X))`
	`Y2=`
	`Y3=`
	`Y4=`
	`Y5=`
	`Y6=`
	`Y7=`

Type in the expression shown to the right to compute the slope of the secant line joining $x = 7.9$ and $x = 8$.	`(Y1(7.9)-Y1(8))/`
	`(7.9-8)`
	`        8458.580519`

Press [2nd] [ENTER] (ENTRY) to recall the last entry, and then use the cursor keys to move the cursor over the 9 in the "7.9". Press [2nd] [DEL] (INS) and press [9] to insert another 9 in <u>both</u> positions where 7.9 appears. When you press [ENTER], you are finding the slope of the secant line joining $x = 7.99$ and $x = 8$.)	`(Y1(7.9)-Y1(8))/`
	`(7.9-8)`
	`        8458.580519`
	`(Y1(7.99)-Y1(8))`
	`/(7.99-8)`
	`        8466.184863`

Continue in this manner, recording each result on paper, until you can determine the value the slopes from the left seem to be approaching.	`        8466.573547`
	`(Y1(7.9999)-Y1(8`
	`))/(7.9999-8)`
	`        8466.60869`
	`(Y1(7.99999)-Y1(`
	`8))/(7.99999-8)`
	`        8466.6122`

We now evaluate the slopes joining nearby close points to the *right* of $x = 8$:
 	
Clear the screen with [CLEAR], recall the last expression with [2nd] [ENTER] (ENTRY), and edit it with [DEL] so that the nearby point is $x = 8.1$.
	`(Y1(8.1)-Y1(8))/`
	`(8.1-8)`
	`        8466.290978`

Continue in this manner as before, recording each result on paper, until you can determine the value the slopes from the right seem to be approaching. When the slopes from the left and the slopes from the right get closer to the same value, that value is the slope of the tangent line at $x = 8$.	`8466.290978`
	`(Y₁(8.01)-Y₁(8))`
	`/(8.01-8)`
	`          8466.956663`
	`(Y₁(8.001)-Y₁(8))`
	`)/(8.001-8)`
	`          8466.650728`

The above process can be done in fewer steps using the TABLE. Recall that we want to evaluate the slope formula $\dfrac{f(x+h)-f(x)}{(x+h)-x} = \dfrac{f(8+h)-f(8)}{h}$ at $x = 8$ for various values of h where h is the distance from 8 to the nearby point. Also remember that when using the TABLE, the output function must be entered in the graphing list.

However, in the graphing list, you must use x as the input variable. Thus, since h is what is varying in the slope formula, replace h by X and enter the slope formula in Y2. Turn Y1 off since we are looking only at the output from Y2.	`Y₁=44000/(1+484e`
	`^(-.7698X))`
	`Y₂⬛(Y₁(8+X)-Y₁(8`
	`))/X`
	`Y₃=`
	`Y₄=`
	`Y₅=`
	`Y₆=`

Press [2nd] [WINDOW] (TblSet) and choose the settings on the right. (Since we are using the ASK feature, the settings for TblMin and ΔTbl do not matter.)	`TABLE SETUP`
	`  TblMin=0`
	`  ΔTbl=1`
	`Indpnt: Auto ASK`
	`Depend: AUTO Ask`

Access the table with [2nd] [GRAPH] (TABLE) and either delete or type over any previous entries. Let X (really h) take on values that move the nearby point on the left closer and closer to 8.	X : Y2 -.1 : 8458.6 -.01 : 8466.2 -.001 : 8466.6 -1E-4 : 8466.6 -1E-5 : 8466.6 -1E-6 : 8466.6 `Y₂=8466.60869`

- Notice that the calculator switches your input values to scientific notation and displays rounded output values so that the numbers can fit in the table. You should position the cursor over each output value and record the complete decimal value in order to determine the limit from the left to the desired degree of accuracy.

| Repeat the process, letting X (really h) take on values that move the nearby point on the right closer and closer to 8. View the entire decimal value for each output and determine the limit from the right. | X : Y2
.1 : 8466.3
.01 : 8467
.001 : 8466.7
1E-4 : 8466.6
1E-5 : 8466.6
1E-6 : 8466.6
`Y₂=8466.613` |

SECTION 4.3: SLOPE FORMULAS

4.3.1 Discovering Slope Formulas:
You can often see a pattern in a table of values for the slopes of a function at indicated values of the input variable and discover a formula for the slope (derivative). The process of calculating the slopes uses the calculator's formula for finding slopes, nDeriv(f (X), X, X). The correspondence between our notation $\frac{d f(x)}{dx}$ and the calculator's notation nDeriv(f (X), X, X) is shown below:

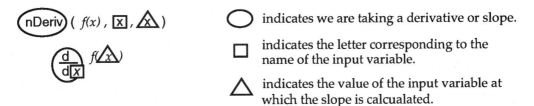

⭕	indicates we are taking a derivative or slope.
▢	indicates the letter corresponding to the name of the input variable.
△	indicates the value of the input variable at which the slope is calcualated.

Return to the home screen and type the expression on the right. Access nDeriv(with MATH 8 (nDeriv(). nDeriv(X², X, 2) = $\frac{dy}{dx}$ for $y = x^2$ evaluated at $x = 2$.	`nDeriv(X²,X,2)` `                  4`

Suppose you are asked to construct a table of values for $y = x^2$ evaluated at different values of x. There are two ways to do this illustrated below:

One way to do this is to recall the last entry and edit the expression nDeriv(x², x, 2) by changing the "2".	`nDeriv(X²,X,-3)`
	 `              -6`
	 `nDeriv(X²,X,-2)`
	 `              -4`
	 `nDeriv(X²,X,-1)`
	 `              -2`

You might prefer to use the TABLE. If so, recall that the expression being evaluated must be in the Y= list.
 	
 If you enter the slope formula as indicated on the right, you will only have to change Y1 when you work another problem with a different function.
	`Y1▤X²`
	 `Y2▤nDeriv(Y1,X,X`
	 `)`
	 `Y3=`
	 `Y4=`
	 `Y5=`
	 `Y6=`
	 `Y7=`

You can either type in the x-values using the ASK feature of the table or you can set TblMin = ⁻3 and ΔTbl = 1 with the AUTO setting chosen.	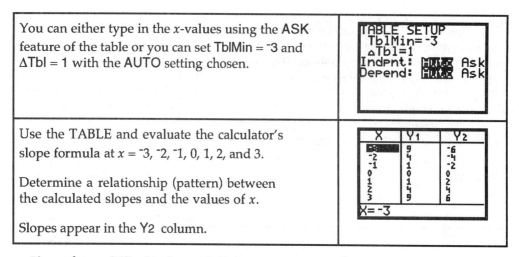
Use the TABLE and evaluate the calculator's slope formula at x = ⁻3, ⁻2, ⁻1, 0, 1, 2, and 3. Determine a relationship (pattern) between the calculated slopes and the values of x. Slopes appear in the Y2 column.	

- If you have difficulty determining a pattern, enter the x-values at which you are evaluating the slope in list L1 and the evaluated values of nDeriv in list L2. Draw a scatterplot of the x-values and the calculated slope formula values. The shape of the scatterplot should give you a clue as to the equation of the slope formula. If not, try drawing another scatterplot where L1 contains the values of y = f(x) and L2 contains the calculated slope formula values. Note that this method might help only if you consider a variety of values for x in list L1.

- The TI-82 only calculates numerical values of slopes -- it does not give the slope in formula form.

SECTION 4.4: THE SUM RULE

4.4.1 Numerically Checking Slope Formulas:
When you use a formula to find the derivative of a function, it is possible to check your answer using the calculator's numerical derivative nDeriv. The basic idea of the checking process is that if you evaluate your derivative and the calculator's derivative at several randomly chosen values of the input variable and the output values are the same, your derivative is *probably* correct.

Let $g(t) = 0.775t^2 - 140.460t + 6868.818$. Applying the sum, power, and constant multiplier rules for derivatives, suppose you determine $g'(t) = 1.55t - 140.460$. Now, let us numerically check this answer.

Enter the function you are taking the derivative of in Y1, the calculator's derivative in Y2, and your derivative formula, $\frac{dg}{dt} = g'(t)$, in Y3.	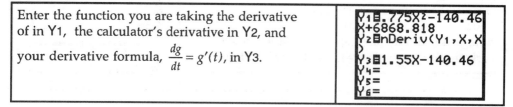

Since the $g(t)$ model represents average fuel consumption per car where $t = 80$ in 1980, it makes sense to check using only positive values of t (that are now denoted as x since we are using the Y= graphing list).	In TABLE SETUP, choose ASK in the independent variable location. Turn off Y1 since you are checking to see if Y2 =Y3.
Press [2nd] [GRAPH] (TABLE) and check to see that Y2 and Y3 are the same at least three values of x.	<table><tr><th>X</th><th>Y2</th><th>Y3</th></tr><tr><td>80</td><td>-16.46</td><td>-16.46</td></tr><tr><td>81</td><td>-14.91</td><td>-14.91</td></tr><tr><td>86</td><td>-7.16</td><td>-7.16</td></tr><tr><td>89</td><td>-2.51</td><td>-2.51</td></tr></table> Y3=

4.4.2 Graphing Checking Slope Formulas:

Another method of checking your answer for a slope formula (derivative) is to draw the calculator's graph of the derivative and draw the graph of your derivative. If the graphs appear identical *in the same viewing window,* your derivative is probably correct.

Again use $g(t) = 0.775t^2 - 140.460t + 6868.818$, and suppose you have calculated your $g'(t) = 1.55t - 140.460$.

Enter the function you are taking the derivative of in Y1, the calculator's derivative in Y2, and your derivative formula, $\frac{dg}{dt} = g'(t)$, in y3.	Y1=.775X²-140.46X+6868.818 Y2=nDeriv(Y1,X,X) Y3=1.55X-140.46 Y4= Y5= Y6=
Turn off Y1 and Y2 so that only the graph of Y3 will draw. Set an appropriate viewing window such as x between 80 and 90 and y between ⁻25 and 25.	 X=85 Y=-8.71
Now, turn off Y3, turn on Y2, and draw the graph of Y2 in the same viewing window. (The graph of the calculator's derivative takes slightly longer to draw because the TI-82 computes the output before plotting each point.)	 X=85 Y=-8.71

To be certain the graphs appear identical, turn on Y3 and draw the graphs of both Y2 and Y3 in this same viewing window. If you see only *one* graph on the screen after both graphs finish drawing, your derivative is very likely correct.

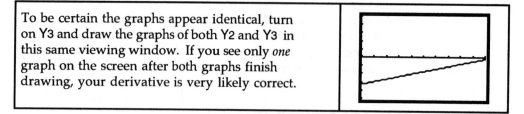

- When you are trying to determine an appropriate viewing window, use the range of the input data for x. If you do not have data, but an equation, use your knowledge of the general shape of the function to find appropriate values for Xmin and Xmax. Recall that you can trace on the graph to see some of the output values to help you determine values for Ymin and Ymax.

- It is tempting to try to shorten the above process for graphically checking your derivative formula by drawing only the graphs of your derivative and the calculator's derivative at the same time without first graphing each separately. If your derivative is such that it cannot be seen in the viewing window in which you see the calculator's derivative or vice versa, you will see only one graph and think that your slope formula is correct. It is better to perform a numerical check on the derivatives than to incorrectly use the graphical checking process.

CHAPTER 5. ANALYZING CHANGE: EXTREMA AND POINTS OF INFLECTION

SECTION 5.1: OPTIMIZATION

5.1.1 Finding Local Maxima and/or Minima: Finding where a function has a high point or a low point is an easy task for the TI-82.

Consider, for example, the model for the average price (per 1000 ft^3) of natural gas for residential use from 1980 to 1991:

$$price = p(x) = 0.012436x^3 - 0.242086x^2 + 1.406993x + 3.444545 \text{ dollars}$$

where x is the number of years since 1980.

Enter this model in the Y1 location of the Y= graphing list. (If you have other equations in the graphing list, turn them off or clear them.)	```Y1◻.012436X^3-.2 42086X²+1.406993 X+3.444545 Y2=nDeriv(Y1,X,X) Y3= Y4= Y5=```
Graph the model in an appropriate viewing window, say x between 0 and 11 and y between 3 and 7.	
Prepare to find the local (relative) maximum by pressing 2nd TRACE (CALC) 4 (maximum). Next, press ◀ to move the blinking cursor that appears to a position to the *left* of the high point. Press ENTER to mark the *lower* bound for x.	Lower Bound? X=2.8085106 Y=5.7620823
Next, press ▶ to move the blinking cursor to a position to the *right* of the high point. Press ENTER to mark the *upper* bound for x.	Upper Bound? X=5.7340426 Y=5.8972694
Use ◀ to move the cursor near your estimate of the high point and press ENTER. The TI-82 uses your guess to locate the highest point in the region between the two bound marks and displays the maximum and the x-value at which it occurs at the bottom of the screen.	Guess? X=4.5638298 Y=6.0056634

Thus, the maximum price was $6.01 per 1000 ft^3 and the price peaked in May, 1984 (4.393 months after January 1, 1980).

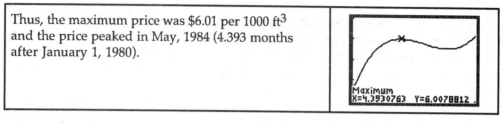

- Note that this maximum is a local or relative maximum, but it is not *the* highest average price of natural gas from 1980 to 1991. Look at the graph and see that the price in January of 1991 ($x = 11$) is the highest price at $6.18 per 1000 ft^3 .

We use a similar method to find the minimum price and when it occurred.

Prepare to find the local (relative) minimum by pressing 2nd TRACE (CALC) 3 (minimum).

Use ▶ to move to the left of the minimum, ENTER to mark the location of the lower bound, ▶ to move to the right of the minimum, ENTER to mark the location of the upper bound, and ◀ to provide a guess.

Press ENTER and the TI-82 uses your guess to locate the lowest point in the region between the two bounds and displays the minimum and the x-value at which it occurs at the bottom of the screen.

Thus, the minimum price was $5.55 per 1000 ft^3 and the price declined to a low point in August, 1988 (8.585 months after January 1, 1980).

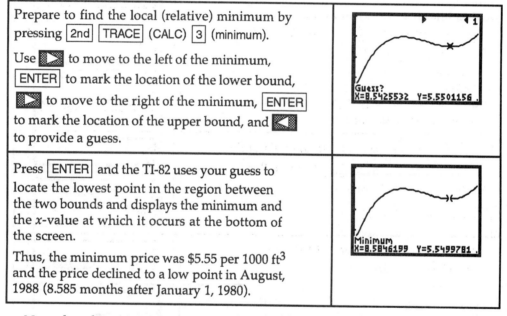

- Note that this minimum is a local or relative minimum, but it is not *the* lowest average price of natural gas from 1980 to 1991. View the graph and see that the price in January of 1980 ($x = 0$) is the lowest price at $3.44 per 1000 ft^3 .

5.1.2 Finding x-Intercepts of Slope Graphs:
Where the graph of a function has a local maximum or minimum, the slope graph has a horizontal tangent. Where the tangent is horizontal, the derivative is zero. Thus, finding where the slope graph crosses the x-axis is the same as finding the location of the local maxima and minima.

We emphasize this fact by finding the x-intercepts of the derivative (where the slope graph crosses the x-axis) and showing those intercepts occur at the local maximum and minimum of the graph of $p(x) = 0.012436x^3 - 0.242086x^2 + 1.406993x + 3.444545$.

Enter $p(x)$ in the Y1 location of the Y= graphing list and either the calculator's derivative *or* your derivative in the Y2 location. Turn off Y1. (Hopefully, you have checked to see that your derivative and the calculator's derivative are the same!)	``` Y1=.012436X^3-.2 42086X²+1.406993 X+3.444545 Y2=nDeriv(Y1,X,X) Y3= Y4= Y5= ```
Choose a viewing window that gives a good view of the slope graph, say x between 0 and 11 and y between ⁻1 and 1.5. Draw the slope graph.	
Find the x-intercepts of the slope graph using 2nd TRACE (CALC) 2 (root). Use ◀ to move the cursor to the *left* of the x-intercept and press ENTER to mark the location of the *lower* bound.	Lower Bound? X=3.5106383 Y=.16704572
Use ▶ to move the cursor to the *right* of the x-intercept and press ENTER to mark the location of the *upper* bound. Provide a guess and press ENTER.	Guess? X=4.4468085 Y=⁻.0082948
The location of the x-intercept (root) is displayed.	Root X=4.3930764 Y=0
Repeat the process to find the other x-intercept. Compare the values of the x-intercepts with the x-values of the locations of the local maximum and local minimum found in 5.1.1 of this *Guide*. They are the same! (The slight difference in the trailing decimal places is due to the different numerical processes the TI-82 uses when finding maxima, minima, and roots.)	Root X=8.5846227 Y=0

It is often difficult to find one viewing window that allows a good look at both a function and its derivative. However, look at the graph of $p(x)$ and $p'(x)$ in the view that has x between 0 and 11 and y between ‾1 and 6.5. Notice the relationship between the locations of the local maximum of $p(x)$, the local minimum of $p(x)$, and the x-intercepts of $p'(x)$.	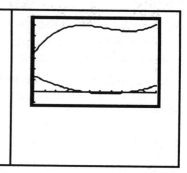

SECTION 5.2: INFLECTION POINTS

5.2.1 Finding Inflection Points: The TI-82 offers two graphical methods of finding an inflection point of a function. To illustrate, consider a model for the percentage of students graduating from high school in South Carolina from 1982 to 1990 who enter post-secondary institutions:

$$f(x) = ‾0.105724x^3 + 1.355375x^2 - 3.672379x + 50.791919 \text{ percent}$$

where $x = 0$ in 1982.

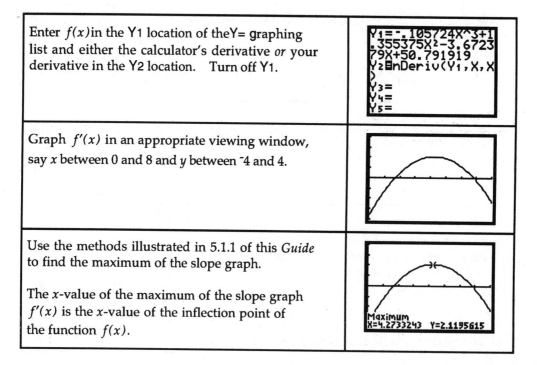

Enter $f(x)$ in the Y1 location of the Y= graphing list and either the calculator's derivative *or* your derivative in the Y2 location. Turn off Y1.	
Graph $f'(x)$ in an appropriate viewing window, say x between 0 and 8 and y between ‾4 and 4.	
Use the methods illustrated in 5.1.1 of this *Guide* to find the maximum of the slope graph. The x-value of the maximum of the slope graph $f'(x)$ is the x-value of the inflection point of the function $f(x)$.	

If you are asked to give the inflection <u>point</u> of $f(x)$, you should give both an x-value and a y-value. Find the y-value by substituting this x-value in the function located in Y1.	X 4.273324258 Y1 51.59923611
Even though it is difficult to find a window that shows a good graph of both the function and its derivative in *this* case, you can often see that the location of the inflection point is at the maximum or minimum of the function.	

Another method you can use to find the x-value of an inflection point is to find the x-intercept (root) of the second derivative of the function. The TI-82 does not have a special function to calculate $f''(x)$, the second derivative. However, you can try to use nDeriv($f'(x)$) for $f''(x)$. Be cautioned, however, that nDeriv($f'(x)$) sometimes "breaks down" and gives invalid results. If this should happen, the graph of nDeriv($f'(x)$) appears very jagged. Of course, when you correctly calculate $f'(x)$ and $f''(x)$ with formulas, entering these in place of the calculator's derivatives should always give reliable results.

Enter $f(x)$ in the Y1 location of the Y= graphing list, either the calculator's derivative *or* your derivative in the Y2 location, and either the calculator's second derivative or your second derivative in the Y3 location. Turn off Y1.	Y1=-.105724X^3+1.355375X²-3.6723 79X+50.791919 Y2◻nDeriv(Y1,X,X) Y3◻nDeriv(Y2,X,X) Y4=
Draw the graphs in a viewing window that gives a good view of the slope graph, $f'(x)$, and its derivative, $f''(x)$, say x between 0 and 8 and y between -4 and 4. (Note that Y3 appears to give good results here.)	

- Notice that the x-intercept of the second derivative occurs at the maximum of the graph of $f'(x)$. Isn't the second derivative the derivative of the first derivative?

Use the methods of 5.1.2 of this *Guide* to find the x-intercept of the second derivative. (Be sure to use ◼ to move to the graph of the line before giving the lower bound for the root.)	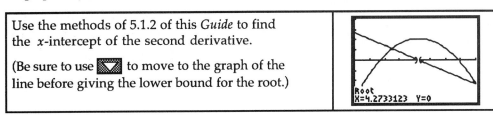 Root X=4.2733123 Y=0

CHAPTER 6. ACCUMULATING CHANGE: LIMITS OF SUMS

SECTION 6.1: RESULTS OF CHANGE

6.1.1 Using a Model to Determine Change:
The TI-82 lists can be used to perform the required calculations to approximate, using left rectangles, the area between the horizontal axis, a (non-negative) rate of change function, and two specific input values. The general procedure for approximating the change in the function $y = f(x)$ between $x = a$ and $x = b$ begins with using the given number, n, of subintervals or determining a suitable value for n. Then, find the equal width of each subinterval, Δx, by using $\Delta x = \frac{b-a}{n}$. Next, when you enter the x-data values in list L1, remember that the x-data values should differ by Δx.

Consider, for example, the model for the number of customers per minute who came to a Saturday sale from 9 AM to 9 PM at a large department store:

$$c(m) = (4.589036*10^{-8})\, m^3 - (7.781267*10^{-5})\, m^2 + 0.033033\, m + 0.887630$$

customers per minute where m is the number of minutes after 9 AM.

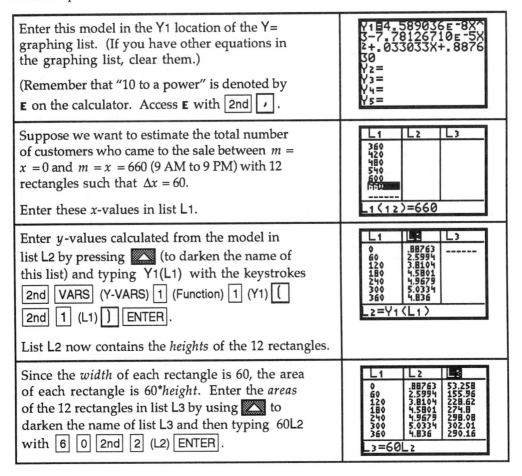

Enter this model in the Y1 location of the Y= graphing list. (If you have other equations in the graphing list, clear them.) (Remember that "10 to a power" is denoted by **E** on the calculator. Access **E** with 2nd , .	Y1◼4.589036E⁻8X^3−7.78126710E⁻5X²+.033033X+.8876 30 Y2= Y3= Y4= Y5=
Suppose we want to estimate the total number of customers who came to the sale between $m = x = 0$ and $m = x = 660$ (9 AM to 9 PM) with 12 rectangles such that $\Delta x = 60$. Enter these x-values in list L1.	L1 L2 L3 360 420 480 540 600 660 ------ L1(12)=660
Enter y-values calculated from the model in list L2 by pressing ◼ (to darken the name of this list) and typing Y1(L1) with the keystrokes 2nd VARS (Y-VARS) 1 (Function) 1 (Y1) (2nd 1 (L1)) ENTER. List L2 now contains the *heights* of the 12 rectangles.	L1 L2 L3 0 .88763 60 2.5994 120 3.8104 180 4.5801 240 4.9679 300 5.0334 360 4.836 L2=Y1(L1)
Since the *width* of each rectangle is 60, the area of each rectangle is 60*height. Enter the *areas* of the 12 rectangles in list L3 by using ◼ to darken the name of list L3 and then typing 60L2 with 6 0 2nd 2 (L2) ENTER.	L1 L2 L3 0 .88763 53.258 60 2.5994 155.96 120 3.8104 228.62 180 4.5801 274.8 240 4.9679 298.08 300 5.0334 302.01 360 4.836 290.16 L3=60L2

Return to the home screen. Find the sum of the areas of the rectangles with [2nd] [STAT] (LIST) [▶] (MATH) [5] (SUM) [2nd] [3] (L3) [ENTER]. We estimate, with 12 rectangles, that 2,574 customers came to the Saturday sale.	``` sum L3 2573.80408 ```

6.1.2 Using Count Data to Determine Change:

This method is very similar to that using a model to determine change. The main difference is that you enter the data values in list L2 instead of using the model to generate the values in that list.

Consider the following data showing the number of aluminum cans that were recycled each year from 1978 to 1988:

year	'78	'79	'80	'81	'82	'83	'84	'85	'86	'87	'88
cans (in billions)	8.0	8.5	14.8	24.9	28.3	29.4	31.9	33.1	33.3	36.6	42.0

Clear all lists. Enter the number of years since 1978 in list L1 and the cans recycled each year (in billions) in list L2.	``` L1 L2 L3 0 8 ------ 1 8.5 2 14.8 3 24.9 4 28.3 5 29.4 6 31.9 L2(1)=8 ```
Suppose we want to estimate the number of cans recycled during the ten year period 1978-1988. Since $\Delta x = 1$ and the heights of the rectangles are in L2, the areas of the 11 rectangles spanning the years 1978 *through* 1988 are the values in L2.	``` L1 L2 L3 5 29.4 6 31.9 7 33.1 8 33.3 9 36.6 10 42 ------ ------ L2(11)=42 ```
Thus, an estimate, given by the 11 rectangles, of the number of cans recycled during the 10 year period is 290.8 billion cans.	``` sum L2 290.8 ```
If you needed an estimate of the number of cans recycled during the 3 year period 1982-1984, copy list L2 to list L3, delete all but those three heights, and sum list L3. The estimate is 89.6 billion cans.	``` L2→L3 {8 8.5 14.8 24… L3 {28.3 29.4 31.9} sum L3 89.6 ```

SECTION 6.2: APPROXIMATING AREA

6.2.1 Left-Rectangle Approximation:
The TI-82 lists can be used to perform the required calculations to find area using left rectangles when given data or a model defining a function $y = f(x)$. For the examples in this section, we consider the function $f(x) = x^3 - 2x^2 + 3x + 1$. Enter this function in the Y1 location of the Y= list.

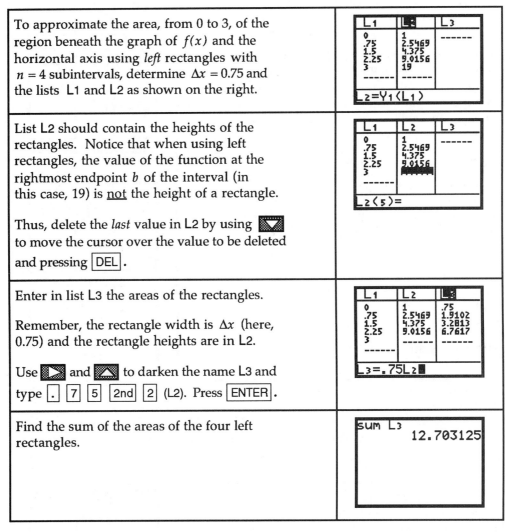

To approximate the area, from 0 to 3, of the region beneath the graph of $f(x)$ and the horizontal axis using *left* rectangles with $n = 4$ subintervals, determine $\Delta x = 0.75$ and the lists L1 and L2 as shown on the right.	
List L2 should contain the heights of the rectangles. Notice that when using left rectangles, the value of the function at the rightmost endpoint b of the interval (in this case, 19) is <u>not</u> the height of a rectangle. Thus, delete the *last* value in L2 by using [▼] to move the cursor over the value to be deleted and pressing [DEL].	
Enter in list L3 the areas of the rectangles. Remember, the rectangle width is Δx (here, 0.75) and the rectangle heights are in L2. Use [▶] and [▲] to darken the name L3 and type [.] [7] [5] [2nd] [2] (L2). Press [ENTER].	
Find the sum of the areas of the four left rectangles.	

- It is always a good idea to draw the graph of the function and sketch the approximating rectangles. By doing so, you should notice that the last y-data value on the right is not the height of a left rectangle and should not be included when determining area *up to* that value.

6.2.2 Right-Rectangle Approximation: The TI-82 lists can be used to perform the required calculations to find area using right rectangles when given data or a model defining a function $y = f(x)$. Enter $f(x) = x^3 - 2x^2 + 3x + 1$ in Y1.

To approximate the area, from 0 to 3, of the region beneath the graph of $f(x)$ and the horizontal axis using *right* rectangles with $n = 4$ subintervals, determine $\Delta x = 0.75$ and the lists L1 and L2 as shown on the right.	L1: 0, .75, 1.5, 2.25, 3 L2: 1, 2.5469, 4.375, 9.0156, 19 L2=Y1(L1)
List L2 should contain the heights of the rectangles. Notice that when using right rectangles, the value of the function at the leftmost endpoint a of the interval (in this case, 1) is <u>not</u> the height of a rectangle. Thus, delete the first value in L2.	L1: 0, .75, 1.5, 2.25, 3 L2: 1, 4.375, 9.0156, 19 L2(1)=2.546875
Enter in list L3 the areas of the rectangles. Remember, the rectangle width is Δx (here, 0.75) and the rectangle heights are in L2.	L1: 0, .75, 1.5, 2.25, 3 L2: 2.5469, 4.375, 9.0156, 19 L3: 1.9102, 3.2813, 6.7617, 14.25 L3=.75L2
Find the sum of the areas of the four right rectangles. (Use the last-entry feature to recall the statement sum L3.)	sum L3 26.203125

6.2.3 Trapezoid Approximation: The TI-82 lists are used to perform the required calculations to find area using trapezoids when given data or a model defining a function $y = f(x)$. Enter $f(x) = x^3 - 2x^2 + 3x + 1$ in Y1.

To approximate the area, from 0 to 3, of the region beneath the graph of $f(x)$ and the horizontal axis using $n = 4$ *trapezoids*, determine $\Delta x = 0.75$ and the lists L1 and L2 as shown on the right.	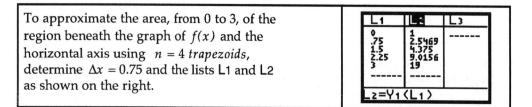

List L2 contains the heights of the sides of the trapezoids. Notice that when using trapezoids, all heights occur twice except for the leftmost and rightmost endpoints a and b. Thus, enter list L3 with first and last values of 1 and all other values 2.	L1: 0, .75, 1.5, 2.25, 3; L2: 1, 2.5469, 4.375, 9.0156, 19; L3: 1, 2, 2, 2, 2; L3(6)=
Determine the "function values portion" of the trapezoid area formula T_n in list L4 as L4 = L2 *L3.	L2: 1, 2.5469, 4.375, 9.0156, 19; L3: 1, 2, 2, 2, 1; L4: 1, 5.0938, 8.75, 18.031, 19; L4=L2*L3
Find the area of the trapezoids using the formula $T_n = (\Delta x\,/\,2)$ sum L4. $T_4 = (0.75/2)$ sum L4 = 19.453125	(.75/2)sum L4 19.453125

6.2.4 Midpoint-Rectangle Approximation:

The TI-82 lists can be used to perform the required calculations to find area using midpoint rectangles when given a model defining a function $y = f(x)$. Enter $f(x) = x^3 - 2x^2 + 3x + 1$ in Y1.

- If you are using the data points and *not* a model for function values and there are no data points given at the midpoint x-values, this method should not be used.

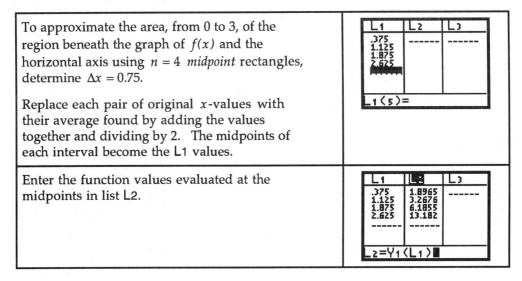

To approximate the area, from 0 to 3, of the region beneath the graph of $f(x)$ and the horizontal axis using $n = 4$ *midpoint* rectangles, determine $\Delta x = 0.75$. Replace each pair of original x-values with their average found by adding the values together and dividing by 2. The midpoints of each interval become the L1 values.	L1: .375, 1.125, 1.875, 2.625; L2: ------; L3: ------; L1(5)=
Enter the function values evaluated at the midpoints in list L2.	L1: .375, 1.125, 1.875, 2.625; L2: 1.8965, 3.2676, 6.1855, 13.182; L3: ------; L2=Y1(L1)

L2 contains the heights of the rectangles. Since the width of each rectangle is $\Delta x = 0.75$, enter the area of each midpoint rectangle in L3 as L3 = 0.75L2.	L1 L2 **L3** .375 1.8965 1.4224 1.125 3.2676 2.4507 1.875 6.1855 4.6392 2.625 13.182 9.8862 ------ ------ ------ L3=.75L2
Find the sum of the areas of the four midpoint rectangles.	sum L3 18.3984375

6.2.5 Simpson's Rule:
The TI-82 lists are used to perform the required calculations to find area approximations using Simpson's Rule when given data or a model defining a function $y = f(x)$. Enter $f(x) = x^3 - 2x^2 + 3x + 1$ in Y1.

- The number, n, of subintervals must be an *even* number in order to use the method presented below.

- If the number, n, of subintervals is *odd*, use this form of Simpson's Rule:
$$S = \frac{2}{3} \text{ (Midpoint Area)} + \frac{1}{3} \text{ (Trapezoid Area)}$$

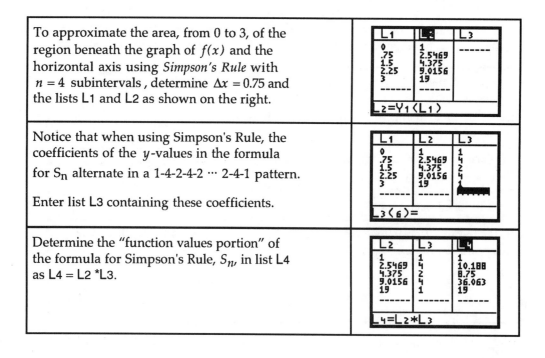

To approximate the area, from 0 to 3, of the region beneath the graph of $f(x)$ and the horizontal axis using *Simpson's Rule* with $n = 4$ subintervals, determine $\Delta x = 0.75$ and the lists L1 and L2 as shown on the right.	L1 **L2** L3 0 1 .75 2.5469 1.5 4.375 2.25 9.0156 3 19 ----- ----- L2=Y1(L1)
Notice that when using Simpson's Rule, the coefficients of the y-values in the formula for S_n alternate in a 1-4-2-4-2 ⋯ 2-4-1 pattern. Enter list L3 containing these coefficients.	L1 L2 L3 0 1 1 .75 2.5469 4 1.5 4.375 2 2.25 9.0156 4 3 19 1 ---- ---- L3(6)=
Determine the "function values portion" of the formula for Simpson's Rule, S_n, in list L4 as L4 = L2 *L3.	L2 L3 **L4** 1 1 1 2.5469 4 10.188 4.375 2 8.75 9.0156 4 36.063 19 1 19 ------ ---- ------ L4=L2*L3

| Find the area using Simpson's Rule formula $S_n = (\Delta x\,/\,3)$ sum L4. $S_4 = (0.75/3)$ sum L4 = 18.75 | (.75/3)sum L4
                    18.75 |

SECTION 6.3: LIMITS OF SUMS

6.3.1 Simplifying Area Calculations: The above procedures using lists are very time consuming when the number, n, of subintervals is large. When you are using a model $y = f(x)$ entered in the Y1 location of the Y= graphing list, you will find program NUMINTG very helpful in determining left-rectangle, right-rectangle, midpoint-rectangle, trapezoid, and Simpson's Rule numerical approximations for area. Program NUMINTG is listed in the TI-82 Appendix.

Enter $f(x) = x^3 - 2x^2 + 3x + 1$ in Y1. If you wish to view the approximating rectangles and/or trapezoids, first construct a graph of $f(x)$. A suitable window is x between 0 and 3 and y between 0 and 19.	
Access program NUMINTG by pressing PRGM followed by the number corresponding to the location of the program. At this point, if you did not enter in Y1 (or did not draw the graph), enter 2 to exit the program. Do what needs to be done and re-run the program. If all is okay, press 1 to continue.	ENTER F(X) IN Y1 DRAW GRAPH OF F CONTINUE? YES(1) NO(2)
At the next prompt, press 1 ENTER to draw the approximating figures or press 2 ENTER to obtain only the numerical approximations to the area between $f(x)$ and the horizontal axis between 0 and 3. Let's view some pictures.	ENTER F(X) IN Y1 DRAW GRAPH OF F CONTINUE? YES(1) NO(2) 1 DRAW PICTURES? YES(1) NO(2) 1
At the LOWER LIMIT? prompt, type 0 ENTER and at the UPPER LIMIT? prompt, 3 ENTER. You are next shown a menu of choices. Press 2 ENTER to find a right-rectangle approximation.	ENTER CHOICE: LEFT RECT (1) RIGHT RECT (2) TRAPEZOIDS (3) MIDPT RECT (4) SIMPSONS (5)

Input 4 at the N? prompt and press ENTER. The four approximating right-rectangles are shown. Notice that the right-rectangle sum overestimates the area under the curve.	
The right-rectangle sum is displayed when you press ENTER.	TRAPEZOIDS (3) MIDPT RECT (4) SIMPSONS (5) 2 N? 4 SUM= 26.203125
Press ENTER once more and more choices are displayed. Suppose we now want to find and see the approximating area using 8 trapezoids. Press 2 and then press 3 ENTER to choose trapezoids.	ENTER CHOICE 1:CHANGE N 2:CHANGE METHOD 3:QUIT
Enter 8 at the N? prompt and view the trapezoids.	
Again press ENTER and the trapezoid sum is displayed. This is certainly a better approximation than the right-rectangle sum with 4 rectangles. Press ENTER again and choose 3 to QUIT.	TRAPEZOIDS (3) MIDPT RECT (4) SIMPSONS (5) 3 N? 8 SUM= 18.92578125

- When n, the number of subintervals, is large, it is not advisable to draw pictures.

- Program NUMINTG informs you that there is "no picture for Simpson's Rule" if you choose the draw picture and Simpson's options.

- The program also informs you that "N is odd. Simpson's Rule not calculated" when you choose an odd number of subintervals. In such a case, you need to find the midpoint and trapezoid approximations and use the formula given at the beginning of this section to find the Simpson's Rule approximation.

- Program NUMINTG cannot be used with data unless you use a model you fit to the data.

6.3.2 Limits of Sums: When finding the trend in the midpoint approximations to the area between a non-negative function and the horizontal axis between two values of the input variable, program NUMINTG is extremely helpful!

To construct a chart of midpoint approximations for the area between $f(x) = x^3 - 2x^2 + 3x + 1$ and the x-axis between x=0 and x=3, first enter $f(x)$ in Y1.
 	
 Run program NUMINTG. Since many subintervals will be used, do not choose to draw the pictures. After entering 0 and 3 as the respective lower and upper limits, choose option 4.
	```ENTER CHOICE:```
	 ```LEFT RECT (1)```
	 ```RIGHT RECT (2)```
	 ```TRAPEZOIDS (3)```
	 ```MIDPT RECT (4)```
	 ```SIMPSONS (5) 4```

Input some number of subintervals, say N = 4.
 	
 Record the midpoint approximation 18.3984375.
	```N? 4```
	 ```SUM=```
	 ``` 18.3984375```

Press ENTER and choose option 1: CHANGE N. Double the number of subintervals to N = 8.
 	
 Record the midpoint approximation 18.66210938.
	```N? 8```
	 ```SUM=```
	 ``` 18.66210938```

Continue on in this manner, each time choosing option 1: CHANGE N and doubling N until a trend is evident.
 	
 (Finding a trend means that you can tell what specific number the values are getting closer and closer to without having to run the program ad infinitum!)
	```N? 128```
	 ```SUM=```
	 ``` 18.74965668```

SECTION 6.4: INDEFINITE INTEGRALS

6.4.1 Finding Integral Formulas: The TI-82 performs the required calculations to help you find integral formulas. You can create a table of values for the definite integral and look for a pattern in those values to help determine an indefinite integral formula. The process of calculating the definite integral uses the calculator's formula for finding the value of the integral, fnInt(f(X), X, a, b).

The correspondence between our definite integral notation $\int_{a}^{b} f(x)\, dx$ and the calculator's definite integral notation fnInt(f(X), X, a, b) is as shown below:

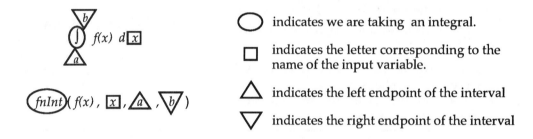

$\bigcirc$ indicates we are taking an integral.

$\square$ indicates the letter corresponding to the name of the input variable.

$\triangle$ indicates the left endpoint of the interval

$\triangledown$ indicates the right endpoint of the interval

We first investigate creating a list of values for the indefinite integral $\int_{a}^{x} f(t)\, dt$ for varying values of x where a is a specific constant. Clear the graphing list. In general, enter Y1 = $f(x)$ and Y2 = fnInt(Y1, X, a, X).

Specifically, if you are investigating $\int_{0}^{x} t\, dt$, use $a = 0$ and $f(t) = t$. Enter the function in Y1. In the Y2 location, type the instruction fnInt(with the keystrokes MATH 9 (fnInt(). Remember to use 2nd VARS (Y-VARS) 1 (Function) 1 (Y1) for the function Y1.	```Y1=X Y2=fnInt(Y1,X,0, X) Y3= Y4= Y5= Y6= Y7=``` Since you are using the graphing list to enter the functions, you must call t by the name x.
Clear lists L1 and L2. Enter the values shown on the right in L1. Position the cursor over the L2 at the top of the second list, and evaluate Y2 at the x-values in L1 as L2 = Y2 (L1)	L1: 0 1 2 3 4 5 L2: 0 .5 2 4.5 8 12.5 L3: ------ L2=Y2(L1)
You will often find it easier to see a pattern if the L2 values are fractions. Many times the TI-82 can do this conversion for you. Return to the home screen and convert using the "to a fraction" key found with MATH 1 (▸Frac). The list scrolls to the right or left with ▸ or ◂.	L2▸Frac {0 5 2 9/2 8 25... L2 ..5 2 4.5 8 12.5}

Finding the L2 values might take a short time since the calculator is determining several definite integral values. Now, all you need do is find the pattern in the L2 values.

- You could have used the TABLE instead of the lists to enter the x-values and evaluate Y2 at those x-values.

- If you have difficulty determining a pattern, draw a scatterplot of the x-values and the calculated definite integral values. The shape of the scatterplot should give you a clue as to the equation of the indefinite integral formula. Note that this method might help only if you consider a variety of values for x in list L1.

- The TI-82 only calculates numerical values of definite integrals -- it does not give formula that is the indefinite integral.

To create a list of values for the indefinite integral $\int_{a}^{x} f(t)\, dt$ for varying values of a, use basically the same procedure as illustrated above. Suppose we want to compare, for various values of a, $\int_{a}^{x} t\, dt$ to $\int_{0}^{x} t\, dt$. Let us use the TABLE to evaluate the output of Y2.

Enter the functions as shown on the right. That is, let $a = 1$.
 	
How do the values of Y2 relate to the output for $\int_{0}^{x} t\, dt$?
	`Y1■X`
	`Y2■fnInt(Y1,X,1,`
	`X)`
	`Y3=`
	`Y4=`
	`Y5=`
	`Y6=`
	`Y7=`

Set the table to either ASK or AUTO and generate the output values for Y2 shown to the right.	X | Y1 | **Y2** 0 | 0 | -.5 1 | 1 | 0 2 | 2 | 1.5 3 | 3 | 4 4 | 4 | 7.5 5 | 5 | 12 `Y2■fnInt(Y1,X,1...`

To find the output values for Y2 when $a = 2$, press Y= and change the lower limit to 2.	`Y1■X`
	`Y2■fnInt(Y1,X,2,`
	`X)`
	`Y3=`
	`Y4=`
	`Y5=`
	`Y6=`
	`Y7=`

Press 2nd GRAPH (TABLE) and view the table. Compare these values to those you found when Y2 = fnInt(Y1, X, 0, X). Repeat for other values of *a* if necessary.		X	Y1	Y2
---	---	---
0	0	-2
1	1	-1.5
2	2	0
3	3	2.5
4	4	6
5	5	10.5	 Y2=fnInt(Y1,X,2...

SECTION 6.5: THE FUNDAMENTAL THEOREM

6.5.1 The Fundamental Theorem of Calculus: This theorem tells us that the derivative of an antiderivative of a function is the function itself. Let us view this theorem both numerically and graphically.

Consider $F'(x) = \dfrac{d}{dx}\left(\displaystyle\int_{1}^{x} 3t^2 + 2t - 5 \, dt\right)$. The FTC tells us $F'(x)$ should equal $f(x) = 3x^2 + 2x - 5$. Enter the functions shown to the right.	Y1⯅3X²+2X-5 Y2⯅nDeriv(fnInt(Y1,X,1,X),X,X) Y3= Y4= Y5= Y6= Y7=
Press 2nd GRAPH (TABLE) and input some different values of x. Other than a small bit of roundoff error due to the numerical nature of the calculator, Y1 and Y2 are identical!		X	Y1	Y2
---	---	---
-5	60	60
-3	16	16
-1	-4	-4
0	-5	-5
1	0	1E-6
2	11	11
4	51	51	 Y1⯅3X²+2X-5
Find a suitable viewing window such as x between ⁻4.7 and 4.7 and y between ⁻6 and 3.1. Draw the graphs of Y1 and Y2 separately in this same window and then draw them together. Only one graph appears! (The graph of Y2 will take a while to draw.)	

- Enter several other functions in Y1 and perform the same explorations as above. Confirm your results with derivative and integral formulas. Are you convinced?

CHAPTER 7.   MEASURING THE EFFECTS OF CHANGE:
THE DEFINITE INTEGRAL

SECTION 7.2: THE DEFINITE INTEGRAL

7.2.1 Antiderivatives: All antiderivatives of a specific function differ only by a constant. We explore this idea using the function $f(x) = 3x^2 - 1$ and its antiderivative $F(x) = x^3 - x + C$.

Enter $f(x)$ in Y1, fnInt(Y1, X, 0, X) in Y2, and $F(x)$ in Y3, Y4, Y5, Y6, and Y7 (using a different value of C in each location) (You can try different values of C than those shown on the right.)	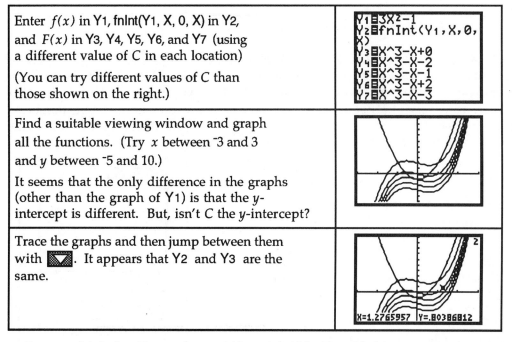
Find a suitable viewing window and graph all the functions. (Try x between ⁻3 and 3 and y between ⁻5 and 10.) It seems that the only difference in the graphs (other than the graph of Y1) is that the y-intercept is different. But, isn't C the y-intercept?	
Trace the graphs and then jump between them with [image]. It appears that Y2 and Y3 are the same.	

- Do you think that if you changed Y2 to fnInt(Y1, X, 2, X) that you would find the graphs of Y2 and Y6, or maybe Y2 and Y4, the same? Can you justify your answer with antiderivative formulas? Explore!

7.2.2 Evaluating a Definite Integral on the Home Screen: The TI-82 finds

a numerical approximation for the definite integral $\int_a^b f(x)\,dx$. All you have to do is, on the home screen, type fnInt($f(x)$, x, a, b) for a specific function $f(x)$ and specific values of a and b, and press ENTER.

- If you evaluate a definite integral using antiderivative formulas and check you answer using the calculator, you may sometimes find a slight difference in the trailing decimal places. Remember, the TI-82 is evaluating the definite integral using an approximation technique.

Find $\displaystyle\int_1^5 (2^x - x)\, dx$.
 	
 Notice that as long as you specify the variable you are using in the position after the function, you can use any letter to represent the variable.
	`fnInt(2^X-X,X,1,`
	 `5)`
	 `        31.28085123`
	 `fnInt(2^T-T,T,1,`
	 `5)`
	 `        31.28085123`

7.2.3 Rates into Amounts: The integral, between to input values, say a and b, of a rate of change is the change in amount of the antiderivative from a to b. Suppose you have modeled marginal cost data to find the rate of change in the marginal cost of ovens to be $C'(x) = -1.12744 + 6137.6892\, x^{-1}$ dollars per oven where x is the number of ovens produced per day. What is the change in cost if production is increased from 300 to 500 ovens per day?

Enter $C'(x)$ in Y1.
 	
 The change in amount is \$2909.80.
	`fnInt(Y₁,X,300,5`
	 `00)`
	 `        2909.800914`

Now, let us prepare to put the amount function in Y2:
 	
 Press [Y=], and move the cursor to the Y2 location. Clear any previously-entered function. Press [2nd] [STO▸] (RCL) [2nd] [VARS] (Y-VARS) [ENTER] [ENTER].
	`Y₁=-1.12744+6137`
	 `.6892X⁻¹`
	 `Y₂=-1.12744+6137`
	 `.6892X⁻¹█`
	 `Y₃=`
	 `Y₄=`
	 `Y₅=`
	 `Y₆=`

Use [2nd] [DEL] (INS) and your knowledge of integral formulas to edit Y2 to the expression on the right.
 	
 The antiderivative of the rate of change (with the constant equal to 0) is now in Y2.
	`Y₁=-1.12744+6137`
	 `.6892X⁻¹`
	 `Y₂=-1.12744X+613`
	 `7.6892ln X`
	 `Y₃=`
	 `Y₄=`
	 `Y₅=`
	 `Y₆=`

Return to the home screen and evaluate the change $C(500) - C(300)$.	`fnInt(Y₁,X,300,5`
	 `00)`
	 `        2909.800914`
	 `Y₂(500)-Y₂(300)`
	 `        2909.800914`

• You should find this method very helpful when the model coefficients are long decimal values. Also, if you use this method, errors in your answer to rounding the coefficients will be eliminated.

7.2.4 Integrals and Area:
Finding the area between two functions utilizes the ideas presented in preceding sections. Suppose we want to find the area between the functions $f(x) = 2 - x$ and $g(x) = -x^3 + 2x + 2$.

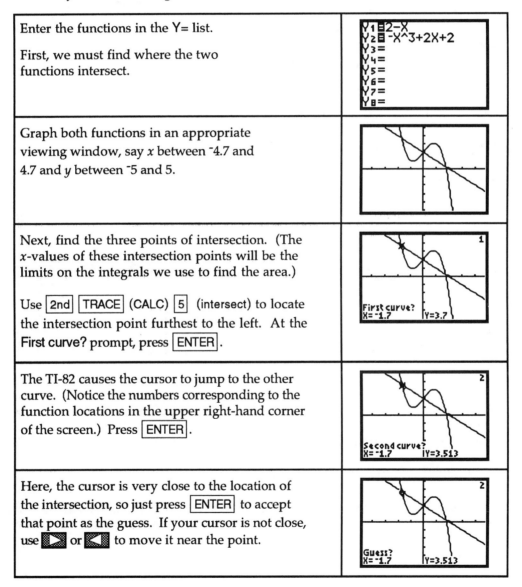

Enter the functions in the Y= list. First, we must find where the two functions intersect.	Y1**=**2-X Y2**=** -X^3+2X+2 Y3= Y4= Y5= Y6= Y7= Y8=
Graph both functions in an appropriate viewing window, say x between ‾4.7 and 4.7 and y between ‾5 and 5.	
Next, find the three points of intersection. (The x-values of these intersection points will be the limits on the integrals we use to find the area.) Use 2nd TRACE (CALC) 5 (intersect) to locate the intersection point furthest to the left. At the **First curve?** prompt, press ENTER.	First curve? X=‾1.7 Y=3.7
The TI-82 causes the cursor to jump to the other curve. (Notice the numbers corresponding to the function locations in the upper right-hand corner of the screen.) Press ENTER.	Second curve? X=‾1.7 Y=3.513
Here, the cursor is very close to the location of the intersection, so just press ENTER to accept that point as the guess. If your cursor is not close, use ▶ or ◀ to move it near the point.	Guess? X=‾1.7 Y=3.513

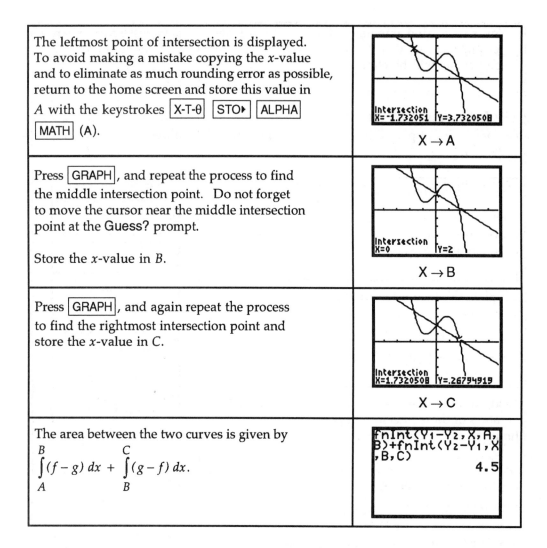

The leftmost point of intersection is displayed. To avoid making a mistake copying the x-value and to eliminate as much rounding error as possible, return to the home screen and store this value in A with the keystrokes X-T-θ STO► ALPHA MATH (A).	Intersection X=-1.732051 Y=3.7320508 X → A
Press GRAPH , and repeat the process to find the middle intersection point. Do not forget to move the cursor near the middle intersection point at the **Guess?** prompt. Store the x-value in B.	Intersection X=0 Y=2 X → B
Press GRAPH , and again repeat the process to find the rightmost intersection point and store the x-value in C.	Intersection X=1.7320508 Y=.26794919 X → C
The area between the two curves is given by $$\int_A^B (f-g)\,dx + \int_B^C (g-f)\,dx.$$	fnInt(Y₁-Y₂,X,A, B)+fnInt(Y₂-Y₁,X ,B,C) 4.5

7.2.5 Evaluating a Definite Integral from the Graphics Screen: You can graphically find the definite integral $\int_a^b f(x)\,dx$ provided that a and b are possible x-values displayed when you trace on the graphics screen.

- For "nice" numbers, you can often find the exact x-value you need if you graph in the ZDecimal screen or set the viewing window so that Xmax – Xmin equals a multiple of 9.4.)

Find $\displaystyle\int_{1}^{5}(2^{x}-x)\,dx$. Turn the **STATPLOTS** off, enter Y1 = 2^X − X, and set the viewing window on the right.	``` WINDOW FORMAT Xmin=-2 Xmax=7.4 Xscl=1 Ymin=-10 Ymax=30 Yscl=10 ```
Graph Y1 with GRAPH . Press 2nd TRACE (CALC) 7 (∫f(x)dx).	Lower Limit? X=2.7 . Y=3.7980192
Press and hold ◀ until you reach X = 1. Press ENTER to set the lower limit on the integral and have the calculator ask for the upper limit.	Upper Limit? X=1 L Y=1
Press and hold ▶ until you reach X = 5. Press ENTER to calculate the numerical value of the definite integral. Notice that the area this integral represents is shaded when the value of the definite integral is displayed.	∫f(x)dx=31.280851

SECTION 7.3: AVERAGES

7.3.1 Average Value of a Function: Use the TI-82 to find the numerical value of and aid in your geometric interpretation of the average value of a function. Consider a model for the average daytime temperature between 7 AM and 7 PM:

$$f(t) = -0.65684t^2 + 9.38212t + 45.54945 \text{ degrees } t \text{ hours after 7 AM.}$$

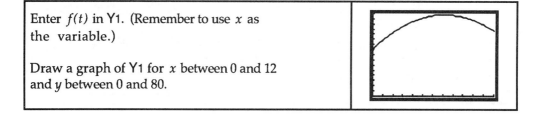

Enter $f(t)$ in Y1. (Remember to use x as the variable.) Draw a graph of Y1 for x between 0 and 12 and y between 0 and 80.	

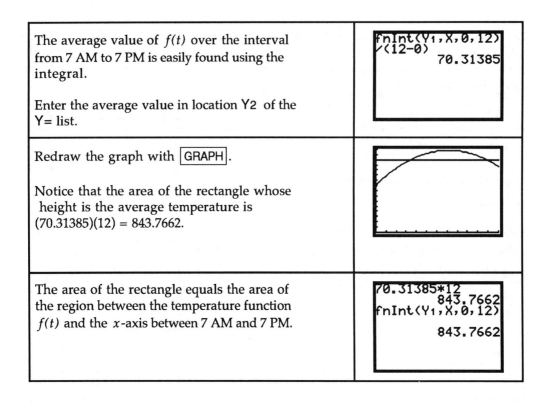

The average value of $f(t)$ over the interval from 7 AM to 7 PM is easily found using the integral. Enter the average value in location Y2 of the Y= list.	fnInt(Y₁,X,0,12) /(12-0) 70.31385
Redraw the graph with GRAPH. Notice that the area of the rectangle whose height is the average temperature is $(70.31385)(12) = 843.7662$.	

The area of the rectangle equals the area of the region between the temperature function $f(t)$ and the x-axis between 7 AM and 7 PM.	70.31385*12
	      843.7662
	fnInt(Y₁,X,0,12)
	      843.7662

SECTION 7.4: INCOME STREAMS

7.4.1 Future and Present Value of an Income Stream: Since future and present value of an income stream are defined by definite integrals, finding these values is easily done with your calculator.

Suppose we want to find the present and future values of an investment of $3.3 million each year that earns continuously compounded interest at a rate of 19.4% annually for a period of 10 years.

The *future value* of the investment is the amount to which the $3.3 million invested each year and the interest it earns would accumulate to at the end of 10 years. (We assume the $3.3 million is flowing in continuously.)

Future value = $e^{0.194(10)} \displaystyle\int_{0}^{10} 3.3e^{-0.194t}\, dt$ which equals $101.360 million.	e^(.194*10)fnInt (3.3e^(-.194X),X ,0,10) 101.3601969

The *present value* of the investment is the amount that would have to be deposited <u>now</u> and remain untouched (except for accumulating interest) to equal the amount to which the $3.3 million invested each year and the interest it earns would accumulate to at the end of 10 years. (We assume the investment is flowing in continuously.)

Present value = $\int_{0}^{10} 3.3 e^{-0.194t}\, dt$
 	
 which equals $14.566 million.
	`e^(.194*10)fnInt`
	 `(3.3e^(-.194X),X`
	 `,0,10)`
	 `          101.3601969`
	 `Ans/(e^(.194*10)`
	 `          14.56586065`

7.4.2 Present Value in Perpetuity:
Your calculator only provides numerical values for definite integrals, not an integral whose upper limit approaches infinity. You can, however, evaluate, using integral formulas, the present value in perpetuity integral for a fixed T and consider what happens numerically and graphically as T gets larger and larger.

Suppose we want to evaluate $\int_{0}^{\infty} 10000 e^{-0.135t}\, dt = \lim_{T\to\infty} \int_{0}^{T} 10000 e^{-0.135t}\, dt =$

$\lim_{T\to\infty} 74074.07(1 - e^{-0.135T})$. We find $\lim_{T\to\infty} (1 - e^{-0.135T})$ and multiply by 74074.07.

To investigate this limit *numerically*, first enter Y1 = 1 − e^(-.135X).
 	
 Access the TABLE SETUP and choose settings similar to those shown on the right.
	`TABLE SETUP`
	 `  TblMin=0`
	 `  ΔTbl=10`
	 `Indpnt: AUTO  Ask`
	 `Depend: AUTO  Ask`

Press 2nd GRAPH (TABLE) and scroll down through the table with ▼. It appears that Y1 is getting closer and closer to 1 as T = X gets larger and larger.	<table><tr><td>X</td><td>Y1</td></tr><tr><td>40</td><td>.99548</td></tr><tr><td>50</td><td>.99883</td></tr><tr><td>60</td><td>.9997</td></tr><tr><td>70</td><td>.99992</td></tr><tr><td>80</td><td>.99998</td></tr><tr><td>90</td><td>.99999</td></tr><tr><td>100</td><td></td></tr></table> `Y1=.999998629041`
To investigate this limit *graphically*, have Y1 = 1 − e^(-.135X). Set a suitable window, such as x between 0 and 100 and y between 0 and 2. Draw the graph and trace it to observe that the Y1 values appear to be getting closer to 1 as T = X gets larger and larger.	 `X=92.553191  Y=.99999625`

Thus, $\lim_{T\to\infty} 74074.07(1 - e^{-0.135T}) = 74074.07 \lim_{T\to\infty} (1 - e^{-0.135T}) = 74074.07*1 = 74074.07$.

SECTION 7.5: INTEGRALS IN ECONOMICS

7.5.1 Consumers' and Producers' Surplus: Consumers' and producers' surplus, being defined by definite integrals, are easy to do using the calculator. You should always draw a graph of the demand and supply functions to better understand the activity. Suppose the demand curve is $D(q) = {}^-0.06q + 71.863$ and the supply curve is $S(q) = 16.977(1.001117)^q$ where q is the number of units of the product and we want to find the social gain at the equilibrium price.

Enter $D(q) = {}^-0.06q + 71.863$ in Y1 and $S(q) = 16.977(1.001117)^q$ in Y2.	```Y1B-.06X+71.863 Y2B16.977(1.0011 17)^X Y3= Y4= Y5= Y6= Y7=```
Graph Y1 and Y2 in a suitable viewing window, say x between 0 and 1000 and y between 0 and 80. Use the methods of 7.2.4 of this *Guide* to find the intersection of the demand and supply functions. $q = 628$ and $D(q) = S(q) \approx 34.21$ is the equilibrium point. (Note that since $x = q$ is the number of units of a product, it should be a whole number.)	```Intersection X=627.57661 ⌐Y=34.208404⌐```
The consumers' surplus at equilibrium is $$\int_0^{628} -0.06x + 71.863\, dx - 628(34.21) = 11{,}814.56$$	```fnInt(Y1,X,0,628)-628(34.21) 11814.564```
The producers' surplus at equilibrium is $$\int_0^{628} 16.977(1.001117)^x\, dx - 628(34.21) = 6{,}034.28$$	```628(34.21)-fnInt (Y2,X,0,628) 6034.275958```
Thus, the social gain is 11,814.56 + 6,034.28 = 17,848.84. Note that you could have calculated the social gain as the area between the demand and supply curves.	```fnInt(Y1-Y2,X,0, 628) 17848.83996```

TI-82 Calculator Appendix

Programs listed below are referenced in *Part A* of this *Guide*. They should be typed in your calculator, transferred to you via a cable using the LINK mode of TI-82, or transferred to your calculator using the TI-GRAPH LINK™ cable and software for a PC or Macintosh computer and a disk containing these programs. Refer to your owner's manual for instructions on typing in the programs or transferring them via a cable from another calculator.

```
DIFF              • Program
 :ClrHome
 :ClrList L₃,L₄,L₅
 :Disp "HAVE X IN L₁"
 :Disp "HAVE Y IN L₂-SEE"
 :Disp "1ST DIFF IN L₃,
 :Disp "2ND DIFF IN L₄,"
 :Disp "PERCENT CHANGE"
 :Disp " IN L₅"
 :1→A
 :dim L₂→M:M-1→dim L₃
 :For(A,1,M-1,1)
 :L₂(A+1)-L₂(A)→L₃(A)
 :End
 :M-2→dim L₄
 :1→B
 :For(B,1,M-2,1)
 :L₃(B+1)-L₃(B)→L₄(B)
 :End
 :M-1→dim L₅
 :1→E
 :For(E,1,M-1,1)
 :(L₃(E)/L₂(E))*100→L₅(E)
 :End
```

```
LOGISTIC              • Program
  :ClrHome
  :Disp "DATA IN L₁,L₂"
  :Disp ""
  :Disp ""
  :Disp "PROGRAM"
  :Disp "CLEARS L₃ L₄"
  :Disp "LEAVES EQ IN Y₀"
  :Disp "ENTER CONTINUES"
  :Pause
  :ClrHome
  :dim L₁→N
  :FnOff
  :PlotsOff
  :Plot1(Scatter,L₁,L₂,□)
  :ZoomStat
  :Pause
  :ClrList (L₃,L₄)
  :For(I,1,N-2)
  :L₂(I+1)→L₃(I)
  :(L₂(I+2)-L₂(I))/((L₁(I+2)-
  L₁(I))L₂(I+1))→L₄(I)
  :End
  :LinReg(a+bx) L₃,L₄
  :a/⁻b→U
  :max(L₂)+.0001→V
  :max(U,V)→L
  :0→W
  :mean(L₂)→M
  :For(J,1,N)
  :W+(M-L₂(J))²→W
  :End
  :Disp "SSY=",W
  :Disp "L=",L
  :Goto 9
  :Lbl A
  :Prompt L
  :Lbl 9
  :ClrList (L₃,L₄)
  :For(I,1,N)
  :L₁(I)→L₃(I)
  :L-L₂(I)→Z
  :If Z>0
  :Then
  :ln (Z/L₂(I))→L₄(I)
  :Else
  :Disp "BAD VALUE FOR L"
  :Disp "...INCREASE L"
  :Goto A
  :End
  :End
  :LinReg(a+bx) L₃,L₄
  :a→C
  :⁻b→B
  :e^C→A
  :ClrDraw
  :DrawF L/(1+Ae^(⁻BX)
  :Pause
  :0→S
```

(Program LOGISTIC continued)

```
  :For(K,1,N)
  :L/(1+Ae^(⁻BL₁(K)))→H
  :S+(L₂(K)-H)²→S
  :End
  :Disp "SSE=",S
  :Pause
  :Menu("SELECT ONE","CHANGE
      L",A,"QUIT ON
      GRAPH",B,"QUIT ON
      SSE",C,"QUIT ON MODEL",D)
  :Lbl B
  :"L/(1+Ae^⁻BX)"→Y₀
  :DrawF L/(1+Ae^⁻BX)
  :Stop
  :Lbl C
  :Stop
  :Lbl D
  :ClrHome
  :Disp "Y=L/(1+Ae^⁻BX)"
  :Output(2,3,"L=")
  :Output(2,6,L)
  :Output(3,3,"A=")
  :Output(3,6,A)
  :Output(4,3,"B=")
  :Output(4,6,B)
  :Output(5,1,"SSE=")
  :Output(5,6,S)
  :Output(6,1,"SSY="
  :Output(6,6,W)
  :Stop
```

```
LSLINE                    • Program
  :0→A:0→B:1→C
  :"A+BX"→Y₁
  :Ymax-Ymin→H
  :.2H+Ymax→Ymax
  :FnOff
  :Text(0,0,"X TICK=",Xscl,"   Y TICK=",Yscl)
  :Pause
  :ClrHome
  :Lbl 1
  :Text(0,0,"GUESS  SLOPE,  Y-INTERCEPT")
  :Pause
  :FnOn
  :Input "SLOPE=",B
  :Input "Y INTERCEPT=",A
  :2-Var Stats
  :Lbl 2
  :0→S
  :For(K,1,n)
  :L₁(K)→X
  :(L₂(K)-Y₁)²+S→S
  :Line(L₁(K),L₂(K),X,Y₁)
  :End
  :Pause
  :Disp ""
  :Disp "SSE=",S
  :Pause
  :If C=2
  :Goto 3
  :Input "TRY AGAIN? 1Y 2N",C
  :If C=1
  :Goto 1
  :LinReg(a+bx)
  :"a+bX"→Y₂
  :Disp ""
  :Disp "PRESS ENTER TO"
  :Disp "SEE YOUR LINE"
  :Disp "AND BESTFIT LINE"
  :Pause
  :DispGraph
  :Pause
  :ClrHome
  :Disp "NOW,PRESS ENTER"
  :Disp "TO SEE ERRORS"
  :Disp "FOR BESTFIT LINE"
  :Pause
  :a→A:b→B
  :Goto 2
  :Lbl 3
  :Disp "Y INTERCEPT",a
  :Disp "SLOPE=",b
  :Disp "r=",r
  :FnOff
```

NUMINTG   • Program

```
:ClrHome
:PlotsOff
:Disp "ENTER F(X) IN Y1"
:Disp "DRAW GRAPH OF F"
:Disp ""
:Disp "CONTINUE?"
:Input "YES(1) NO(2) ",G
:If G=2:Stop
:Disp ""
:Disp "DRAW PICTURES?"
:Input "YES(1) NO(2) ",H
:ClrHome
:Input "LOWER LIMIT? ",A
:Input "UPPER LIMIT? ",B
:0→Ymin
:min(Y1(A),Y1(B))→θ
:If θ<0:θ→Ymin
:Lbl 0
:ClrHome
:Disp "ENTER CHOICE:"
:Disp "LEFT RECT   (1)"
:Disp "RIGHT RECT  (2)"
:Disp "TRAPEZOIDS  (3)"
:Disp "MIDPT RECT  (4)"
:Input "SIMPSONS    (5) ",R
:Lbl 1
:ClrDraw
:Input "N? ",N
:(B-A)/N→W
:0→S:1→C
:Lbl 2
:If R=1:Goto 3
:If R=2:Goto 4
:If R=3:Goto 3
:If R=4:Goto 5
:If R=5:Goto 6
:Lbl 3
:A+(C-1)W→X
:X→J:X+W→L
:Goto 7
:Lbl 4
:A+CW→X
:X-W→J:X→L
:Goto 7
:Lbl 5
:If H≠1:Then
:If N>5:Then
:1→Z:W/2→H:A→X
:Lbl 8
:X+H→X:Y1+S→S
:A+ZW→X
:IS>(Z,N):Goto 8
:SW→S:Goto T
:End:End
:A+CW-W/2→X
:X-W/2→J
:X+W/2→L
:Goto 7
```

(Program NUMINTG continued)

```
:Lbl 6
:If fPart (N/2)≠0:Then:
:Disp "N IS ODD"
:Disp "SIMPSONS RULE"
:Disp "NOT CALCULATED."
:Pause :Goto E
:End
:If H=1:Then
:Disp "NO PICTURE FOR"
:Disp "SIMPSONS RULE"
:End
:A→G:G+W→G:G→V
:Lbl 9
:V→X:Y1→Y:V+W→X:4Y+2Y1+S→S
:V+2W→V
:If V<B:Goto 9
:G-W→X:Y1→E
:B→X:Y1→F
:(W/3)(S+E-F)→S
:Goto T
:Lbl 7
:Y1→K:K+S→S
:If H=1:Goto D
:Lbl I
:IS>(C,N)
:Goto 2
:If R=3:Then
:A→X:Y1→P
:B→X:Y1→Q
:S+(Q-P)/2→S
:End
:W*S→S
:Lbl T
:Disp "SUM=",S
:Pause
:ClrHome
:Lbl E
:Menu("ENTER CHOICE","CHANGE
    N",1,"CHANGE
    METHOD",0,"QUIT",F)
:Lbl F
:Stop
:Lbl D
:If R=3:Then
:Y1(L)→M
:Else:K→M
:End
:Line(J,0,J,K)
:Line(J,K,L,M)
:Line(L,M,L,0)
:If C=N:Pause
:Goto I
```

Part B   Texas Instruments TI-85 Advanced Scientific Calculator

Chapter 1.   The Ingredients of Change: Functions and Linear Models

Setup: Before you begin, check the TI-85's basic setup with [2nd] [MORE] (MODE). Choose the settings shown in Figure 1. Check the graphics screen setup with [GRAPH] [MORE] [F3] (FORMT). Choose the settings shown in Figure 2.

- If you do not have the darkened choices shown in each of the figures below, use the arrow keys to move the blinking cursor over the setting you want to choose and press [ENTER].

- Press [EXIT] or [2nd] [EXIT] (QUIT) to return to the home screen.

Figure 1. Basic Setup

Figure 2. Graphics Screen Setup

SECTION 1.1 FUNDAMENTALS OF MODELING

1.1.1 Calculating: You can type in lengthy expressions; just make sure that you use parentheses when you are not sure of the calculator's order of operations. As a general rule, numerators and denominators of fractions and powers consisting of more than one term should be enclosed in parentheses.

Evaluate $\dfrac{1}{4*15+\frac{895}{7}}$.
 	
 Evaluate $\dfrac{(\text{-}3)^4-5}{8+1.456}$. (Use [(-)] for the negative symbol and [−] for the subtraction sign.)
	`1/(4*15+895/7)`
	 `                .005323193916`
	 `((-3)^4-5)/(8+1.456)`
	 `                 8.0372250423`

Evaluate $e^3*0.027$ and $e^{3*0.027}$.
 	
 The calculator will assume you mean the first expression unless you use parentheses around the two values in the exponent. (It is not necessary to type in the 0 *before* the decimal point.)
	`e^3*.027`
	 `                .542309496926`
	 `e^(3*.027)`
	 `                 1.08437089657`

1.1.2 Using the ANS Memory: Instead of again typing an expression that was evaluated immediately prior, use the answer memory by pressing [2nd] [(-)] (ANS).

Calculate $\left(\dfrac{1}{4*15 + \dfrac{895}{7}}\right)^{-1}$ using this nice shortcut.
 	
 (If you wish to clear the home screen, press [CLEAR].)
	```895/7```
	 ``` 127.857142857```
	 ```1/(4*15+Ans)```
	 ``` .005323193916```
	 ```Ans⁻¹```
	 ``` 187.857142857```

1.1.3 Answer Display: When the denominator of a fraction has no more than three digits, the TI-85 can provide the calculated answer as a fraction. When an answer is very large or very small, the calculator displays the result in scientific notation.

The "to a fraction" key is obtained by pressing [2nd] [X] (MATH) [F5] (MISC) [MORE] [F1] (▶Frac).	```2/5+1/3```
	 ``` .733333333333```
	 ```Ans▶Frac```
	 ``` 11/15```
	 ```.3875▶Frac```
	 ``` 31/80```

The calculator's symbol for "times 10^{12}" is **E12**. Thus, 7.945**E**12 means 7,945,000,000,000.
 	
 The result 1.4675**E** $^{-}$6 means $1.4675*10^{-6}$, the scientific notation expression for 0.0000014675.
	```5600000000000+2345000```
	 ```000000```
	 ``` 7.945E12```
	 ```.00025*.00587```
	 ``` 1.4675E-6```

1.1.4 Storing Values: Sometimes it is beneficial to store numbers or expressions for later recall. To store a number, type the number on the display and press [STO▶]. (Note that the cursor automatically changes to alphabetic mode when you press [STO▶].) Next, press the key corresponding to the letter in which you wish to store the value, and then press [ENTER]. To join several short commands together, use [2nd] [.] (:).

Store 5 in A and 3 in B.
 Calculate $4A - 2B$.
 	
 To recall a value stored in a variable, use [ALPHA] to type the letter in which the expression or value is stored and then press [ENTER]. The value remains stored until you change it.
	```5→A:3→B```
	 ``` 3```
	 ```4A-2B```
	 ``` 14```
	 ```A```
	 ``` 5```

1.1.5 Error Messages: When your input is incorrect, an error message is displayed.

If you have more than one command on a line without the commands separated by a colon (:), an error message results when you press ENTER.	`2→A x+2→B█`

Choose F1 (Goto) to position the cursor to the place the error occurred so that you can correct the mistake or choose F5 (Quit) to begin a new line on the home screen.	`ERROR 07 SYNTAX`
	
	`GOTO` ⎯⎯⎯⎯ `QUIT`

1.1.6 Entering an Equation in the Graphing List: Press GRAPH F1 (y(x)=)
to access the graphing list. Up to 99 equations can be entered in the graphing list, and the output variables are called by the names y1, y2, etc. When you intend to graph an equation you enter in the list, you must use x as the input variable.

If there are any previously entered equations that you will no longer use, clear them out of the graphing list.	Position the cursor on the line containing the equation and press CLEAR or F4 (DELf).

Enter $A = 1000(1 + 0.05t)$ in the graphing list.
 	
For convenience, we use the first, or y1 , location in the list. We intend to graph this equation, so enter the right hand side as $1000(1 + 0.05x)$. (Type x by pressing x-VAR or F1 (x), not the times sign X .)
	`y1█1000(1+.05 x)`
	
	`Y(X)= RANGE ZOOM TRACE GRAPH`
	`x   y   INSf DELf SELCT`

1.1.7 Drawing a Graph: Follow the basic procedures shown next to draw a graph
with your calculator. Always begin by entering the equation in the y(x)= list using x as the input variable. Let us draw the graph of y1 = $1000(1 + 0.05x)$.

Remove the lower menu with EXIT , and press F3 (ZOOM) MORE ZOOM F4 (ZDECM).
 	
Notice that the graphics screen is blank.
	`y1█1000(1+.05x)`
	
	`Y(X)= RANGE ZOOM TRACE GRAPH`
	`ZFIT ZSQR ZTRIG ZDECM ZRCL ▶`

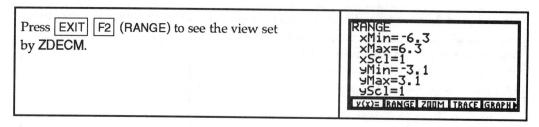

- xMin and xMax are the settings of the left and right edges of the viewing screen, and yMin and yMax are the settings for the lower and upper edges of the viewing screen. xScl and yScl set the spacing between the tick marks on the *x*- and *y*-axes.

1.1.8 Changing the View of the Graph:
If your view of the graph is not good or if you do not see the graph, change the view with one of the ZOOM options or manually set the RANGE. (We later discuss the ZOOM options.)

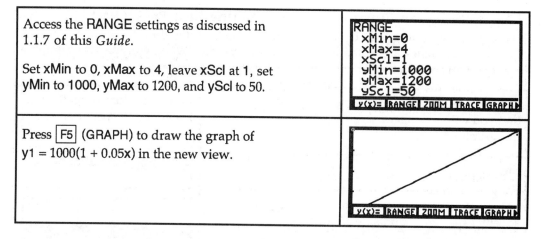

1.1.9 Tracing:
You can display the coordinates of certain points on the graph by *tracing* the graph. The *x*-values shown when you trace are dependent on the horizontal view that is set for the graph, and the *y*-values are calculated by substituting the *x*-values into the equation that is being graphed.

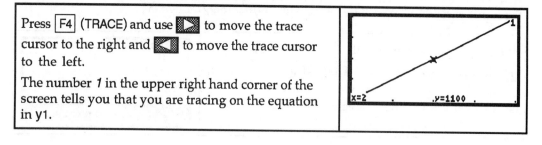

Trace past the edge of the screen and notice that even though you cannot see the trace cursor, x and y values of points on the line are still displayed at the bottom of the screen. Also notice that the graph scrolls to the left or right as you move the cursor past the edge of the current viewing screen.

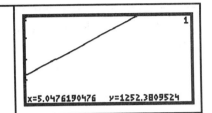

x=5.0476190476   y=1252.3809524

1.1.10 Estimating Outputs: You can estimate outputs from the graph of an equation in the graphing list using **TRACE**. It is important to realize that such outputs are *never* exact values unless the displayed x-value is *identically* the same as the value of the input variable.

Estimate the value of A where $A = 1000(1 + 0.05x)$ when $x = 5$, $x = 7$, and $x = 10$.
 	
 Press EXIT F2 (RANGE). If you do not have the settings shown to the right, reset those values.
	RANGE
	  xMin=0
	  xMax=4
	  xScl=1
	  yMin=1000
	  yMax=1200
	  yScl=50
	 y(x)= RANGE ZOOM TRACE GRAPH

Press F3 (ZOOM) F3 (ZOUT) ENTER. After the graph finishes being drawn, again press ENTER to enlarge your view of the graph. (Press EXIT F2 (RANGE) and observe the values now defining the graphics screen.)	x=2 y=1100
Press F4 (TRACE) and use ▶ to move as close as you can to $x = 5$. (Your displayed coordinates may not be exactly the same as the ones shown on the right.) An *estimate* for A when $x = 5$ is 1252.38. Continue pressing ▶ to obtain an *estimate* for A when $x = 7$ to be approximately 1356.97.	x=5.0476190476 y=1252.3809524

- If your RANGE has xMax=10, you should obtain from tracing the *exact* value $A = 1500$ when $x = 10$ because 10, not a value "close to" 10, is the displayed x-value.

- If you want "nice, friendly" values displayed for x when tracing, set xMin and xMax so that xMax–xMin is a multiple of 12.6, the width of the ZDECM viewing screen. For instance, if you set xMin = 0 and xMax = 12.6 in the example above, the *exact* values when $x = 5$, $x = 7$, and $x = 10$ are displayed when you trace. Another view that gives friendly values is xMin = ‾5 and xMax = 20.2 since 25.2 = 2(12.6). Try it!

1.1.11 Evaluating Outputs: The TI-85 evaluates outputs from an equation in the graphing list from the graph or from the home screen. Begin by entering the equation whose output you want to evaluate in the *y(x)* = list. Even though you can use any of the locations, let us say for this illustration you have y1 = 1000(1 + 0.05*x*).

To evaluate an output while the graph is on the screen:

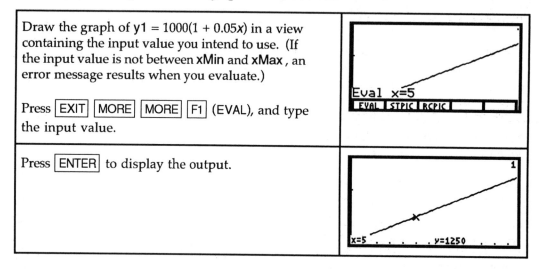

Draw the graph of y1 = 1000(1 + 0.05*x*) in a view containing the input value you intend to use. (If the input value is not between xMin and xMax, an error message results when you evaluate.) Press [EXIT] [MORE] [MORE] [F1] (EVAL), and type the input value.	
Press [ENTER] to display the output.	

To evaluate an output from the home screen:

First, press [EXIT] until you are on the home screen. Store the input value, say 5, in *x* by pressing 5 [STO▸] [x-VAR] [ENTER]. Next, type the location in the *y(x)*= list in which the equation is stored with [2nd] [ALPHA] y 1. Note that the second function key is pressed before typing the letter *y* in order to type lower-case *y*.	
The TI-85 distinguishes between lower-case and upper-case variable names. Locations in which equations are stored in the graphing list are referred to with *lower-case* letters. If you had entered Y1, you are either using another variable or a different equation stored in the calculator's memory. (Your values may be different from these.)	

| To evaluate another output, simply store the input value in x, type y1 and press ENTER.  Evaluate y1 = 1000(1 + 0.05x) at x = 2.5 and x = 7. | ```
                        2.5
y1
                       1125
7→x
                          7
y1
                       1350
``` |
|---|---|

- The values obtained by either of these evaluation processes are *actual* output values of the equation, not *estimated* values such as those generally obtained by tracing.

SECTION 1.2 FUNCTIONS AND GRAPHS

1.2.1 Evaluating Functions: Function outputs can be determined by evaluating from the graph or the home screen as discussed in 1.1.11 of this *Guide*. You can also evaluate functions using the TABLE program found in the TI-85 Appendix.

Program TABLE automates the process of evaluating from the home screen. It is illustrated below for finding outputs of the function $A = 1000(1 + 0.05x)$. *The function to be evaluated must be entered in the y1 location of the y(x)= graphing list before using the program.*

| Enter 1000(1 + 0.05x) in the y1 location of the *y(x)=* list.  Press PRGM and then press F1 (NAMES). An alphabetical list of the programs you have entered in your TI-85 appears on the bottom menu. | ```



NAMES EDIT
``` |
|---|---|
| Find the name TABLE (press MORE if necessary). Press the F-key corresponding to the location of the program to "run" the program.  If you have entered the function in y1, press 1 ENTER to continue.  Otherwise, enter 2 to exit the program, enter the function, and again run the program. | ```
TABLE
Enter equation in y1
Continue? Yes 1 No 2
``` |
| Type in the input value, press ENTER, and the evaluated function value is displayed.  Continue this process until you have finished your evaluation.  Enter ALPHA Q to end the program. | ```
Enter Q for x to end
x=5
y1=
                    1250
x=6
y1=
                    1300
x=█
``` |

1.2.2 Solving for Input Values:
Your calculator solves for input values of an equation that you enter in the SOLVER. You can use any letter you wish for the input variable when using the SOLVER. You can even enter an equation consisting of several variables!

Press 2nd GRAPH (SOLVER) to access the SOLVER.
 	
Any equations you have recently used are listed on the bottom menu. (Your list may be different than that shown to the right.)
	```eqn:█```
	
	```[ReqEq] y1 [ ][ ][ ]```

You can access a function stored in another location, such as y1 = 1000(1 + 0.05x), by pressing the F-key corresponding to the equation or you can type in a new equation.	```eqn:y1```
	
	```[ReqEq] y1 [ ][ ][ ]```

Press ENTER and you will see the last values the calculator used for y1 and x. (Your values may not be the same as those on the right.)
 	
Suppose we want to solve $A = 1000(1 + 0.05x)$ for x when $A = 1800$.
	```exp=y1```
	``` exp=1500```
	``` x=-9999999999```
	``` bound=(-1E99,1E99)```
	
	```[GRAPH][RANGE][ZOOM][TRACE][SOLVE]```

Enter 1800 for y1. (Use [▼] and/or [▲] to move between locations in the SOLVER.)
 	
The displayed bound gives the values between which the TI-85 will look for the solution to the equation.
	```exp=y1```
	``` exp=1800```
	``` x=█9999999999```
	``` bound=(-1E99,1E99)```
	
	```[GRAPH][RANGE][ZOOM][TRACE][SOLVE]```

Position the blinking cursor on the row corresponding to the variable for which you want to solve and press F5 (SOLVE).
 	
The left side of the equation, y1, evaluated at x = 16 and the right side of the equation, 1800, are subtracted and displayed in the *left-rt* row. Since this value is 0, an exact solution was found.
	```exp=y1```
	``` exp=1800```
	```•x=16```
	``` bound=(-1E99,1E99)```
	```•left-rt=0```
	
	```[GRAPH][RANGE][ZOOM][TRACE][SOLVE]```

• It is possible to change the bound and the tolerance if the calculator has trouble finding a solution to a particular equation. Refer to your Owner's Manual for details.

Suppose you want to solve the equation $-2p^3 + 8p^2 + 4p - 4 = (p + 3)^2 - 8$ for p.

Press ▲ as many times as necessary to return to the eqn location in the SOLVER. Press CLEAR.
 	
Enter the equation $-2p^3 + 8p^2 + 4p - 4 = (p + 3)^2 - 8$.
 	
The variable can be entered as either upper-case P or lower-case p, but be consistent.
	```eqn:...^2+4P-4=(P+3)²-8```
	
	 ```Re9E9 y1```
	
	 Long equations scroll to the left as you enter the symbols.

Press ENTER, be sure the blinking cursor is on the P line, and press F5 (SOLVE). There are several solutions to this equation, and the one found by the calculator is the one closest to the value that was in P before you pressed F5.
 	
Note that left–rt = 0.0000000000001, a value close enough to 0 for our purposes.
	```-2P^3+8P^2+4P-4=(P+3...```
	 `■P=-.66401564474781`
	 ` bound=(-1E99,1E99)`
	 `■left-rt=1E-13`
	
	 ```GRAPH RANGE ZOOM TRACE SOLVE```

To see that there are several solutions to this equation, let's graph it. Press F2 (RANGE) F3 (ZOOM) F5 (ZSTD). The graph that appears is the graph of the left side of the equation minus the right side of the equation, $-2p^3 + 8p^2 + 4p - 4 - (p + 3)^2 + 8$. The solutions to the original equation are where this graph crosses the horizontal axis.	 ```EDIT RANGE ZOOM TRACE SOLVE``` Notice there are three values of P where the graph of this equation crosses the P-axis.

Press F4 (TRACE) to position the cursor near the first positive solution, press EXIT to return the menu to the bottom of the screen, and then press F5 (SOLVE) to find that solution.
 	
Notice that the bound has changed to the horizontal view set by ZSTD.
	```-2P^3+8P^2+4P-4=(P+3...```
	 `■P=2.836848891301`
	 ` bound=(-10,10)`
	 `■left-rt=0`
	
	 ```GRAPH RANGE ZOOM TRACE SOLVE```

Repeat this process to find the third solution.
 	
The three solutions to the equation, recorded to five decimal places, are $P = -0.66402, 2.83685, 1.327167$.
	```-2P^3+8P^2+4P-4=(P+3...```
	 `■P=1.3271667534469`
	 ` bound=(-10,10)`
	 `■left-rt=0`
	
	 ```GRAPH RANGE ZOOM TRACE SOLVE```

1.2.3 Graphically Finding Intercepts:

To find the y-intercept of a function $y = f(x)$, set $x=0$ and solve the resulting equation. To find the x-intercept of a function $y = f(x)$, set $y=0$ and solve the resulting equation. The solving process can be done graphically as well as by the methods indicated in 1.2.2 of this *Guide*.

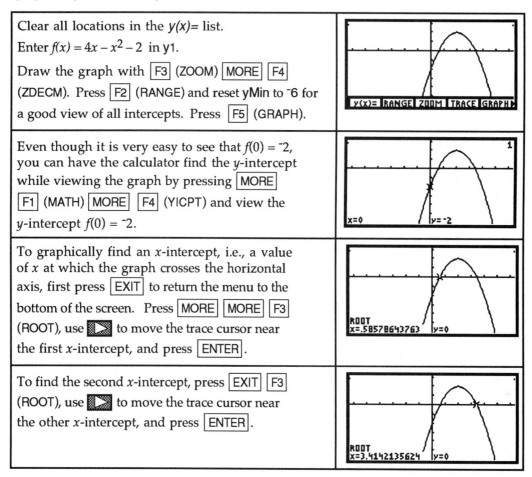

Clear all locations in the $y(x)=$ list. Enter $f(x) = 4x - x^2 - 2$ in y1. Draw the graph with [F3] (ZOOM) [MORE] [F4] (ZDECM). Press [F2] (RANGE) and reset yMin to ⁻6 for a good view of all intercepts. Press [F5] (GRAPH).	
Even though it is very easy to see that $f(0) = $⁻2, you can have the calculator find the y-intercept while viewing the graph by pressing [MORE] [F1] (MATH) [MORE] [F4] (YICPT) and view the y-intercept $f(0) = $⁻2.	
To graphically find an x-intercept, i.e., a value of x at which the graph crosses the horizontal axis, first press [EXIT] to return the menu to the bottom of the screen. Press [MORE] [MORE] [F3] (ROOT), use ▶ to move the trace cursor near the first x-intercept, and press [ENTER].	
To find the second x-intercept, press [EXIT] [F3] (ROOT), use ▶ to move the trace cursor near the other x-intercept, and press [ENTER].	

1.2.4 Combining Functions:

The TI-85 can easily draw the graph of the sum, difference, product, quotient, and composition of two functions. You can use the home screen or program TABLE to determine outputs for function combinations.

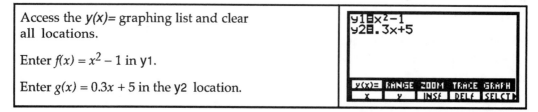

Access the $y(x)=$ graphing list and clear all locations. Enter $f(x) = x^2 - 1$ in y1. Enter $g(x) = 0.3x + 5$ in the y2 location.	

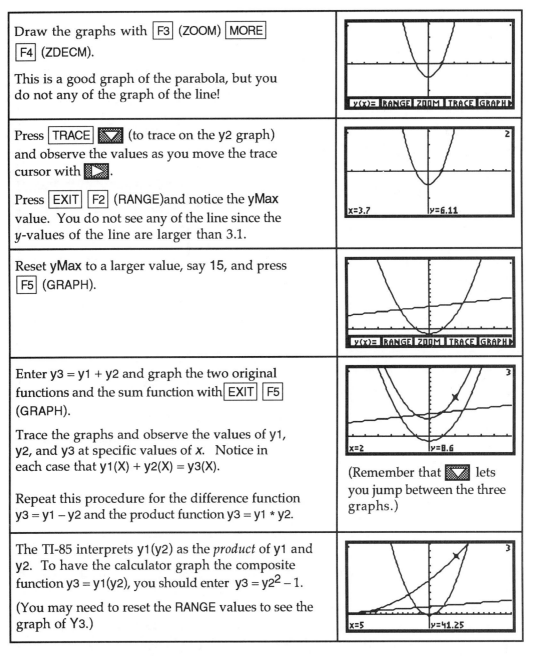

Draw the graphs with [F3] (ZOOM) [MORE] [F4] (ZDECM). This is a good graph of the parabola, but you do not any of the graph of the line!	
Press [TRACE] [▼] (to trace on the y2 graph) and observe the values as you move the trace cursor with [▶]. Press [EXIT] [F2] (RANGE)and notice the yMax value. You do not see any of the line since the *y*-values of the line are larger than 3.1.	
Reset yMax to a larger value, say 15, and press [F5] (GRAPH).	
Enter y3 = y1 + y2 and graph the two original functions and the sum function with [EXIT] [F5] (GRAPH). Trace the graphs and observe the values of y1, y2, and y3 at specific values of *x*. Notice in each case that y1(X) + y2(X) = y3(X). Repeat this procedure for the difference function y3 = y1 − y2 and the product function y3 = y1 * y2.	(Remember that [▼] lets you jump between the three graphs.)
The TI-85 interprets y1(y2) as the *product* of y1 and y2. To have the calculator graph the composite function y3 = y1(y2), you should enter y3 = y2^2 − 1. (You may need to reset the RANGE values to see the graph of Y3.)	

- If you do not want to view the menu at the bottom of the graphics screen when investigating a graph you have drawn, press [CLEAR] to temporarily remove the menu. [EXIT] returns the menu to the bottom of the graphics screen.

SECTION 1.3 LINEAR FUNCTIONS AND MODELS

1.3.1 Entering Data: There are several ways to input data in the TI-85. Two of these, entering data from the home screen and entering data using the list editor, are discussed below.

Enter the following data:

x	1984	1985	1987	1990	1992
y	37	35	29	20	14

To enter data from the home screen,	`(1984,1985,1987,1990,`
	`1992)→L1`
	`(1984 1985 1987 1990…`

Return to the home screen with 2nd EXIT (QUIT).	
Press 2nd − (LIST), press F1 ({) to begin the list, type in each of the x-data values separated by commas, and end the list with F2 (}).	`< { } NAMES EDIT OPS`
Store this list to the name with L1 with STO▸ L ALPHA 1 ENTER.	

To enter data using the list editor,	`LIST:L2`
	`e1=37`
	`e2=35`
	`e3=29`

Press 2nd − (LIST) F4 (EDIT) to access the list editor. Enter the name L2 at the name prompt and press ENTER.	`e4=20`
	`e5=14`
	`e6=`
	`INSi DELi ▸REAL`

If there are data values in this list, see 1.3.3 of this *Guide* and first delete the "old" data.	
Enter the first y-value as e1, press ENTER or ▼, enter the second y-value as e2, etc.	

1.3.2 Editing Data: If you incorrectly type a data value, access the data with the list editor and use the cursor keys to move to the value you wish to correct. Type the correct value and press ENTER.

To *insert* a data value, put the cursor over the value that will be directly below the one you will insert, and press F1 (INSi). The values in the list below the insertion point move down one location and a 0 is filled in at the insertion point. Type the data value to be inserted and press ENTER. The 0 is replaced with the new value.

To *delete* a single data value, move the cursor to the value you wish to delete, and press F2 (DELi). The values in the list below the deleted value move up one location.

1.3.3 Deleting Old Data: Whenever you enter new data in your calculator, you should first delete any previously-entered data using one of the following methods:

Whenever you enter data from the home screen, previously-entered data is automatically replaced with new data. Thus, {1, 2, 3} STO▸ L2 replaces the "old" L2.

When you enter the list editor and there is "old" data in the list, position the cursor over the e1 value and repeatedly press F2 (DELᵢ) until all data is deleted.

1.3.4 Aligning Data: Suppose you want L1 to contain the number of years since a certain year (here, 1984) instead of actual years. That is, you want to *align* the x-data.

Return to the home screen. Replace the L1 values with L1 − 1984 values by pressing ALPHA L1 − 1984 STO▸ L ALPHA 1 ENTER. L1 now contains the aligned x-values.	`L1-1984→L1` `          ⟨0  1  3  6  8⟩`

1.3.5 Plotting Data: The TI-85 command Scatter L1, L2 draws a scatterplot of L1 versus L1. However, you must set an appropriate RANGE before using this command. Program STPLT found in the TI-85 Appendix automates this task. Any functions you have in the y(x)= graphing list will graph when you plot data. Therefore, you should delete them or turn them off before drawing a scatterplot.

Access the y(x)= graphing list. If any entered function is no longer needed, delete it with F4 (DELf) or clear it with CLEAR. If you want the function to remain but do not want it to graph, position the cursor in that function location and press F5 (SELCT).	`y1=x²-1` A "turned off" function.
Press PRGM and then press F1 (NAMES). Find the name STPLT (press MORE if necessary).	Press the F-key corresponding to the location of STPLT to run the program.
Press CLEAR to remove the menu from the bottom of the screen for a better view.	

- Program STPLT sets the *x* and *y*-axis tick marks to 0 so they do not interfere with your view of the scatterplot.

- Because the dots the calculator uses to plot data are sometimes difficult to see when overdrawing the model of best fit, the program places a small box around each data point. (The boxes may appear a slightly different size due to the screen.)

- Even though the TI-85 generally allows you to call lists by any names you want, *you must enter the input data in the list named L1 and the output data in the list named L2* when using program STPLT.

- Lists L1 and L2 must be of the same length or an error message results.

- It is not possible to trace a scatterplot drawn on the TI-85.

1.3.6 Finding First Differences:

When the input values are evenly spaced, use program DIFF to compute first differences in the output values. If the data is perfectly linear (i.e., every data point falls on the linear model), the first differences in the output values are constant. If the first differences are "close" to constant, this is an indication that a linear model *may* be appropriate.

Program DIFF is given in the TI-85 Appendix.
 	
To run the program, press PRGM followed by the F-key under the name of the program and press ENTER.
 	
The message on the right appears on your screen.
	`Store x-values in L1`
	`Store y-values in L2`
	`Continue? Yes 1 No 2`

If you have not entered the data, stop the program by pressing 2 ENTER.
 	
To continue the program, press 1 ENTER.
	`Continue? Yes 1 No 2`
	`1`
	`See the`
	`1st difference in L3`
	`2nd difference in L4`
	`percent change in L5`
	`                Done`

View list L3 containing the first differences in the output data by pressing 2nd – (LIST) F4 (EDIT) F3 (L3) ENTER.	`LIST:L3`
	`e1=-2`
	`e2=-6`
	`e3=-9`
	`e4=-6`
	
	`INSi  DELi  REAL`

- Notice the results of program DIFF are **not valid** for the data in the above example because the *x*-values in this example are *not* evenly spaced. The first differences give no information about a possible linear fit to these data.

- Don't be concerned with the results appearing in lists L4 and L5 -- they are used in later sections.

1.3.7 Finding a Linear Model: Use your calculator to obtain the linear model that best fits two-variable data. The linear model found by the TI-85 is accessed with the command LINR in the statistics menu and is of the form $y = a + bx$.

It is possible to enter data while in the statistics mode of the TI-85. However, the examples in this *Guide* assume that input data is already entered in list L1 and output data is in list L2.
 	
 Press $\boxed{\text{STAT}}$ $\boxed{\text{F1}}$ (CALC) and press the F-keys on the menu to enter L1 as the xlist Name and L2 as the ylist Name. Press $\boxed{\text{ENTER}}$ after each entry.
	```xlist Name=L1```
	 ```ylist Name=L2```
	
	 CALC EDIT DRAW FCST
	 xStat yStat L1 L2 L3 ▶
	
	 Use L1 = {0 1 3 6 8} and
	 L2 = {37 35 29 20 14}.

Choose the linear model with $\boxed{\text{F2}}$ (LINR).
 	
 The y-intercept, a, and the slope, b, of the model is displayed along with the value of the correlation coefficient, corr = r, and the number, n, of data points.
	```LinR```
	 ```a=37.5132743363```
	 ```b=-2.9203539823```
	 ```corr=-.999334915702```
	 ```n=5```
	
	 CALC EDIT DRAW FCST
	 1-VAR LINR LNR EXPR PWRR ▶

1.3.8 Pasting a Model into the Function List: To overdraw the model on the scatterplot of the data, copy the model into the $y(x)=$ graphing list. The values found by the calculator should *not* be rounded. This is not a problem because the calculator will paste the entire model into the function list!

Press $\boxed{\text{MORE}}$ $\boxed{\text{F4}}$ (STREG) and at the Name= prompt, type in y1 with the keystrokes $\boxed{\text{2nd}}$ $\boxed{\text{ALPHA}}$ y $\boxed{\text{ALPHA}}$ $\boxed{\text{ALPHA}}$ 1. Press $\boxed{\text{ENTER}}$.
 	
 Remember that you must use a lower-case *y* to refer to functions in the $y(x)=$ graphing list.
 	
 (Any function currently in y1 will be replaced with the linear model.)
	```LinR```
	 ```a=37.5132743363```
	 ```b=-2.9203539823```
	 ```corr=-.999334915702```
	 ```n=5```
	 ```Name=y1```
	 CALC EDIT DRAW FCST
	 P2REG P3REG P4REG STREG

Press $\boxed{\text{GRAPH}}$ $\boxed{\text{F1}}$ ($y(x)=$) to see the equation of the model in the y1 location. If you cannot see all of the equation, press the right arrow key to scroll the screen to the right.	```y1□...2.9203539823009x``` y(x)= RANGE ZOOM TRACE GRAPH x y INSf DELf SELCT ▶

1.3.9 Graphing a Model: You should always overdraw the model on the scatterplot to check the fit to the data.

After you have copied the model to the *y(x)=* list, run program STPLT to graph the model and the scatter plot on the same screen. The model will graph first and then the scatter plot will appear. (Pressing ENTER should re-run program STPLT.)	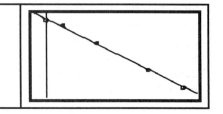

1.3.10 Predictions Using a Model: Use one of the methods described in 1.1.11 or 1.2.1 of this *Guide* to evaluate the linear model at the desired input value. Remember, if you have aligned your data, the input value at which you evaluate the model may not be the value given in the question you are asked.

Predict the value of $y(x) = 37.513274 + {}^{-}2.92036x$ in 1988 from the graphics menu using EVAL. (Remember that you should always use the full model, i.e., the function in y1, for all computations.) Note that 1988 is four years since 1984, so $x = 4$.	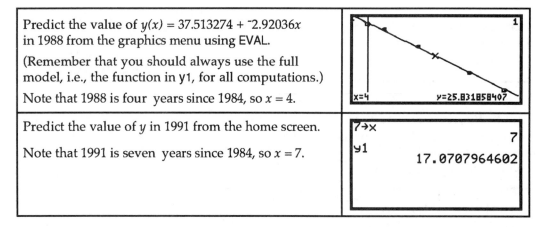
Predict the value of y in 1991 from the home screen. Note that 1991 is seven years since 1984, so $x = 7$.	

1.3.11 Copying Graphs to Paper: Your instructor may ask you to copy what is on your graphics screen to paper. If so, refer to the RANGE set by the calculator in order to help determine values to place on your input and output axes. Place a scale (tick marks) on each axis and plot the data values to draw the scatterplot. To help in drawing the model on paper, do the following:

Press GRAPH to return the graph to the screen. Press F4 (TRACE) to trace the graph. Use ▶ and/or ◀ to locate several values that are as "nice" as possible and mark those points on your paper. Use a ruler to connect the linear model points.	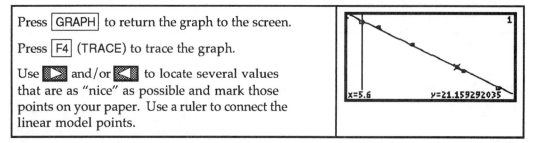

1.3.12 What Is "Best Fit"? Even though the TI-85 easily computes the values a and b for the best fitting linear model $y = a + bx$, it is important to understand the method of least-squares and the conditions necessary for its application if you intend to use this model. You can explore the process of finding the line of best fit with program **LSLINE**. (Program LSLINE is given in the TI-85 Appendix.) For your investigations of the least-squares process with this program, it is better to use data that is not perfectly linear and data for which you do *not* know the best-fitting line.

Before using **LSLINE**, clear the *y(x)=* list and enter your data in lists L1 and L2. Next, use program STPLT to draw a scatterplot. Press `F2` (RANGE) and reset xScl and yScl so that you can use the tick marks to help identify points on the graphics screen.

To run program LSLINE, press `PRGM` `F1` (NAMES) followed by the F-key under the program, and press `ENTER`. (Since the TI-85 "loads" each program in memory when you run it, longer programs such as this one take a moment before anything appears on the screen.)

The program first informs you that you will see the scatterplot of the data and use the tick marks you set to help you guess the slope and y-intercept of *some* line you estimate will go "through" the data. (You should not expect to guess the best fit line on your first try!) The values you set for xScl and yScl are also displayed. Press `ENTER` after you have read the message. The program then displays the scatterplot of the data and pauses for you to view the screen and estimate the slope and y-intercept of the line of best fit.

- While the program is calculating, there is a small vertical line in the upper-right hand corner of the graphics screen that is dashed and "moving". The program pauses several times during execution. Whenever this happens, the small vertical line is "still". You should press `ENTER` to resume execution.

After you enter a guess for the y-intercept and slope, your line is drawn and the errors are shown as vertical line segments on the graph. After you again press `ENTER`, the sum of squares of errors, SSE, is displayed for your line. Choose the **Try again** option by pressing 1 `ENTER`. View the graph and decide whether you want to move the y-intercept of the line or change its slope to improve the fit to the data. After you enter another guess for the y-intercept and/or slope, the process of viewing your line, the errors, and display of SSE is repeated. If the new value of SSE is smaller than the SSE for your first guess, you have improved the fit. When it is felt that an SSE value close to the minimum value is found, you should choose 2 at the **Try again** prompt. The coefficients a and b of the best-fitting linear model $y = ax + b$ are then displayed. `ENTER` causes the program to overdraw the line of best fit on the graph for comparison with your last attempt. Pressing `ENTER` then shows the line of best fit and the errors for the line of best fit. Press `ENTER` once more to display the minimum SSE, and press `ENTER` to end the program. Use program LSLINE to explore finding the line of best fit.

1.3.13 Finding SSE for a Line: The TI-85 lists are useful when finding the deviation (error) of *each* data point from a line entered in the *y(x)=* list and then computing SSE.

Use either the home screen method or the list editor method to enter the following lists: L1 = {0 1 3 6 8} and L2 = {37 35 29 20 14}. Refer to 1.3.7 and 1.3.8 of this *Guide* to find the best fitting linear model to these data and paste it in y1.	```y1■37.513274336284+-…``` y(x)= RANGE ZOOM TRACE GRAPH x y INSf DELf SELCT▶

Delete the "old" values from list L3 with
0 STO▶ L3 ENTER.
 	
Evaluate the model at each of the *x*-values in L1 and store those values in L3 like this:
 	
On the home screen, store 0 in x, evaluate y1, and store that value in the first position of list L3.
	```0→x 0```
	```y1```
	``` 37.5132743363```
	```Ans→L3(1)```
	``` 37.5132743363```
	
	L3(k) is the kth position in L3.

Store 1 in x, evaluate y1, and store that value in the second position of list L3, etc. until all five *x*-values have been evaluated and stored.	``` 37.5132743363```
	```1→x 1```
	```y1```
	``` 34.592920354```
	```Ans→L3(2)```
	``` 34.592920354```

Check that L3 now contains the values shown on the right.
 	
Return to the home screen.
	```LIST:L3```
	```e1=37.513274336284```
	```e2=34.592920353983```
	```e3=28.752212389381```
	```e4=19.991150442479```
	```e5=14.150442477877```
	
	INSi DELi ▶REAL

Enter the deviation = error = $y_{data} - y_{line}$ in L4 by typing L2 – L3 STO▶ L4.
 	
Enter the squares of each of the errors in list L5 with L4 x^2 STO▶ L5.
	```L2-L3→L4```
	```{-.513274336284 .407…```
	```L4²→L5```
	```{.263450544288 .1657…```
	
	{ } NAMES EDIT OPS
	L1 L2 L3 L4 L5 ▶

Return to the home screen and compute SSE, the sum of the squared errors, as sum L5 by pressing 2nd – (LIST) F5 (OPS) MORE F1 (SUM) L5 ENTER.	```sum L5```
	``` .513274336283```
	
	{ } NAMES EDIT OPS
	sum prod seq ▶dvc vc▶li ▶

CHAPTER 2.   THE INGREDIENTS OF CHANGE: NON-LINEAR MODELS

SECTION 2.1: EXPONENTIAL FUNCTIONS AND MODELS

2.1.1 Finding Percentage Change: When the input values are evenly spaced, use program DIFF to compute percentage change in the output values. If the data is perfectly exponential (i.e., every data point falls on the model of best fit), the percentage change in the output values is constant. If the percentage change is "close" to constant, this is an indication that an exponential model *may* be appropriate.

Clear any old data, and enter the following in lists L1 and L2:

x	0	1	2	3	4	5	6	7
y	23	38.4	64	107	179	299	499	833

Run program DIFF and observe the percentage change in list L5. The percentage change is very close to constant, so an exponential model may be a good fit.	LIST:L5 e1=66.95652173913 e2=66.666666666667 e3=67.1875 e4=67.289719626168 e5=67.039106145251 ↓e6=66.889632107023 **INSi DELi ▸REAL**

- You should always construct a scatterplot of the data either before or after using program DIFF. For the data in this example, the scatterplot confirms that an exponential model certainly seems appropriate!

2.1.2 Finding an Exponential Model: Use your calculator to obtain the exponential model that best fits the data. The exponential model found by the TI-85 is accessed with the command EXPR in the statistics menu and is of the form $y = ab^x$.

Press ⬜STAT ⬜F1 (CALC) and press the F-keys on the menu to enter L1 as the xlist Name and L2 as the ylist Name. Press ⬜ENTER after each entry. If these names already appear, just press ⬜ENTER ⬜ENTER.	xlist Name=L1 ylist Name=L2 **CALC EDIT DRAW FCST** **xStat yStat L1 L2 L3 ▸**
Choose the exponential model with ⬜F4 (EXPR). The best fitting exponential model is displayed on the screen. Copy the model to the *y(x)=* list, overdraw the graph on the scatterplot with STPLT, and see that it gives a very good fit to the data.	EXPR a=22.9823536435 b=1.67023009783 corr=.99999972229 n=8 Name=y1 **CALC EDIT DRAW FCST** **P2REG P3REG P4REG STREG**

2.1.3 Finding a Logistics Model: Use your calculator to obtain the logistics model with limiting value L that best fits the data. Use program LOGISTIC to fit the logistic model $y = \dfrac{L}{1 + Ae^{-Bx}}$. (Program LOGISTIC is given in the TI-85 Appendix.)

Clear any old data, and enter the following in lists L1 and L2:

x	0	1	2	3	4	5
y	1	2	4	6	8	9

Construct a scatterplot of the data. A logistics model seems appropriate. Run program LOGISTIC by pressing PRGM followed by the number of the location of the program and press ENTER.	

The program gives you some information.	`Have data in L₁,L₂`
	
	 `Program clears L₃,L₄`
	 `and leaves eq in y2`
	
	 `ENTER continues.`

After again showing a scatterplot of the data, ENTER draws a graph of a *possible* logistics model fit to the data. This may or may not be the best-fitting logistics model. (Usually, it will *not* be the best fit.)	

Press ENTER and observe the values of the quantities shown on the right. SSY is the *total variation* of the output variable. SSY gives the maximum value for SSE, the sum of squared errors. SSE changes with different limiting values L, but SSY remains constant for a particular data set.	`SSY=`
	 `                  52`
	 `L=`
	 `      9.77528089888`
	 `SSE=`
	 `      .053991456092`

Press ENTER and choose option 1: Change L by pressing 1 ENTER. At the L=? prompt, type 11 and press ENTER.	`SELECT ONE:`
	 `Change L        (1)`
	 `Change L,graph  (2)`
	 `Quit on graph   (3)`
	 `Quit on model   (4) 1`
	 `L=?`

The SSE for L=11 along with the previous value for SSE are displayed. The fit is not as good as when using L = 9.77528089888 because the SSE value is higher.	```
	Quit on graph (3)
	Quit on model (4) 1
	L=?11
	Previous SSE=
	          .053991456092
	SSE=
	          .243100779268
	``

Press ENTER and choose option 1: Change L by pressing 1 ENTER. At the L=? prompt, type 10 and press ENTER.
 	
The SSE value and the context of the problem confirm that a limiting value of 10 seems best in this situation.
	``
	Quit on graph (3)
	Quit on model (4) 1
	L=?10
	Previous SSE=
	          .243100779268
	SSE=
	          .033240812293
	``
	You should try different limiting values *L* until the lowest SSE is determined.

To visually verify the fit, press ENTER and choose option 2: Change L, graph. At the L=? prompt, type 10 and press ENTER. (If you want to view the graph each time you change *L*, always choose option 2 instead of option 1.)	

Press ENTER twice, and choose option 4: Quit on Model by pressing 4 ENTER.	```
	y=L/(1+Ae^(-Bx))
	   L= 10
	
	   A= 9.22111412672
	
	   B= .888598347323
	
	SSE= .033240812293
	``

If you now want to *view* the graph of this model or trace it, press GRAPH F1 (y(x)=), move the cursor to the y2 line, and press F5 (SELCT) ENTER F5 (GRAPH). To view the scatterplot and the model, run program STPLT after selecting y2.	``` y2=L/(1+A e^(-B x)) y(x)= RANGE ZOOM TRACE GRAPH X Y INSf DELf SELCT▶ ```
If you choose option 3: Quit on graph instead of option 4, the graph is automatically displayed and selected and the last instruction above is not necessary.	``` SELECT ONE: Change L (1) Change L,graph (2) Quit on graph (3) Quit on model (4) 3 ```

If you want to use this model in program TABLE, it must be in location y1. To copy the equation to y1, use ▨ to move the cursor to that location or press [F3] (INSf) if y1 does not appear the screen.
 	
 [2nd] [STO▸] (RCL) [F2] (y) [ALPHA] [2] [ENTER] recalls the equation to y1.
	```y1=```
	```y2=L/(1+A e^(-B x))```
	
	```Rcl y1```
	`y(x)= RANGE ZOOM TRACE GRAPH`
	`  x    y   INSf DELf SELCT▸`

If you need to recall the values of A and B for the logistics model, return to the home screen and type [ALPHA] [LOG] (A) [ENTER] and then [ALPHA] [SIN] (B) [ENTER].	```A```
	``` 9.22111412672```
	```B```
	``` .888598347323```

- Program DIFF might be helpful when you are trying to determine if a logistics model is appropriate for certain data. If the first differences (in list L3 after running program DIFF) *begin small, peak in the middle,* and *end small,* this is an indication that a logistics model *may* provide a good fit to the data. (For this particular example, there is not enough data for DIFF to be helpful.)

2.1.4 Random Numbers:

Imagine all the real numbers between 0 and 1, including the 0 but not the 1, written on identical slips of paper and placed in a hat. Close your eyes and draw one slip of paper from the hat. You have just chosen a number "at random". Your calculator doesn't offer you a choice of all real numbers between 0 and 1, but it allows you to choose, *with an equal chance of obtaining each one,* any of 10^{14} different numbers between 0 and 1 with its random number generator called rand.

First, "seed" the random number generator. (This is like mixing up all the slips of paper in the hat.)
 	
 Pick some number, <u>not</u> the one shown on the right, and store it as the "seed". (Everyone needs to have a different seed, or the choice will not be random.)
 	
 The random number generator is accessed with [2nd] [X] (MATH) [F2] (PROB) [F4] (rand).
	```2587→rand```
	``` 2587```
	
	`NUM  PROB ANGLE HYP   MISC`
	`  !   nPr  nCr  rand`

Enter rand again and press [ENTER] several times. Your list of random numbers should be different from the one on the right.	```rand```
	``` .765718263504```
	``` .214692618914```
	``` .006287071174```
	``` .895737735569```
	`NUM  PROB ANGLE HYP   MISC`
	`  !   nPr  nCr  rand`

If you want to choose, at random, a whole number between 1 and N, enter int(N rand + 1) by pressing [2nd] [X] (MATH) [F1] (NUM) [F4] (int) [( ] N [2nd] [F2] (PROB) [F4] (rand) [+] [1] [ )] [ENTER] for a specific value of N. Repeatedly press [ENTER] to choose more random numbers. For instance, the screen to the right shows several values that were chosen at random with $N = 10$.	`int (10 rand+1)`
	             5
	             7
	             2
	             9
	`NUM  PROB ANGLE HYP  MISC`
	`  !   nPr  nCr  rand   `

SECTION 2.2 EXPONENTIAL MODELS IN FINANCE

2.2.1 Replay of Previous Entries to Find Formula Outputs: You can recall the last expression you typed using the calculator's last entry feature. Because the TI-85 will not recall more than the last entry, multiple commands must be entered on the same line if you want to recall them all using the last entry feature.

On the home screen, store 1 in n, press [2nd] [.] (:) to join statements on one line, and type the amount formula $\left(1+\frac{1}{n}\right)^{n}$. Press [ENTER]. (You can use either upper-case or lower-case n, but be consistent.)	`1→N:(1+1/N)^N` 2

To find the output when $n = 2$, recall the last entry with [2nd] [ENTER] (ENTRY), use ◄ to position the cursor over the 1 in "1→ N" and type 2. Press [ENTER]. The formula is now evaluated at $n = 2$.
 	
Store 3 in n and repeat the procedure.
	`1→N:(1+1/N)^N`
	               2
	`2→N:(1+1/N)^N`
	            2.25
	`3→N:(1+1/N)^N`
	      2.37037037037

- Since this formula contains only one input variable, you could enter it in the *y(x)=* list, using *x* as the input variable, and find the outputs using program TABLE.

- When the formula contains more than one input variable, it is easier to recall the last entry on the home screen than to try to use program TABLE. To illustrate, consider the simple interest formula -- one that contains several input variables.

   The formula for the amount in an account paying *r*% simple interest on an initial deposit of $P over a period of *t* years is $A = P(1 + rt)$. The value obtained depends on the values stored in *P*, *R*, and *T*.

Store 100 in P, 0.05 in R, 1 in T and type the simple interest formula, using the colon to join all statements. Carefully watch the screen as you type. STO▸ puts the cursor in alphabetic mode, so you must press ALPHA before typing the colon.	``` 100→P:.05→R:1→T:P(1+R *T) 105 ```

Recall the last entry with 2nd ENTER (ENTRY), use ◀ to move the cursor, and edit the statements to determine the accumulated amount if $500 is invested at 5% interest for 3 years.	```
	100→P:.05→R:1→T:P(1+R
	*T)
	                      105
	500→P:.05→R:3→T:P(1+R
	*T)
	                      575
	``

- Use the last entry feature as described above to find future value.

2.2.2 Finding Present Value:
The present value of an investment is easily found with the calculator's SOLVER. For instance, suppose you want to solve the equation

$$9438.40 = P\left(1 + \frac{0.075}{12}\right)^{60}$$ for the present value P.

Refer to 1.2.2 of this *Guide* for instructions on using the TI-85's SOLVER. Enter the equation on the right.	``` 9438.4=P(1+.075/12)^… P=500 bound=(-1E99,1E99) GRAPH RANGE ZOOM TRACE SOLVE ```
Solve for P to obtain the present value $6494.49. If you prefer, you could find the x-intercept of y1 = 9438.4 − x(1+.075/12)^60 to find the present value. Refer to 1.2.3 of this *Guide* for more detailed instructions.	``` 9438.4=P(1+.075/12)^… ■P=6494.4858703432 ■bound=(-1E99,1E99) ■left−rt=1E-10 GRAPH RANGE ZOOM TRACE SOLVE ```

SECTION 2.3 POLYNOMIAL FUNCTIONS AND MODELS

2.3.1 Finding Second Differences: When the input values are evenly spaced, use program DIFF to compute second differences in the output values. If the data is perfectly quadratic (i.e., every data point falls on the quadratic model), the second differences in the output values are constant. If the second differences are "close" to constant, this is an indication that a quadratic model *may* be appropriate.

Clear any old data, and enter the following in lists L1 and L2:

x	0	1	2	3	4	5
y	12	14	22	35	54	80

Run program DIFF and observe the second differences in list L4.
 	
The second differences are close to constant, so a quadratic model may be a good fit.
 	
Construct a scatterplot of the data. A quadratic model seems appropriate!
	LIST:L4
	  e1=6
	  e2=5
	  e3=6
	  e4=7
	
	 INSi DELi ⊳REAL

2.3.2 Finding a Quadratic Model:
Use your calculator to obtain the quadratic model that best fits the data. The quadratic model found by the TI-85 is accessed with the command P2REG in the statistics menu and is of the form $y = ax^2 + bx + c$.

Press STAT F1 (CALC) and press the F-keys on the menu to enter L1 as the xlist Name and L2 as the ylist Name. Press ENTER after each entry. If these names already appear, just press ENTER ENTER.	xlist Name=L1 ylist Name=L2 CALC EDIT DRHW FCST xStat yStat L1 L2 L3 ▸

Choose the quadratic model with MORE F1 (P2REG).
 	
The best fitting quadratic model is displayed.
The coefficients of the model $y = ax^2 + bx + c$ are displayed in the list $\{a,b,c\}$ that can be scrolled with ▸ for viewing.
	P2Reg
	  n=6
	  PRegC=
	  (2.92857142857 -1.12...
	Name=y1
	 CALC EDIT DRHW FCST
	 P2REG P3REG P4REG STREG

Copy the model to the $y(x)=$ list, overdraw the graph on the scatterplot with program STPLT, and see that this model gives a very good fit to the data.	

2.3.3 Finding a Cubic Model: Whenever a scatterplot of the data shows a single change in concavity, a cubic or logistic model is appropriate. If a limiting value is apparent, use the logistic model. Otherwise, a cubic model should be considered. When appropriate, use your calculator to obtain the cubic model that best fits data. The TI-85's cubic model is accessed with **P3REG** and is of the form $y = ax^3 + bx^2 + cx + d$.

Clear any old data, and enter the following in lists L1 and L2:

Year	'80	'81	'82	'83	'84	'85	'86	'87	'88	'89	'90
Price	3.68	4.29	5.17	6.06	6.12	6.12	5.83	5.54	5.47	5.64	5.77

First, align the data so that x represents the number of years since 1980.	L1 {80 81 82 83 84 85 8… L2 {3.68 4.29 5.17 6.06… L1−80→L1 {0 1 2 3 4 5 6 7 8 9… ◄ ► NAMES EDIT OPS
Draw a scatterplot of these data with STPLT. Notice that a concavity change is evident, but there do not appear to be any limiting values. Thus, a cubic model may fit the data.	
Press STAT F1 (CALC) and enter L1 as the xlist Name and L2 as the ylist Name. Choose the cubic model with MORE F2 (P3REG). The best fitting cubic model is displayed. The coefficients of the model $y = ax^3 + bx^2 + cx + d$ are displayed in the list $\{a, b, c, d\}$ that can be scrolled with ▶ for viewing.	P3Reg n=11 PRegC= {.012435897436 -.242… CALC EDIT DRAW FCST P2REG P3REG P4REG STREG
Copy the model to the $y(x)=$ list using the STREG key, and overdraw the graph on the scatterplot with program STPLT.	

CHAPTER 3.   DESCRIBING CHANGE: RATES

SECTION 3.1: AVERAGE RATES OF CHANGE

3.1.1 Finding Average Rates of Change:

Finding the average rate of change using a model is just a matter of evaluating the model at two different values of the input variable and dividing by the difference in those input values. Let us consider the example where the April temperature is given by $temperature = {}^-0.8t^2 + 2t + 79$ $^\circ$F where $t = 0$ at noon and we wish to calculate the average rate of change between 11 a.m. and 6 p.m.

Enter the model in the y1 location of the *y(x)=* graphing list.
 	
(Remember that you must use *x* as the input variable in the graphing list.)
	`y1=-.8 x²+2 x+79`
	
	`y(x)= RANGE ZOOM TRACE GRAPH`
	`  x    y    INSf  DELf  SELCT▶`

Return to the home screen with 2nd EXIT (QUIT).
 	
Store ⁻1 (11 a.m.) in *x* and evaluate the model.
 	
Store this result, for easy recall, in some variable, say *A*.
	`-1→x`
	`                   -1`
	`y1`
	`                 76.2`
	`Ans→A`
	`                 76.2`

Store 6 (6 p.m.) in *x* and evaluate the model.
 	
Store this result, for easy recall, in another variable, say *B*.
	`6→x`
	`                    6`
	`y1`
	`                 62.2`
	`Ans→B`
	`                 62.2`

Evaluate the average rate of change $\dfrac{B-A}{6-{}^-1}$. Remember that you must enclose the numerator and denominator of a fraction in parentheses when either consists of more than one term.	`(B-A)/(6--1)` `                   -2`

You could use program **TABLE** to evaluate the model at the input values. However, when the output values are not "nice" numbers, you will find the above described method results in less chance of making an error.	`x=6`
	`y1=`
	`                 62.2`
	`x=Q`
	`               Done`
	`(62.2-76.2)/(6--1)`
	`                   -2`

SECTION 3.4: DERIVATIVES

3.4.1 Magnifying a Portion of a Graph:
The ZOOM menu of the TI-85 allows you to magnify any portion of the graph of a function. Suppose we are investigating the graph of $y = {}^-x^2 + 40x + 50$ and the tangent line, $y = 20x + 150$, to the graph of this function at $x = 10$.

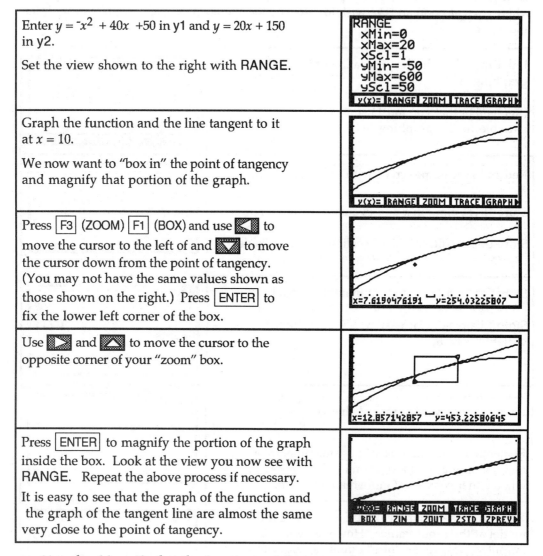

Enter $y = {}^-x^2 + 40x + 50$ in y1 and $y = 20x + 150$ in y2.

Set the view shown to the right with RANGE.

Graph the function and the line tangent to it at $x = 10$.

We now want to "box in" the point of tangency and magnify that portion of the graph.

Press F3 (ZOOM) F1 (BOX) and use ◄ to move the cursor to the left of and ▼ to move the cursor down from the point of tangency. (You may not have the same values shown as those shown on the right.) Press ENTER to fix the lower left corner of the box.

Use ► and ▲ to move the cursor to the opposite corner of your "zoom" box.

Press ENTER to magnify the portion of the graph inside the box. Look at the view you now see with RANGE. Repeat the above process if necessary.

It is easy to see that the graph of the function and the graph of the tangent line are almost the same very close to the point of tangency.

- You should verify that the function and its tangent have close output values near the point of tangency by tracing the graphs near the point of tangency. Recall that you jump from one function to the other with ▲ or ▼ and that the number in the upper right-hand corner of the screen tells you on which function you are tracing.

SECTION 3.5: PERCENTAGE CHANGE AND PERCENTAGE RATES OF CHANGE

3.5.1 Percentage Change and Percentage Rates of Change: Recall that program DIFF stores percentage change in data in list L5. Consider the following data giving quarterly earnings for a business:

Quarter ending	Mar '93	June '93	Sept '93	Dec '93	Mar '94	June '94
Earnings (in millions)	27.3	28.9	24.6	32.1	29.4	27.7

Align the input data so that x is the number of quarters since March, 1993, and input x in L1 and earnings (in millions) in L2.	(0,1,2,3,4,5)→L1 (0 1 2 3 4 5) (27.3,28.9,24.6,32.1, 29.4,27.7)→L2 (27.3 28.9 24.6 32.1…
Run program DIFF and view the percentage change in list L5. Notice that the percentage change from the end of Sept '93 through Dec '93 is approximately 30.5%. Also, from the end of March '94 through June '94, the percentage change is approximately ⁻5.8%.	LIST:L5 e₁=5.8608058608059 e₂=⁻14.878892733564 e₃=30.487804878049 e₄=⁻8.411214953271 e₅=⁻5.7823129251701
You may find it easier to calculate these using the percentage change formula than have the program do it for you.	(32.1−24.6)/24.6:Ans∗ 100 30.487804878 (27.7−29.4)/29.4:Ans∗ 100 ⁻5.78231292517

To evaluate percentage rate of change at a point, suppose you are told or otherwise find that the rate of change at the end of the June, 1993 is 1.8 million dollars per quarter.

Divide the rate of change at the end of June, 1993 by the earnings, in millions, at the end of June, 1993 and multiply by 100 to obtain the percentage rate of change at that point. The percentage rate of change in earnings at the end of June, 1993 is approximately 6.2% per quarter.	1.8/28.9 .062283737024 Ans∗100 6.22837370242

CHAPTER 4.   DETERMINING CHANGE: DERIVATIVES

SECTION 4.1: NUMERICALLY FINDING SLOPES

4.1.1 Numerically Investigating Slopes:
Finding slopes of secant lines joining the point at which the tangent line is drawn to increasingly "close" points on a function to the left and right of the point of tangency is easily done using your calculator. Suppose we want to find the slope of the tangent line at $t = 8$ to the graph of the function $y = \dfrac{44000}{1 + 484e^{-0.7698\,t}}$.

Enter the equation in the y1 location of the *y(x) =* graphing list. (Carefully check the entry of your equation.
 	
 We now evaluate the slopes joining nearby points to the *left* of $x = 8$:
	`y1=44000/(1+484e^( -.…`
	
	 `y(x)= RANGE ZOOM TRACE GRAPH`
	 `x   y   INSf DELf SELCT▶`

Store the point at which the tangent is drawn in x and evaluate y1. Store the result in A for easy recall.
 	
 Type in the second expression shown to the right to compute the slope of the secant line joining the points where $x = 7.9$ and $x = 8$. *Be very careful that you watch the screen as you type and turn the alphabetic cursor off and on as needed.*
	`8→x:y1→A`
	          `21739.4782049`
	 `-.1→H:8+H→x:y1→B:(B-A`
	`)/H`
	        `8458.58051863`

Press [2nd] [ENTER] (ENTRY) to recall the last entry, and then use [▲] [◀] to move the cursor over the 1 in the first statement.
 	
 Press [2nd] [DEL] (INS) and press [0] to insert another 0. (When $H = {}^-.01$, you are evaluating the slope of the secant line joining $x = 7.99$ and $x = 8$, etc.)
	`8458.58051863`
	 `-.01→H:8+H→x:y1→B:(B-`
	`A)/H`
	        `8466.1848628`
	 `-.001→H:8+H→x:y1→B:(B`
	`-A)/H`
	        `8466.573547`

Continue in this manner, recording each result on paper, until you can determine the value the slopes from the left seem to be approaching.	`8466.573547`
	 `-.0001→H:8+H→x:y1→B:(`
	`B-A)/H`
	        `8466.60869`
	 `-.00001→H:8+H→x:y1→B:`
	`(B-A)/H`
	        `8466.6122`

We now evaluate the slopes joining nearby points to the *right* of $x = 8$:
 	
Clear the screen with CLEAR , recall the last expression with 2nd ENTER (ENTRY), and edit it with DEL so that $H = .1$.
	`.1→H:8+H→x:y1→B:(B-A)`
	`/H`
	`          8466.29097848`

Recall the last entry, and then use ▲ ◄ to move the cursor over the 1 in the first statement.
 	
Press 2nd DEL (INS) and press 0 to insert another 0. (When $H = .01$, you are evaluating the slope of the secant line joining $x = 8.01$ and $x = 8$, etc.)
	`          8466.29097848`
	`.01→H:8+H→x:y1→B:(B-A`
	`)/H`
	`           8466.9566628`
	`.001→H:8+H→x:y1→B:(B-`
	`A)/H`
	`            8466.650728`

Continue in this manner as before, recording each result on paper, until you can determine the value the slopes from the right seem to be approaching.
 	
When the slopes from the left and the slopes from the right get closer to the same value, that value is the slope of the tangent line at $x = 8$.
	`            8466.650728`
	`.0001→H:8+H→x:y1→B:(B`
	`-A)/H`
	`             8466.61641`
	`.00001→H:8+H→x:y1→B:(`
	`B-A)/H`
	`              8466.6129`

SECTION 4.3: SLOPE FORMULAS

4.3.1 Discovering Slope Formulas: You can often see a pattern in a table of values for the slopes of a function at indicated values of the input variable and discover a formula for the slope (derivative). The process of calculating the slopes uses the calculator's formula[1] for finding slopes, nDer($f(x)$, x, x). The correspondence between our notation $\frac{df(x)}{dx}$ and the calculator's notation nDer($f(x)$, x, x) is shown below:

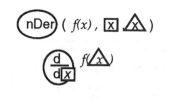

◯ indicates we are taking a derivative or slope.

▢ indicates the letter corresponding to the name of the input variable.

△ indicates the value of the input variable at which the slope is calcualated.

---

[1]The TI-85 has another numerical derivative, der1. Refer to your owner's manual for the distinction between these two forms. We use nDer throughout this *Guide*.

| Return to the home screen and type the expression on the right. Access nDer(with $\boxed{\text{2nd}}$ $\boxed{\div}$ (CALC) $\boxed{\text{F2}}$ (nDer).

nDer(x^2, x, 2) = $\frac{dy}{dx}$ for $y = x^2$ evaluated at $x = 2$. | nDer(x²,x,2)

4

evalF nDer der1 der2 fnInt |

Suppose you are asked to construct a table of values for $y = x^2$ evaluated at different values of x. There are two ways to do this illustrated below:

One way to do this is to recall the last entry and edit the expression nDer(x^2, x, 2) by changing the "2".	4 nDer(x²,x,⁻3) -6 nDer(x²,x,⁻2) -4 nDer(x²,x,⁻1) -2
You might prefer to use program **TABLE**. If so, remember that the expression being evaluated must be in location y1 of the *y(x)=* graphing list. If you enter the slope formula as indicated on the right, you will only have to change y2 when you work another problem with a different function.	y1=nDer(y2,x,x) y2=x² INSF DELF SELCT evalF nDer der1 der2 fnInt
Run program **TABLE** and evaluate the calculator's slope formula at $x = ⁻3, ⁻2, ⁻1, 0, 1, 2,$ and 3. Record these values as they are displayed and try to determine a relationship (pattern) between the calculated slopes and the values of x.	2 x=2 y1= 4 x=3 y1= 6 x=Q

- If you have difficulty determining a pattern, enter the x-values at which you are evaluating the slope in list L1 and the evaluated values of nDer in list L2. Use program **STPLT** to draw a scatterplot of the x-values and the calculated slope formula values. The shape of the scatterplot should give you a clue as to the equation of the slope formula. If not, try drawing another scatterplot where L1 contains the values of $y = f(x)$ and L2 contains the calculated slope formula values. Note that this method might help only if you consider a variety of values for x.

- The TI-85 only calculates numerical values of slopes -- it does not give the slope in formula form.

SECTION 4.4: THE SUM RULE

4.4.1 Numerically Checking Slope Formulas: When you use a formula to find the derivative of a function, it is possible to check your answer using the calculator's numerical derivative nDer. The basic idea of the checking process is that if you evaluate your derivative and the calculator's derivative at several randomly chosen values of the input variable and the output values are the same, your derivative is *probably* correct.

Let $g(t) = 0.775t^2 - 140.460t + 6868.818$. Applying the sum, power, and constant multiplier rules for derivatives, suppose you determine $g'(t) = 1.55t - 140.460$. Now, let us numerically check this answer.

Enter the calculator's derivative in y1, the function you are taking the derivative of in y2, and your derivative formula, $\frac{dg}{dt} = g'(t)$, in y3.	`y1=nDer(y2,x,x)`
	`y2=.775x²-140.46x+68…`
	`y3=1.55x-140.45`
	
	`y(x)= RANGE ZOOM TRACE GRAPH`
	`  x   y   INSf DELf SELCT▶`

Since the $g(t)$ model represents average fuel consumption per car where $t = 80$ in 1980, it makes sense to check using only positive values of t (that are now denoted as x since we are using the $y(x)=$ graphing list).	`80→x:y1`
	`                    -16.46`
	`80→x:y3`
	`                    -16.46`
	`86→x:y1`
	`                     -7.16`

Return to the home screen, and check to see that y1 and y3 are the same at least 3 values of x.
 	
(Hint: Use the last entry feature.)
	`                     -7.16`
	`86→x:y3`
	`                     -7.16`
	`89→x:y1`
	`                     -2.51`
	`89→x:y3`
	`                     -2.51`

4.4.2 Graphically Checking Slope Formulas: Another method of checking your answer for a slope formula (derivative) is to draw the calculator's graph of the derivative and draw the graph of your derivative. If the graphs appear identical *in the same viewing window*, your derivative is probably correct.

Again use $g(t) = 0.775t^2 - 140.460t + 6868.818$ and $g'(t) = 1.55t - 140.460$.

Enter the calculator's derivative in y1, the function you are taking the derivative of in y2, and your derivative formula in y3.	`y1=nDer(y2,x,x)`
	`y2=.775x²-140.46x+68…`
	`y3=1.55x-140.45`
	
	`y(x)= RANGE ZOOM TRACE GRAPH`
	`  x   y   INSf DELf SELCT▶`

Turn off y1 and y2 using [F5] (SELCT) so that only the graph of y3 will draw. Set an appropriate viewing window such as *x* between 80 and 90 and *y* between ⁻25 and 25.	
Now, turn off y3, turn on y1, and draw the graph of y1 in the same viewing window. (The graph of the calculator's derivative takes slightly longer to draw because the TI-85 computes the output before plotting each point.)	
To be certain the graphs appear identical, turn on y3 and draw the graphs of both y1 and y3 in this same viewing window. If you see only *one* graph on the screen after both graphs finish drawing, your derivative is very likely correct.	

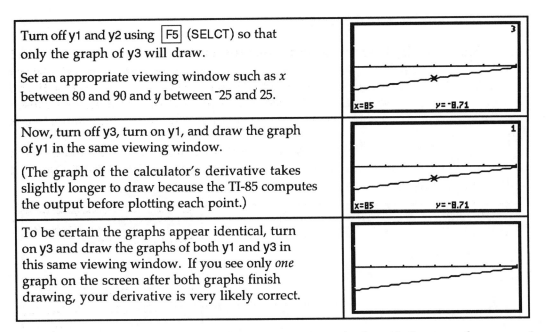

- When you are trying to determine an appropriate viewing window, use the range of the input data for *x*. If you do not have data, but an equation, use your knowledge of the general shape of the function to find appropriate values for xMin and xMax. Recall that you can trace on the graph to see some of the output values to help you determine values for yMin and yMax.

- It is tempting to try to shorten the above process for graphically checking your derivative formula by drawing only the graphs of your derivative and the calculator's derivative at the same time without first graphing each separately. If your derivative is such that it cannot be seen in the viewing window in which you see the calculator's derivative or vice versa, you will see only one graph and think that your slope formula is correct. It is better to perform a numerical check on the derivatives than to incorrectly use the graphical checking process.

CHAPTER 5.   ANALYZING CHANGE: EXTREMA AND POINTS OF INFLECTION

SECTION 5.1: OPTIMIZATION

5.1.1 Finding Local Maxima and/or Minima:
Finding where a function has a high point or a low point is an easy task for the TI-85.

Consider, for example, the model for the average price (per 1000 ft^3) of natural gas for residential use from 1980 to 1991:

$$price = p(x) = 0.012436x^3 - 0.242086x^2 + 1.406993x + 3.444545 \text{ dollars}$$

where x is the number of years since 1980.

Enter this model in the y2 location of the $y(x) =$ graphing list. (If you have another equation in y1, turn it off.)	`y1=nDer(y2,x,x)`
	 `y2█.012436x^3-.24208...`
	
	 `y(x)= RANGE ZOOM TRACE GRAPH`
	 `x   y   INSf  DELf  SELCT▶`

Graph the model in an appropriate viewing window, say x between 0 and 11 and y between 3 and 7.	`y(x)= RANGE ZOOM TRACE GRAPH▶`
Prepare to find the local (relative) maximum by pressing MORE F1 (MATH) MORE F2 (FMAX). Next, press ◀ to move the blinking cursor that appears to your *estimate* of the high point.	² `x=4.3650793651 . y=6.0078196481`
Press ENTER and the TI-85 uses your estimate to locate the highest point in the region around your value and displays the maximum and the x-value at which it occurs at the bottom of the screen. Thus, the maximum price was $6.01 per 1000 ft^3 and the price peaked in May, 1984 (4.393 months after January 1, 1980).	`FMAX` `x=4.3930775795 . y=6.0078B120B`

- Note that this maximum is a local or relative maximum, but it is not *the* highest average price of natural gas from 1980 to 1991. Look at the graph and see that the price in January of 1991 ($x = 11$) is the highest price at $6.18 per 1000 ft^3 .

We use a similar method to find the minimum price and when it occurred.

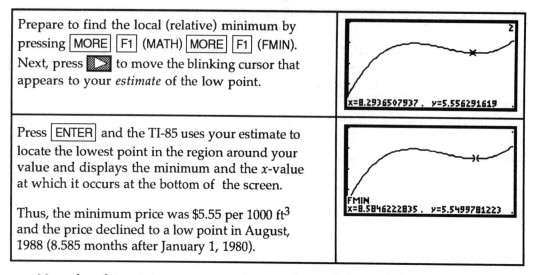

Prepare to find the local (relative) minimum by pressing MORE F1 (MATH) MORE F1 (FMIN). Next, press ▶ to move the blinking cursor that appears to your *estimate* of the low point.	x=8.2936507937 , y=5.556291619
Press ENTER and the TI-85 uses your estimate to locate the lowest point in the region around your value and displays the minimum and the x-value at which it occurs at the bottom of the screen. Thus, the minimum price was $5.55 per 1000 ft³ and the price declined to a low point in August, 1988 (8.585 months after January 1, 1980).	FMIN x=8.5846222835 , y=5.5499781223

- Note that this minimum is a local or relative minimum, but it is not *the* lowest average price of natural gas from 1980 to 1991. View the graph and see that the price in January of 1980 ($x = 0$) is the lowest price at $3.44 per 1000 ft³ .

5.1.2 Finding x-Intercepts of Slope Graphs:
Where the graph of a function has a local maximum or minimum, the slope graph has a horizontal tangent. Where the tangent is horizontal, the derivative is zero. Thus, finding where the slope graph crosses the x-axis is the same as finding the location of the local maxima and minima.

We emphasize this fact by finding the x-intercepts of the derivative (where the slope graph crosses the x-axis) and showing those intercepts occur at the local maximum and minimum of the graph of $p(x) = 0.012436x^3 - 0.242086x^2 + 1.406993x + 3.444545$.

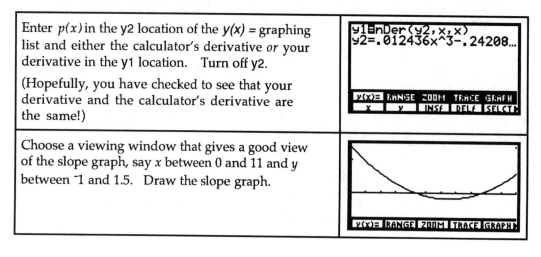

Enter $p(x)$ in the y2 location of the $y(x) =$ graphing list and either the calculator's derivative *or* your derivative in the y1 location. Turn off y2. (Hopefully, you have checked to see that your derivative and the calculator's derivative are the same!)	y1=nDer(y2,x,x) y2=.012436x^3-.24208...
Choose a viewing window that gives a good view of the slope graph, say x between 0 and 11 and y between ¯1 and 1.5. Draw the slope graph.	

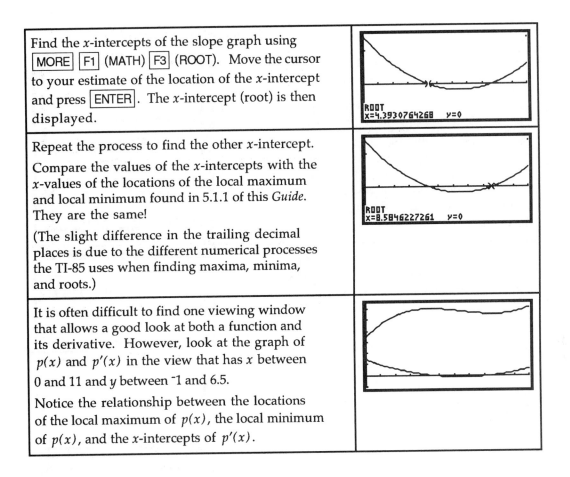

Find the x-intercepts of the slope graph using MORE F1 (MATH) F3 (ROOT). Move the cursor to your estimate of the location of the x-intercept and press ENTER. The x-intercept (root) is then displayed.	ROOT x=4.3930764268 y=0
Repeat the process to find the other x-intercept. Compare the values of the x-intercepts with the x-values of the locations of the local maximum and local minimum found in 5.1.1 of this *Guide*. They are the same! (The slight difference in the trailing decimal places is due to the different numerical processes the TI-85 uses when finding maxima, minima, and roots.)	ROOT x=8.5846227261 y=0
It is often difficult to find one viewing window that allows a good look at both a function and its derivative. However, look at the graph of $p(x)$ and $p'(x)$ in the view that has x between 0 and 11 and y between ⁻1 and 6.5. Notice the relationship between the locations of the local maximum of $p(x)$, the local minimum of $p(x)$, and the x-intercepts of $p'(x)$.	

SECTION 5.2: INFLECTION POINTS

5.2.1 Finding Inflection Points: The TI-85 offers three graphical methods of finding an inflection point of a function. To illustrate, consider a model for the percentage of students graduating from high school in South Carolina from 1982 to 1990 who enter post-secondary institutions:

$$f(x) = {}^-0.105724x^3 + 1.355375x^2 - 3.672379x + 50.791919 \text{ percent}$$

where $x = 0$ in 1982.

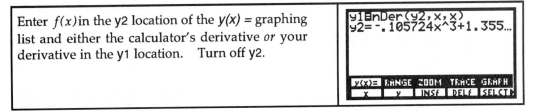

Enter $f(x)$ in the y2 location of the $y(x) =$ graphing list and either the calculator's derivative *or* your derivative in the y1 location. Turn off y2.	y1=nDer(y2,x,x) y2=-.105724x^3+1.355...

Graph $f'(x)$ in an appropriate viewing window, say x between 0 and 8 and y between ⁻4 and 4.	
Use the methods illustrated in 5.1.1 of this *Guide* to find the maximum of the slope graph. The x-value of the maximum of the slope graph $f'(x)$ is the x-value of the inflection point of the function $f(x)$.	 FMAX X=4.2733128321 y=2.1195615155
If you are asked to give the inflection <u>point</u> of $f(x)$, you should give both an x-value and a y-value. Find the y-value by substituting this x-value in the function located in y2.	x y2 4.27331283207 51.5992118947
Even though it is difficult to find a window that shows a good graph of both the function and its derivative in *this* case, you can often see that the location of the inflection point is at the maximum or minimum of the function.	

Another method you can use to find the x-value of an inflection point is to find the x-intercept (root) of the second derivative of the function. The calculator's notation for $f''(x)$, the second derivative, is der2 accessed with 2nd ÷ (CALC) F4 (der2).

Enter $f(x)$ in the y2 location of the $y(x) =$ list, either the calculator's derivative *or* your derivative in the y1 location, and either the calculator's second derivative or your second derivative in the y3 location. Turn off y2.	y1=nDer(y2,x,x) y2=-.105724x^3+1.355... y3=der2(y2,x,x) y(x)= RANGE ZOOM TRACE GRAPH x y INSf DELf SELCT
Draw the graphs in a viewing window that gives a good view of the slope graph, $f'(x)$, and its derivative, $f''(x)$, say x between 0 and 8 and y between ⁻4 and 4.	

- Notice that the x-intercept of the second derivative occurs at the maximum of the graph of $f'(x)$. Isn't the second derivative the derivative of the first derivative?

Use the methods of 5.1.2 of this *Guide* to find the x-intercept of the second derivative. (Be sure to use 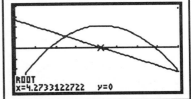 to move to the graph of the line before giving the estimate of the root.)	ROOT x=4.2733122722 y=0

A third method is to use the TI-85's built-in numerical routine to find inflection points.

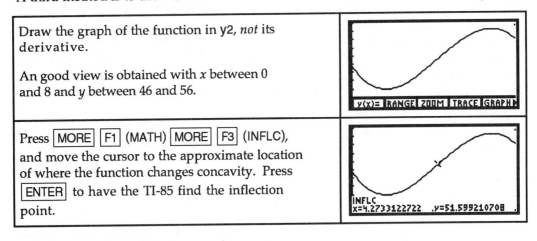

Draw the graph of the function in y2, *not* its derivative. An good view is obtained with x between 0 and 8 and y between 46 and 56.	y(x)= RANGE ZOOM TRACE GRAPH
Press MORE F1 (MATH) MORE F3 (INFLC), and move the cursor to the approximate location of where the function changes concavity. Press ENTER to have the TI-85 find the inflection point.	INFLC x=4.2733122722 y=51.599210708

CHAPTER 6. ACCUMULATING CHANGE: LIMITS OF SUMS

SECTION 6.1: RESULTS OF CHANGE

6.1.1 Using a Model to Determine Change:
The TI-85 lists can be used to perform the required calculations to approximate, using left rectangles, the area between the horizontal axis, a (non-negative) rate of change function, and two specific input values. The general procedure for approximating the change in the function $y = f(x)$ between $x = a$ and $x = b$ begins with using the given number, n, of subintervals or determining a suitable value for n. Then, find the equal width of each subinterval, Δx, by using $\Delta x = \dfrac{b - a}{n}$. Next, when you enter the x-data values in list L1, remember that the x-data values should differ by Δx. Program MDVAL simplifies computations by evaluating the model at the L1 values and storing the evaluated values in L2.

Consider, for example, the model for the number of customers per minute who came to a Saturday sale from 9 AM to 9 PM at a large department store:

$$c(m) = (4.589036*10^{-8})\,m^3 - (7.781267*10^{-5})\,m^2 + 0.033033\,m + 0.887630$$

customers per minute where m is the number of minutes after 9 AM.

Enter this model in the y1 location of the *y(x)=* graphing list. (If you have other equations in the graphing list, clear them.) (Remember that "10 to a power" is denoted by **E** on the calculator. Access **E** with EE .)	`y1▣4.589036E⁻8x^3-7...` `y(x)= RANGE ZOOM TRACE GRAPH` `x  y  INSf DELf SELCT▸`
Suppose we want to estimate the total number of customers who came to the sale between $m = x = 0$ and $m = x = 660$ (9 AM to 9 PM) with 12 rectangles such that $\Delta x = 60$. Enter these x-values in list L1.	`LIST:L1` `↑e7=360` `e8=420` `e9=480` `e10=540` `e11=600` `e12=660` `INSi DELi ▸REAL`
Enter y-values calculated from the model in list L2 using program MDVAL (model values). You can have the model entered in any of the first four locations of *y(x)=* . Tell the program which y location at the Function location? prompt. L2 now contains the *heights* of the 12 rectangles.	`MDVAL` `Function location? 1` `(.88763 2.5993967021...`
Since the *width* of each rectangle is 60, the area of each rectangle is 60*height*. Enter the *areas* of the 12 rectangles in list L3. Press and hold down ▶ to view all the values in L3 or use the LIST EDIT menu to view them.	`60 L2→L3` `(53.2578 155.9638021...` `<  >  NAMES EDIT OPS▸` `L1  L2  L3  L4  L5 ▸`

Find the sum of the areas of the rectangles with 2nd − (LIST) F5 (OPS) MORE F1 (SUM) EXIT F3 (NAMES) F3 (L3) ENTER .
 	
 We estimate, with 12 rectangles, that 2,574 customers came to the Saturday sale.
	```60 L2→L3```
	 `(53.2578 155.9638021…`
	 `sum L3`
	 `          2573.80408014`
	
	 `  x    y   NAMES EDIT OPS`
	 `  L1   L2   L3   L4   L5`

6.1.2 Using Count Data to Determine Change:

This method is very similar to that using a model to determine change. The main difference is that you enter the data values in list L2 instead of using the model to generate the values in that list.

Consider the following data showing the number of aluminum cans that were recycled each year from 1978 to 1988:

year	'78	'79	'80	'81	'82	'83	'84	'85	'86	'87	'88
cans (in billions)	8.0	8.5	14.8	24.9	28.3	29.4	31.9	33.1	33.3	36.6	42.0

Enter the number of years since 1978 in list L1 and the cans recycled each year (in billions) in list L2.	`L1`
	 `(0 1 2 3 4 5 6 7 8 9…`
	 `L2`
	 `(8 8.5 14.8 24.9 28.…`
	
	 `  x    y   NAMES EDIT OPS`
	 `  L1   L2   L3   L4   L5`

Suppose we want to estimate the number of cans recycled during the ten year period 1978-1988.
 	
 Since $\Delta x = 1$ and the heights of the rectangles are in L2, the areas of the 11 rectangles spanning the years 1978 *through* 1988 are the values in L2.
	`LIST:L2`
	 `↑e6=29.4`
	 `  e7=31.9`
	 `  e8=33.1`
	 `  e9=33.3`
	 `  e10=36.6`
	 `  e11=42`
	 `INSi  DELi  ▶REAL`

Thus, an estimate, given by the 11 rectangles, of the number of cans recycled during the 10 year period is 290.8 billion cans.	`sum L2`
	 `                290.8`
	
	 `  x    y   NAMES EDIT OPS`
	 `  L1   L2   L3   L4   L5`

If you needed an estimate of the number of cans recycled during the 3 year period 1982-1984, copy list L2 to list L3, delete all but those three heights, and sum list L3. The estimate is 89.6 billion cans.	`L2→L3`
	 `(8 8.5 14.8 24.9 28.…`
	 `L3`
	 `       (28.3 29.4 31.9)`
	 `sum L3`
	 `                 89.6`

SECTION 6.2: APPROXIMATING AREA

6.2.1 Left-Rectangle Approximation: The TI-85 lists are used to perform the required calculations to find area using left rectangles when given data or a model defining a function $y = f(x)$. For the examples in this section, we consider the function $f(x) = x^3 - 2x^2 + 3x + 1$. Enter this function in the y1 location of the $y(x)=$ list.

To approximate the area, from 0 to 3, of the region beneath the graph of $f(x)$ and the horizontal axis using *left* rectangles with $n = 4$ subintervals, determine $\Delta x = 0.75$ and the list L1 as shown on the right. Use program MDVAL to generate list L2.	```L1 (0 .75 1.5 2.25 3) MDVAL Function location? 1 (1 2.546875 4.375 9....```
List L2 should contain the heights of the rectangles. Notice that when using left rectangles, the value of the function at the rightmost endpoint b of the interval (in this case, 19) is <u>not</u> the height of a rectangle. Thus, delete the *last* value in L2 by positioning the cursor over the last value, and pressing F2 (DELi).	```LIST:L2 e1=1 e2=2.546875 e3=4.375 e4=9.015625 e5=█ INSi DELi REAL```
Enter in list L3 the areas of the rectangles. Remember, the rectangle width is Δx (here, 0.75) and the rectangle heights are in L2.	```.75 L2→L3 (.75 1.91015625 3.28...```
Find the sum of the areas of the four left rectangles.	```.75 L2→L3 (.75 1.91015625 3.28... sum L3 12.703125```

- It is always a good idea to draw the graph of the function and sketch the approximating rectangles. By doing so, you should notice that the last y-data value on the right is not the height of a left rectangle and should not be included when determining area *up to* that value.

6.2.2 Right-Rectangle Approximation: The TI-85 lists are used to perform the required calculations to find area using right rectangles when given data or a model defining a function $y = f(x)$. Enter $f(x) = x^3 - 2x^2 + 3x + 1$ in y1.

To approximate the area, from 0 to 3, of the region beneath the graph of $f(x)$ and the horizontal axis using *right* rectangles with $n = 4$ subintervals, determine $\Delta x = 0.75$ and the list L1 as shown on the right. Use program MDVAL to determine list L2.	L1 　(0 .75 1.5 2.25 3) MDVAL Function location? 1 (1 2.546875 4.375 9.…
List L2 should contain the heights of the rectangles. Notice that when using right rectangles, the value of the function at the leftmost endpoint a of the interval (in this case, 1) is <u>not</u> the height of a rectangle. Thus, delete the *first* value in L2.	LIST:L2 　e1=2.546875 　e2=4.375 　e3=9.015625 　e4=19 INSi　DELi　REAL
Enter in list L3 the areas of the rectangles. Remember, the rectangle width is Δx (here, 0.75) and the rectangle heights are in L2.	.75L2→L3 (1.91015625 3.28125 … NAMES EDIT OPS L1 L2 L3 L4 L5
Find the sum of the areas of the four right rectangles.	.75L2→L3 (1.91015625 3.28125 … sum L3 　　　　　26.203125 NAMES EDIT OPS L1 L2 L3 L4 L5

6.2.3 Trapezoid Approximation: The TI-85 lists are used to perform the required calculations to find area using trapezoids when given data or a model defining a function $y = f(x)$. Enter $f(x) = x^3 - 2x^2 + 3x + 1$ in y1.

To approximate the area, from 0 to 3, of the region beneath the graph of $f(x)$ and the horizontal axis using $n = 4$ *trapezoids*, determine $\Delta x = 0.75$ and the list L1 as shown on the right. Use program MDVAL to determine list L2.	L1 　(0 .75 1.5 2.25 3) MDVAL Function location? 1 (1 2.546875 4.375 9.…

List L2 contains the heights of the sides of the trapezoids. Notice that when using trapezoids, all heights occur twice except for the leftmost and rightmost endpoints a and b. Thus, enter list L3 with first and last values of 1 and all other values 2.	{1,2,2,2,1}→L3 {1 2 2 2 1}

Determine the "function values portion" of the trapezoid area formula T_n in list L4 as L4 = L2 *L3.	LIST:L4
	  e1=1
	  e2=5.09375
	  e3=8.75
	  e4=18.03125
	  e5=19
	
	  INSi DELi ▸REAL

Find the area of the trapezoids using the formula $T_n = (\Delta x \, / \, 2)$ sum L4. $T_4 = (0.75/2)$ sum L4 = 19.453125	{1 2 2 2 1} L2*L3→L4 {1 5.09375 8.75 18.0... (.75/2)sum L4 19.453125

6.2.4 Midpoint-Rectangle Approximation: The TI-85 lists can be used to perform the required calculations to find area using midpoint rectangles when given a model defining a function $y = f(x)$. Enter $f(x) = x^3 - 2x^2 + 3x + 1$ in y1.

- If you are using the data points and *not* a model for function values and there are no data points given at the midpoint x-values, this method should not be used.

To approximate the area, from 0 to 3, of the region beneath the graph of $f(x)$ and the horizontal axis using $n = 4$ *midpoint* rectangles, determine $\Delta x = 0.75$.
 	
Replace each pair of original x-values with their average found by adding the values together and dividing by 2. The midpoints of each interval become the L1 values.
	{.375,1.125,1.875,2.6
	25}→L1
	{.375 1.125 1.875 2....
	
	  ‹ › NAMES EDIT OPS
	  L1 L2 L3 L4 L5 ▸

Use program MDVAL to generate and store in list L2 the function values evaluated at the midpoints.	LIST:L2
	  e1=1.896484375
	  e2=3.267578125
	  e3=6.185546875
	  e4=13.181640625
	
	  INSi DELi ▸REAL

| L2 contains the heights of the rectangles.<br><br>Since the width of each rectangle is $\Delta x = 0.75$, enter the area of each midpoint rectangle in L3 as L3 = 0.75L2. | ```
LIST:L3
 e1=1.42236328125
 e2=2.45068359375
 e3=4.63916015625
 e4=9.88623046875


 INSi  DELi  ▶REAL
``` |
| Find the sum of the areas of the four midpoint rectangles. | ```
.75 L2→L3
{1.42236328125 2.450...
sum L3
              18.3984375

      x  :  NAMES EDIT  OPS
 sum  prod  seq  li▶vc  vc▶li▶
``` |

6.2.5 Simpson's Rule: The TI-85 lists are used to perform the required calculations to find area approximations using Simpson's Rule when given data or a model defining a function $y = f(x)$. Enter $f(x) = x^3 - 2x^2 + 3x + 1$ in y1.

- The number, n, of subintervals must be an *even* number in order to use the method presented below.

- If the number, n, of subintervals is *odd*, use this form of Simpson's Rule:
  $$S = \frac{2}{3} \text{ (Midpoint Area)} + \frac{1}{3} \text{ (Trapezoid Area)}$$

| To approximate the area, from 0 to 3, of the region beneath the graph of $f(x)$ and the horizontal axis using *Simpson's Rule* with $n = 4$ subintervals, determine $\Delta x = 0.75$ and the list L1 as shown on the right. Use program MDVAL to determine list L2. | ```
{0,.75,1.5,2.25,3}→L1
   {0 .75 1.5 2.25 3}
MDVAL
Function location? 1
{1 2.546875 4.375 9....
``` |
| Notice that when using Simpson's Rule, the coefficients of the $y$-values in the formula for $S_n$ alternate in a 1-4-2-4-2 ⋯ 2-4-1 pattern.<br><br>Enter list L3 containing these coefficients. | ```
{1,4,2,4,1}→L3
       {1 4 2 4 1}



 x  :  NAMES EDIT  OPS
 L1   L2   L3   L4   L5
``` |
| Determine the "function values portion" of the formula for Simpson's Rule, $S_n$, in list L4 as L4 = L2 *L3. | ```
LIST:L4
 e1=1
 e2=10.1875
 e3=8.75
 e4=36.0625
 e5=19
 INSi  DELi  ▶REAL
``` |
```

Find the area using Simpson's Rule formula
 	
$S_n = (\Delta x / 3)$ sum L4.
 	
$S_4 = (0.75/3)$ sum L4 $= 18.75$
	`(1,4,2,4,1)→L3`
	`          (1 4 2 4 1)`
	`L2*L3→L4`
	`(1 10.1875 8.75 36.0…`
	`(.75/3)sum L4`
	`                   18.75`

SECTION 6.3: LIMITS OF SUMS

6.3.1 Simplifying Area Calculations: The above procedures using lists are very time consuming when the number, n, of subintervals is large. When you use a model $y = f(x)$ entered in the y1 location of the $y(x)=$ graphing list, you will find program NUMINTG very helpful in determining left-rectangle, right-rectangle, midpoint-rectangle, trapezoid, and Simpson's Rule numerical approximations for area. Program NUMINTG is listed in the TI-85 Appendix.

Enter $f(x) = x^3 - 2x^2 + 3x + 1$ in y1. If you wish to view the approximating rectangles and/or trapezoids, first construct a graph of $f(x)$. A suitable **RANGE** is x between 0 and 3 and y between 0 and 19.	

Press 2nd EXIT (QUIT) and access program NUMINTG by pressing PRGM NAMES followed by the F-key under the location of the program.
 	
At this point, if you did not enter in y1 (or did not draw the graph), enter 2 to exit the program. Do what needs to be done and re-run the program.
 	
If all is okay, press 1 to continue.
	`Enter f(x) in y1.`
	
	`Draw graph of f.`
	
	`Continue?`
	`Yes (1) No (2)`

At the next prompt, press 1 ENTER to draw the approximating figures or press 2 ENTER to obtain only the numerical approximations to the area between $f(x)$ and the horizontal axis between 0 and 3. Let's view some pictures.	`Draw graph of f.`
	
	`Continue?`
	`Yes (1) No (2) 1`
	
	`Draw Pictures?`
	`Yes(1) No(2) 1`

At the LOWER LIMIT? prompt, type 0 ENTER and at the UPPER LIMIT? prompt, 3 ENTER.
 	
You are next shown a menu of choices. Press 2 ENTER to find a right-rectangle approximation.
	`Enter Choice:`
	`Left Rect   (1)`
	`Right Rect  (2)`
	`Trapezoids  (3)`
	`Midpt Rect  (4)`
	`Simpsons    (5)`

Input 4 at the N? prompt and press ENTER.	
The four approximating right-rectangles are shown. Notice that the right-rectangle sum overestimates the area under the curve.	
The right-rectangle sum is displayed when you press ENTER.	Trapezoids (3) Midpt Rect (4) Simpsons (5) 2 N? 4 SUM= 26.203125
Press ENTER once more and more choices are displayed. Suppose we now want to find and see the approximating area using 8 trapezoids. Press 2 and then press 3 ENTER to choose trapezoids.	Enter Choice: Change N (1) Change Method (2) Quit (3) 2
Enter 8 at the N? prompt and view the trapezoids.	
Again press ENTER and the trapezoid sum is displayed. This is certainly a better approximation than the right-rectangle sum with 4 rectangles. Press ENTER again and press 3 ENTER to QUIT.	Trapezoids (3) Midpt Rect (4) Simpsons (5) 3 N? 8 SUM= 18.92578125

- When n, the number of subintervals, is large, it is not advisable to draw pictures.

- Program NUMINTG informs you that there is "no picture for Simpson's Rule" if you choose the draw picture and Simpson's options.

- The program also informs you that "N is odd. Simpson's Rule not calculated" when you choose an odd number of subintervals. In such a case, you need to find the midpoint and trapezoid approximations and use the formula given at the beginning of this section to find the Simpson's Rule approximation.

- Program NUMINTG cannot be used with data unless you use a model you fit to the data.

6.3.2 Limits of Sums: When finding the trend in the midpoint approximations to the area between a non-negative function and the horizontal axis between two values of the input variable, program NUMINTG is extremely helpful!

To construct a chart of midpoint approximations for the area between $f(x) = x^3 - 2x^2 + 3x + 1$ and the x-axis between x=0 and x=3, first enter $f(x)$ in y1. Run program NUMINTG. Since many subintervals will be used, do not choose to draw the pictures. After entering 0 and 3 as the respective lower and upper limits, choose option 4.	```Enter Choice:↵ Left Rect (1) Right Rect (2) Trapezoids (3) Midpt Rect (4) Simpsons (5) 4```
Input some number of subintervals, say N = 4. Record the midpoint approximation 18.3984375.	```Trapezoids (3) Midpt Rect (4) Simpsons (5) 4 N? 4 SUM= 18.3984375```
Press ENTER and choose option 1: CHANGE N. Double the number of subintervals to N = 8. Record the midpoint approximation 18.66210938.	```Change N (1) Change Method (2) Quit (3) 1 N? 8 SUM= 18.662109375```
Continue on in this manner, each time choosing option 1: CHANGE N and doubling N until a trend is evident. (Finding a trend means that you can tell what specific number the values are getting closer and closer to without having to run the program ad infinitum!)	```Change N (1) Change Method (2) Quit (3) 1 N? 128 SUM= 18.7496566772```

SECTION 6.4: INDEFINITE INTEGRALS

6.4.1 Finding Integral Formulas: The TI-85 performs the required calculations to help you find integral formulas. You can create a table of values for the definite integral and look for a pattern in those values to help determine an indefinite integral formula. The process of calculating the definite integral uses the calculator's formula for finding the value of the integral, fnInt(f(X), X, a, b).

The correspondence between our definite integral notation $\int_a^b f(x)\,dx$ and the calculator's definite integral notation fnInt(f(X), X, a, b) is as shown below:

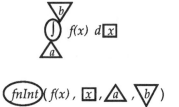

○ indicates we are taking an integral.

□ indicates the letter corresponding to the name of the input variable.

△ indicates the left endpoint of the interval

▽ indicates the right endpoint of the interval

We first create a list of values for the indefinite integral $\int_a^x f(t)\,dt$ for varying values of x where a is a specific constant. Clear the graphing list. In general, enter y1 = $f(x)$ and y2 = fnInt(y1, X, a, X).

Specifically, if you are investigating $\int_0^x t\,dt$, use $a = 0$ and $f(t) = t$. Enter the function in y1.
 	
In the Y2 location, type the instruction fnInt(with the keystrokes 2nd ÷ (CALC) F5 (fnInt(). Remember to use a lower-case *y* when entering the function y1.
	`y1=x`
	`y2=fnInt(y1,x,0,x)`
	
	Y(X)= RANGE ZOOM TRACE GRAPH
	x y INSf DELf SELCT
	
	Since you are using the graphing list to enter the functions, you must call *t* by the name *x*.

Exit the graphing list with EXIT EXIT or with 2nd EXIT (QUIT).
 	
Enter the values shown on the right in L1.
	`{0,1,2,3,4,5}→L1`
	`{0 1 2 3 4 5}`
	
	NAMES EDIT OPS
	L1 L2 L3 L4 L5

Use program MDVAL to evaluate y2 at each of the values in L1. Remember to type in 2 at the Function location? prompt.
 	
Seeing the fractional form of the L1 values may help in determining the pattern. The "to a fraction" key is found with 2nd × (MATH) F5 (MISC) MORE F1 (▸Frac).
	`MDVAL`
	`Function location? 2`
	`{0 .5 2 4.5 8 12.5}`
	`L2▸Frac`
	`{0 1/2 2 9/2 8 25/2}`
	
	NUM PROB ANGLE HYP MISC
	▸Frac 2 PEval xr eval

Finding the L2 values might take a short time since the calculator is determining several definite integral values. Now, all you need do is find the pattern in the L2 values.

- If you have difficulty determining a pattern, draw a scatterplot of the x-values and the calculated definite integral values. The shape of the scatterplot should give you a clue as to the equation of the indefinite integral formula. Note that this method might help only if you consider a variety of values for x in list L1.

- The TI-85 only calculates numerical values of definite integrals -- it does not give formula that is the indefinite integral.

To create a list of values for the indefinite integral $\int_a^x f(t)\,dt$ for varying values of a, use basically the same procedure as illustrated above. Suppose we want to compare, for various values of a, $\int_a^x t\,dt$ to $\int_0^x t\,dt$. The quickest way to evaluate the output of Y2 is with program MDVAL.

Enter the functions as shown on the right. That is, let $a = 1$.

How do the values of y2 relate to the output for $\int_0^x t\,dt$?

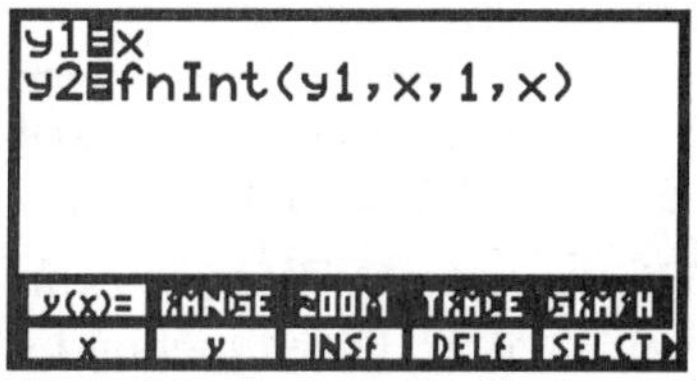
y1=x
y2=fnInt(y1,x,1,x)
y(x)= RANGE ZOOM TRACE GRAPH
x y INSf DELf SELCT

Run program MDVAL. Remember to type in 2 at the Function location? prompt.

Look at the values the program generated and stored in list L2. (Remember, ▷ scrolls the list to the right for viewing.)

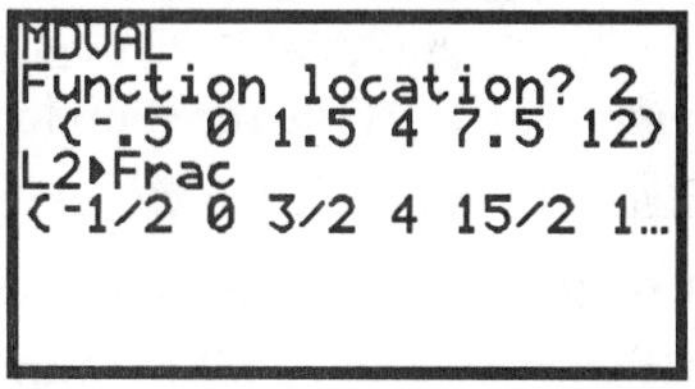
MDVAL
Function location? 2
{-.5 0 1.5 4 7.5 12}
L2▸Frac
{-1/2 0 3/2 4 15/2 1...

To find the output values for y2 when $a = 2$, press GRAPH F1 (y(x)=) and change the lower limit to 2.

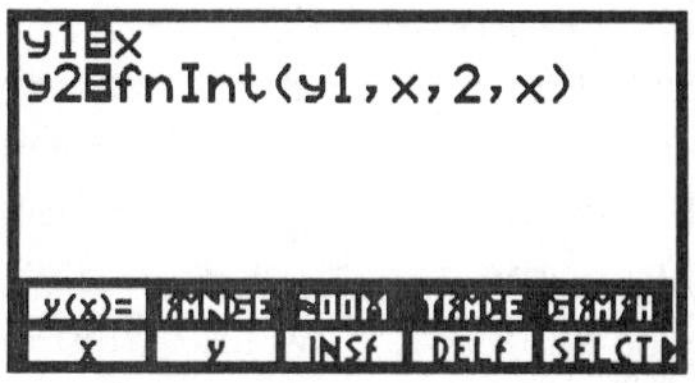
y1=x
y2=fnInt(y1,x,2,x)
y(x)= RANGE ZOOM TRACE GRAPH
x y INSf DELf SELCT

Run program MDVAL. Remember to type in 2 at the Function location? prompt. Compare these values to those you found when y2 = fnInt(y1, X, 0, X). Repeat for other values of a if necessary.	``` MDVAL Function location? 2 (-2 -1.5 0 2.5 6 10.... L2▸Frac (-2 -3/2 0 5/2 6 21/... ```

SECTION 6.5: THE FUNDAMENTAL THEOREM

6.5.1 The Fundamental Theorem of Calculus: This theorem tells us that the derivative of an antiderivative of a function is the function itself. Let us view this theorem both numerically and graphically.

Consider $F'(x) = \dfrac{d}{dx}\left(\displaystyle\int_1^x 3t^2 + 2t - 5\ dt\right)$. The FTC tells us $F'(x)$ should equal $f(x) = 3x^2 + 2x - 5$. Enter the functions shown to the right.	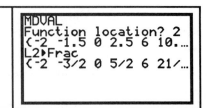 y2 = nDer(fnInt(y1,x,1,x), x, x)
Store some different values of x in list L1, say -5, -3, -1, 0, 1, 2, and 4. Use program MDVAL to evaluate y1 at these values of x. (The function location is 1.) Record, on paper, the y1 values.	``` (-5, -3, -1,0,1,2,4)→L1 (-5 -3 -1 0 1 2 4) MDVAL Function location? 1 (60 16 -4 -5 0 11 51) ```
Use program MDVAL to evaluate y2 at these values of x. (The function location is 2.) Record, on paper, the y2 values. Compare the outputs from y1 and y2. Other than a small bit of roundoff error due to the numerical nature of the calculator, y1 and y2 are identical!	``` LIST:L2 e1=60.000001 e2=16.0000010004 e3=-3.999999 e4=-4.999999 e5=9.9999998635E-7 ↓e6=11.00000100005 INSi DELi ▸REAL ```
Find a suitable viewing window such as x between -6.3 and 6.3 and y between -6 and 3.1. Draw the graphs of y1 and y2 separately in this same window and then draw them together. Only one graph appears! (The graph of y2 will take a while to draw.)	

CHAPTER 7.   MEASURING THE EFFECTS OF CHANGE: THE DEFINITE INTEGRAL

SECTION 7.2: THE DEFINITE INTEGRAL

7.2.1 Antiderivatives: All antiderivatives of a specific function differ only by a constant. We explore this idea using the function $f(x) = 3x^2 - 1$ and its antiderivative $F(x) = x^3 - x + C$.

Enter $f(x)$ in y1, fnInt(y1, x, 0, x) in y2, and $F(x)$ in y3, y4, y5, y6, and y7 (using a different value of C in each location) (You can try different values of C than those shown on the right.)	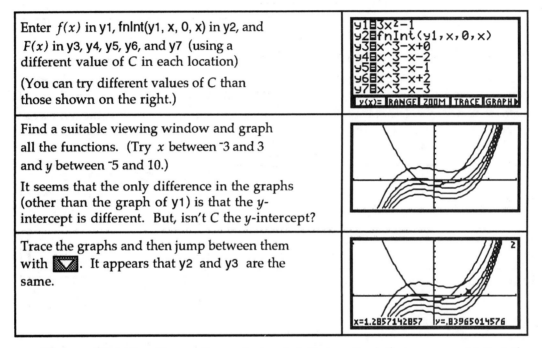
Find a suitable viewing window and graph all the functions. (Try x between ⁻3 and 3 and y between ⁻5 and 10.) It seems that the only difference in the graphs (other than the graph of y1) is that the y-intercept is different. But, isn't C the y-intercept?	
Trace the graphs and then jump between them with . It appears that y2 and y3 are the same.	

- Do you think that if you changed y2 to fnInt(y1, x, 2, x) that you would find the graphs of y2 and y6, or maybe y2 and y4, the same?   Can you justify your answer with antiderivative formulas? Explore!

7.2.2 Evaluating a Definite Integral on the Home Screen: The TI-85 finds a numerical approximation for the definite integral $\int_a^b f(x)\,dx$. All you have to do is, on the home screen, type fnInt($f(x)$, x, a, b) for a specific function $f(x)$ and specific values of a and b, and press ENTER .

- If you evaluate a definite integral using antiderivative formulas and check you answer using the calculator, you may sometimes find a slight difference in the trailing decimal places. Remember, the TI-85 is evaluating the definite integral using an approximation technique.

Find $\displaystyle\int_{1}^{5}(2^{x}-x)\,dx$.
 	
Notice that as long as you specify the variable you are using in the position after the function, you can use any letter to represent the variable.
	`fnInt(2^x-x,x,1,5)`
	`            31.2808512267`
	`fnInt(2^T-T,T,1,5)`
	`            31.2808512267`
	
	`evalF  nDer  der1  der2  fnInt ▸`

7.2.3 Rates into Amounts: The integral, between two input values, say a and b, of a rate of change is the change in amount of the antiderivative from a to b. Suppose you have modeled marginal cost data to find the rate of change in the marginal cost of ovens to be $C'(x) = {}^{-}1.12744 + 6137.6892\,x^{-1}$ dollars per oven where x is the number of ovens produced per day. What is the change in cost if production is increased from 300 to 500 ovens per day?

Enter $C'(x)$ in y1. The change in amount is \$2909.80.	`fnInt(y1,x,300,500)` `            2909.80091407`

Now, let us prepare to put the amount function in y2:
 	
Access the $y(x)=$ list, and move the cursor to the y2 location. Clear any previously-entered function. Press `2nd` `STO▸` (RCL) `F2` (y) `ALPHA` `1` `ENTER` .
	`y1B-1.12744+6137.689...`
	`y2B...44+6137.6892x^-1■`
	
	`y(x)=  RANGE  ZOOM  TRACE  GRAPH`
	`  x      y      INSf  DELf  SELCT▸`

Use `2nd` `DEL` (INS) and your knowledge of integral formulas to edit y2 to the expression on the right.
 	
The antiderivative of the rate of change (with the constant equal to 0) is now in y2 .
	`y1=-1.12744+6137.689...`
	`y2B...4x+6137.6892ln x`
	`y3=`
	
	`y(x)=  RANGE  ZOOM  TRACE  GRAPH`
	`  x      y      INSf  DELf  SELCT▸`

Return to the home screen and evaluate the change $C(500) - C(300)$.	`500→x:y2→A`
	`            37579.6130079`
	`300→x:y2→B`
	`            34669.8120938`
	`A-B`
	`            2909.80091407`

- You should find this method very helpful when the model coefficients are long decimal values. Also, if you use this method, errors in your answer to rounding the coefficients will be eliminated.

7.2.4 Integrals and Area: Finding the area between two functions utilizes the ideas presented in preceding sections. Suppose we want to find the area between the functions $f(x) = 2 - x$ and $g(x) = -x^3 + 2x + 2$.

Enter the functions in the *y(x)=* list. First, we must find where the two functions intersect.	y1=2-x y2=-x^3+2x+2 **Y(x)= RANGE ZOOM TRACE GRAPH** **x y INSf DELf SELCT**
Graph both functions in an appropriate viewing window, say *x* between ⁻6.3 and 6.3 and *y* between ⁻5 and 5.	
Next, find the three points of intersection. (The *x*-values of these intersection points will be the limits on the integrals we use to find the area.) Press MORE F1 (MATH) MORE F5 (ISECT) and then use ◄ to move the cursor close to the intersection point furthest to the left.	x=⁻1.7 y=3.7
Press ENTER. The TI-85 causes the cursor to jump to the other curve. (Notice the numbers corresponding to the function locations in the upper right-hand corner of the screen.)	x=⁻1.7 y=3.513
Press ENTER. The leftmost point of intersection is displayed. To avoid making a mistake copying the *x*-value and to eliminate as much rounding error as possible, return to the home screen with 2nd EXIT (QUIT) and store this value in *A* with the keystrokes X-VAR STO► LOG (A) ENTER.	ISECT x=⁻1.732050808 y=3.732050808076 x → A

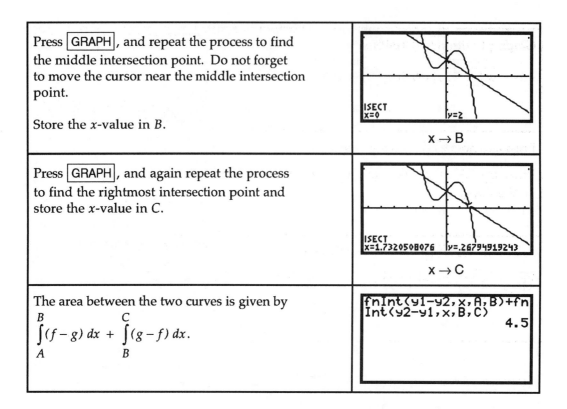

Press ⎡GRAPH⎤, and repeat the process to find the middle intersection point. Do not forget to move the cursor near the middle intersection point. Store the x-value in B.	ISECT X=0 y=2 x → B
Press ⎡GRAPH⎤, and again repeat the process to find the rightmost intersection point and store the x-value in C.	ISECT X=1.7320508076 y=.26794919243 x → C
The area between the two curves is given by $$\int_A^B (f-g)\,dx \ + \ \int_B^C (g-f)\,dx.$$	fnInt(y1-y2,x,A,B)+fn Int(y2-y1,x,B,C) 4.5

7.2.5 Evaluating a Definite Integral from the Graphics Screen: You can graphically find the definite integral $\int_a^b f(x)\,dx$ provided that a and b are possible x-values displayed when you trace on the graphics screen.

- For "nice" numbers, you can often find the exact x-value you need if you graph in the ZDECM screen or set the viewing window so that xMax − xMin equals a multiple of 12.6.)

Find $\int_1^5 (2^x - x)\,dx$.
 	
Enter y1 = 2^x − x , and set the viewing window on the right.
	RANGE
	  xMin=-3
	  xMax=9.6
	  xScl=1
	  yMin=-10
	  yMax=30
	  yScl=10
	  y(x)= RANGE ZOOM TRACE GRAPH▶

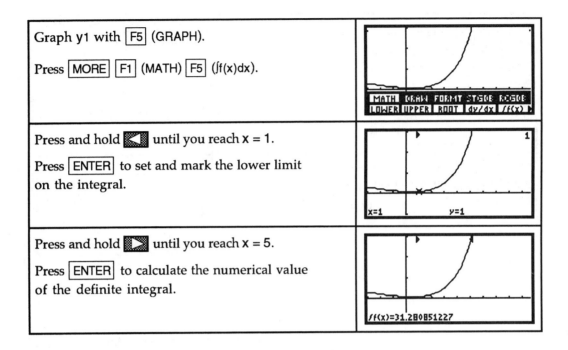

Graph y1 with F5 (GRAPH). Press MORE F1 (MATH) F5 (∫f(x)dx).	
Press and hold ◄ until you reach x = 1. Press ENTER to set and mark the lower limit on the integral.	
Press and hold ► until you reach x = 5. Press ENTER to calculate the numerical value of the definite integral.	

SECTION 7.3: AVERAGES

7.3.1 Average Value of a Function: Use the TI-85 to find the numerical value of and aid in your geometric interpretation of the average value of a function. Consider a model for the average daytime temperature between 7 AM and 7 PM:

$$f(t) = -0.65684t^2 + 9.38212t + 45.54945 \text{ degrees } t \text{ hours after 7 AM.}$$

Enter $f(t)$ in y1. (Remember to use x as the variable.) Draw a graph of y1 for x between 0 and 12 and y between 0 and 80.	
The average value of $f(t)$ over the interval from 7 AM to 7 PM is easily found using the integral. Enter the average value in location y2 of the *y(x)*= list.	fnInt(y1,x,0,12)/(12-0) 70.31385

Redraw the graph with GRAPH . Notice that the area of the rectangle whose height is the average temperature is $(70.31385)(12) = 843.7662$.	
| The area of the rectangle equals the area of the region between the temperature function $f(t)$ and the $x$-axis between 7 AM and 7 PM. | ```
70.31385*12
              843.7662
fnInt(y1,x,0,12)
              843.7662

evalF nDer der1 der2 fnInt ▸
``` |

SECTION 7.4: INCOME STREAMS

7.4.1 Future and Present Value of an Income Stream: Since future and present value of an income stream are defined by definite integrals, finding these values is easily done with your calculator.

Suppose we want to find the present and future values of an investment of $3.3 million each year that earns continuously compounded interest at a rate of 19.4% annually for a period of 10 years.

The *future value* of the investment is the amount to which the $3.3 million invested each year and the interest it earns would accumulate to at the end of 10 years. (We assume the $3.3 million is flowing in continuously.)

| Future value = $e^{0.194(10)} \displaystyle\int_{0}^{10} 3.3e^{-0.194t}\, dt$  which equals $101.360 million. | ```
e^(.194*10)fnInt(3.3
e^(-.194 x),x,0,10)
           101.360196923

evalF nDer der1 der2 fnInt ▸
``` |

The *present value* of the investment is the amount that would have to be deposited now and remain untouched (except for accumulating interest) to equal the amount to which the $3.3 million invested each year and the interest it earns would accumulate at the end of 10 years. (We assume the investment is flowing in continuously.)

Present value = $\displaystyle\int_{0}^{10} 3.3e^{-0.194t}\, dt$

which equals $14.566 million.

```
e^(.194*10)fnInt(3.3
e^(-.194 x),x,0,10)
             101.360196923
Ans/(e^(.194*10))
             14.5658606481
```
evalF nDer der1 der2 fnInt

7.4.2 Present Value in Perpetuity: Your calculator only provides numerical values for definite integrals, not an integral whose upper limit approaches infinity. You can, however, evaluate, using integral formulas, the present value in perpetuity integral for a fixed T and consider what happens numerically and graphically as T gets larger and larger.

Suppose we want to evaluate $\displaystyle\int_{0}^{\infty} 10000e^{-0.135t}\, dt = \lim_{T\to\infty} \int_{0}^{T} 10000e^{-0.135t}\, dt =$

$\lim_{T\to\infty} 74074.07(1 - e^{-0.135T})$. We find $\lim_{T\to\infty} (1 - e^{-0.135T})$ and multiply by 74074.07.

To investigate this limit *numerically*, first enter y1 $= 1 - e^{\wedge}(-.135x)$.
 	
Run program TABLE to evaluate y1 at increasingly larger values of x. (You may want to begin at $x = 0$ and let x increase by 10 each time.)
	`.740759739354`
	`x=20`
	`y1=`
	`           .93279448726`
	`x=30`
	`y1=`
	`          .982577625361`
	`x=40`

It appears that y1 is getting closer and closer to 1 as T = x gets larger and larger.	`.999979600497`
	`x=90`
	`y1=`
	`          .999994711627`
	`x=100`
	`y1=`
	`          .999998629041`
	`x=Q`

To investigate this limit *graphically*, have y1 $= 1 - e^{\wedge}(-.135x)$. Set a suitable window, such as x between 0 and 100 and y between 0 and 2. Draw the graph and trace it to observe that the y1 values appear to be getting closer to 1 as T = x gets larger and larger.	 `x=92.063492064  y=.99999599742`

Thus, $\displaystyle\lim_{T\to\infty} 74074.07(1 - e^{-0.135T}) = 74074.07 \lim_{T\to\infty} (1 - e^{-0.135T}) = 74074.07*1 = 74074.07.$

SECTION 7.5: INTEGRALS IN ECONOMICS

7.5.1 Consumers' and Producers' Surplus: Consumers' and producers' surplus, being defined by definite integrals, are easy to do using the calculator. You should always draw a graph of the demand and supply functions to better understand the activity. Suppose the demand curve is $D(q) = -0.06q + 71.863$ and the supply curve is $S(q) = 16.977(1.001117)^q$ where q is the number of units of the product. We want to find the social gain at the equilibrium price.

Enter $D(q) = -0.06q + 71.863$ in y1 and $S(q) = 16.977(1.001117)^q$ in y2.	`y1=-.06 x+71.863`
	`y2=...977(1.001117)^x`
	
	`y(x)= RANGE ZOOM TRACE GRAPH`
	`x  y  INSf DELf SELCT`

Graph y1 and y2 in a suitable viewing window, say x between 0 and 1000 and y between 0 and 80. Use the methods of 7.2.4 of this *Guide* to find the intersection of the demand and supply functions. $q = 628$ and $D(q) = S(q) \approx 34.21$ is the equilibrium point. (Note that since $x = q$ is the number of units of a product, it should be a whole number.)	`ISECT` `X=627.57660514 _y=34.208403692 _`

The consumers' surplus at equilibrium is
$$\int_0^{628} -0.06x + 71.863\, dx - 628(34.21) = 11{,}814.56$$
	`fnInt(y1,x,0,628)-628`
	`(34.21)`
	`            11814.564`
	
	`evalF nDer der1 der2 fnInt`

The producers' surplus at equilibrium is
$$\int_0^{628} 16.977(1.001117)^x\, dx - 628(34.21) = 6{,}034.28$$
	`628(34.21)-fnInt(y2,x`
	`,0,628)`
	`        6034.27595821`

Thus, the social gain is $11{,}814.56 + 6{,}034.28 = 17{,}848.84$.
 	
Note that you could have calculated the social gain as the area between the demand and supply curves.
	`fnInt(y1-y2,x,0,628)`
	`        17848.8399582`
	
	`evalF nDer der1 der2 fnInt`

TI-85 Calculator Appendix

Programs listed below are referenced in *Part B* of this *Guide*. They should be typed in your calculator, transferred to you via a cable using the LINK mode of TI-85, or transferred to your calculator using the TI-GRAPH LINK™ cable and software for a PC or Macintosh computer and a disk containing these programs. Refer to your owner's manual for instructions on typing in the programs or transferring them via a cable from another calculator.

```
TABLE                • Program
  :Disp "Enter equation in y1"
  :Input "Continue? Yes 1 No 2
    ",C
  :Disp "Enter Q for x to end"
  :If C==2:Stop
  :-9999999999→Q
  :Lbl M
  :Input "x=",x
  :If x==Q:Stop
  :Disp "y1=",y1
  :Goto M


STPLT                • Program
  :dimL L1→N
  :min(L1)→A1
  :max(L1)→B1
  :min(L2)→C1
  :max(L2)→D1
  :(B1-A1)/10→X1:(D1-C1)/10→Y1
  :A1-X1→xMin:B1+X1→xMax
  :C1-1.5*Y1→yMin:D1+Y1→yMax
  :0→xScl
  :0→yScl
  :(xMax-xMin)/125.5→P1
  :(xMax-xMin)/128.5→P2
  :(yMax-yMin)/62→P3
  :For(K,1,N,1)
  :L1(K)-P2→W1
  :L1(K)+P1→W2
  :L2(K)-P3→H1
  :L2(K)+P3→H2
  :Line(W1,H2,W2,H2)
  :Line(W2,H2,W2,H1)
  :Line(W2,H1,W1,H1)
  :Line(W1,H1,W1,H2)
  :End
```

```
DIFF                 • Program
  :ClLCD
  :Disp "Store x-values in L1"
  :Disp "Store y-values in L2"
  :Input "Continue? Yes 1 No 2
    ",C
  :If C==2:Stop
  :dimL L1→M
  :dimL L2→N
  :If M≠N:Goto Z
  :Disp "See the"
  :Disp "1st difference in L3"
  :Disp "2nd difference in L4"
  :Disp "percent change in L5"
  :1→A
  :M-1→dimL L3
  :For(A,1,M-1,1)
  :L2(A+1)-L2(A)→L3(A)
  :End
  :M-2→dimL L4
  :1→B
  :For(B,1,M-2,1)
  :L3(B+1)-L3(B)→L4(B)
  :End
  :M-1→dimL L5
  :1→E
  :For(E,1,M-1,1)
  :(L3(E)/L2(E))*100→L5(E)
  :End
  :Stop
  :Lbl Z
  :Disp "Lists are of unequal"
  :Disp "length. Check data."
  :Stop
```

```
LSLINE              • Program
  :FnOff
  :0→A:0→B:1→C
  :y1=A+B x
  :L1→xStat
  :L2→yStat
  :dimL xStat→N
  :ClLCD
  :Disp "You will next view"
  :Disp "the data. Use tick"
  :Disp "marks to guess the"
  :Disp "slope and y-intercept"
  :Disp "of best fit line."
  :Disp "xScl=":Outpt(6,7,xScl)
  :Disp "yScl=":Outpt(7,7,yScl)
  :Pause
  :Lbl A1
  :Scatter
  :Pause
  :Disp ""
  :Input "slope=",B
  :Input "y intercept=",A
  :1→K:0→x:0→S
  :Lbl V
  :xStat(K)→x
  :y1→Y
  :(yStat(K)-Y)²+S→S
  :Line(xStat(K),yStat(K),x,Y)
  :K+1→K
  :If K≤N
  :Goto V
  :Pause
  :Disp "SSE=",S
  :Pause
  :If C==2
  :Goto W
  :Input "Try again? Y(1) N(2) ",C
  :If C==1
  :Goto A1
  :LinR
  :ShwSt
  :Pause
  :DrawF RegEq
  :Pause
  :a→A:b→B
  :1→K:0→x:0→S
  :Goto V
  :Lbl W
  :FnOff
```

```
LOGISTIC            • Program
  :ClLCD
  :Disp "Have data in L1,L2"
  :Disp ""
  :Disp "Program clears L3,L4"
  :Disp "and leaves eq in y2"
  :Disp ""
  :Disp "ENTER continues."
  :Pause
  :Y=1:ClLCD
  :dimL L1→N:dimL L2→D
  :If N≠D:Goto F
  :y2=L/(1+A e^(-B x))
  :FnOff
  :STPLT
  :Pause
  :0→L3:0→L4
  :For(I,1,N-2,1)
  :L2(I+1)→L3(I)
  :(L2(I+2)-L2(I))/((L1(I+2)-
    L1(I))L2(I+1))→L4(I)
  :End
  :LinR (L3,L4)
  :a/-b→U
  :max(L2)+.0001→V
  :max(U,V)→L
  :0→W:0→G
  :(sum L2)/N→M
  :For(J,1,N,1)
  :W+(M-L2(J))²→W
  :End
  :Disp "SSY=",W
  :Disp "L=",L
  :Goto Q
  :Lbl A2
  :0→G
  :Lbl E
  :Prompt L
  :Lbl Q
  :0→L3:0→L4
  :For(I,1,N)
  :L1(I)→L3(I)
  :L-L2(I)→Z
  :If Z>0
  :Then
  :ln (Z/L2(I))→L4(I)
  :Else
  :Disp "BAD VALUE FOR L"
  :Disp "...INCREASE L"
  :Goto A2
  :End
  :End
  :LinR (L3,L4)
  :a→C
  :-b→B
  :e^C→A
  :If G==2:Goto P
  :ClDrw
  :FnOn 2
```

(Program LOGISTIC continued)

```
  :STPLT
  :Pause
  :Lbl P
  :FnOff 2
  :S→T
  :0→S
  :For(K,1,N,1)
  :L1(K)→x
  :y2→H
  :S+(L2(K)-H)²→S
  :End
  :If Y≠1:Disp "previous
    SSE=",T
  :Disp "SSE=",S
  :Y+1→Y
  :Pause
  :ClLCD
  :Disp "SELECT ONE:"
  :Disp "Change L        (1)"
  :Disp "Change L,graph (2)"
  :Disp "Quit on graph  (3)"
  :Input "Quit on model  (4)
    ",R
  :If R==1:Goto A1
  :If R==2:Goto A2
  :If R==3:Goto A3
  :If R==4:Goto A4
  :Lbl A1
  :2→G
  :Goto E
  :Lbl A3
  :FnOn 2
  :STPLT
  :Stop
  :Lbl A4
  :ClLCD
  :Disp "y=L/(1+Ae^(-Bx))"
  :Outpt(2,3,"L=")
  :Outpt(2,6,L)
  :Outpt(4,3,"A=")
  :Outpt(4,6,A)
  :Outpt(6,3,"B=")
  :Outpt(6,6,B)
  :Outpt(8,1,"SSE=")
  :Outpt(8,6,S)
  :Stop
  :Lbl F
  :Disp "Lists are of unequal"
  :Disp "length. Check data."
  :Stop
```

```
NUMINTG          • Program
  :ClLCD
  :Disp "Enter f(x) in y1."
  :Disp ""
  :Disp "Draw graph of f."
  :Disp ""
  :Disp "Continue?"
  :Input "Yes (1) No (2) ",G
  :If G==2:Stop
  :Disp ""
  :Disp "Draw Pictures?"
  :Input "Yes(1) No(2) ",H
  :ClLCD
  :Input "Lower Limit? ",A
  :Input "Upper Limit? ",B
  :0→yMin
  :min(y1(A),y1(B))→θ
  :If θ<0:0→yMin
  :Lbl A0
  :ClLCD
  :Disp "Enter Choice:"
  :Disp "Left Rect   (1)"
  :Disp "Right Rect  (2)"
  :Disp "Trapezoids (3)"
  :Disp "Midpt Rect  (4)"
  :Input "Simpsons    (5) ",R
  :Lbl A1
  :ClDrw
  :Disp ""
  :Input "N? ",N
  :(B-A)/N→W
  :0→S:1→C
  :Lbl A2
  :If R==1:Goto A3
  :If R==2:Goto A4
  :If R==3:Goto A3
  :If R==4:Goto A5
  :If R==5:Goto A6
  :Lbl A3
  :A+(C-1)W→x
  :x→J:x+W→L
  :Goto A7
  :Lbl A4
  :A+C*W→x
  :x-W→J:x→L
  :Goto A7
  :Lbl A5
  :If H≠1:Then
  :If N>5:Then
  :1→Z:W/2→H:A→x
  :Lbl A8
  :x+H→x:y1+S→S
  :A+Z*W→x
  :IS>(Z,N):Goto A8
  :S*W→S:Goto T
  :End:End
  :A+C*W-W/2→x
  :x-W/2→J
  :x+W/2→L
  :Goto A7
  :Lbl A6
  :If fPart (N/2)≠0:Then:
  :Disp ""
  :Disp "N is odd,"
  :Disp "Simpsons Rule"
  :Disp "not calculated."
```

(Program NUMINTG continued)

```
  :Pause :Goto E
  :End
  :If H==1:Then
  :Disp ""
  :Disp "No picture for"
  :Disp "Simpsons Rule"
  :End
  :A→G:G+W→G:G→V
  :Lbl A9
  :V→x:y1→Y:V+W→x
  :4Y+2y1+S→S
  :V+2*W→V
  :If V<B:Goto A9
  :G-W→x:y1→E
  :B→x:y1→F
  :(W/3)*(S+E-F)→S
  :Goto T
  :Lbl A7
  :y1→K:K+S→S
  :If H==1:Goto D
  :Lbl I
  :IS>(C,N)
  :Goto A2
  :If R==3:Then
  :A→x:y1→P
  :B→x:y1→Q
  :S+(Q-P)/2→S
  :End
  :W*S→S
  :Lbl T
  :Disp "SUM=",S
  :Pause
  :ClLCD
  :Lbl E
  :ClLCD
  :Disp "Enter Choice:"
  :Disp "Change N      (1)"
  :Disp "Change Method (2)"
  :Input "Quit         (3)
  ",T
  :If T==1:Goto A1
  :If T==2:Goto A0
  :If T==3:Goto F
  :Lbl F
  :Stop
  :Lbl D
  :If R==3:Then
  :x→I:L→x
  :y1→M:I→x
  :Else:K→M
  :End
  :Line(J,0,J,K)
  :Line(J,K,L,M)
  :Line(L,M,L,0)
  :If C==N:Pause
  :Goto I
```

Part C   Hewlett-Packard HP-48G Series Calculator

CHAPTER 1.   THE INGREDIENTS OF CHANGE: FUNCTIONS AND LINEAR MODELS

Setup: The HP-48G series (48G/48GX) offers a choice of two methods of accessing calculator applications: *screen interface* or *stack interface*. The screen interface, available for use when the green right-shift key $\boxed{\rightarrow}$ is pressed before an application printed in green type, provides access through dialog boxes on the screen. The stack interface uses the standard HP-48 softkeys and the stack to easily approach all commands related to a particular topic when the application key (printed in purple type) is preceded by the purple left-shift $\boxed{\leftarrow}$ key. Both operational methods will be illustrated in this *Guide*.

Turn your HP-48 on. At the top left of the display screen is information telling you where you are in the calculator's directory system. Directories are like file folders that organize information and applications. If only { HOME } is printed in the top left corner, you are in your HOME directory. The menus at the bottom of the screen change depending on the directory you have chosen. Anything you store in the calculator is in the VAR directory. Many directories have a lot of menu items. To see all of these, press $\boxed{\text{NXT}}$ to scroll thorough the menu items when you enter a particular directory.

It is helpful to create a calculus directory to hold the programs given in this *Guide*. Before creating your directory, press $\boxed{\rightarrow}$ $\boxed{\text{'}}$ (HOME) to return to your home directory. To create your calculus concepts directory, first press $\boxed{\rightarrow}$ $\boxed{\text{VAR}}$ (MEMORY) $\boxed{\text{NEW}}$ and $\boxed{\blacktriangledown}$. You should now be in the NAME: location. Although this directory can be given any name, we suggest CALCC. Enter CALCC on the stack.

- All alphabetic characters must be preceded by the alphabetic key $\boxed{\alpha}$. Whenever you are typing several alphabetic characters, you will find it convenient to holddown the $\boxed{\alpha}$ key with one hand and continue holding it while you type in the letters with your other hand. When you finish typing, release the $\boxed{\alpha}$ key.

Press $\boxed{\text{OK}}$ and $\boxed{\sqrt{\text{CHK}}}$ $\boxed{\text{OK}}$. $\boxed{\text{OK}}$ returns you to the stack, and you should see the name of the new directory in your variables ($\boxed{\text{VAR}}$) menu.

Check the HP's basic setup by pressing $\boxed{\rightarrow}$ $\boxed{\text{CST}}$ (MODES). Choose **Std** number format, **Radians** as the angle measure, and **Rectangular** for the coordinate system.

- If a particular setting is not chosen, press $\boxed{\text{CHOOS}}$, use the cursor keys to move to the desired setting, and press $\boxed{\text{OK}}$. Press $\boxed{\text{ON}}$ to return to the stack when done.

SECTION 1.1 FUNDAMENTALS OF MODELING

1.1.1 Calculating: HP calculators offer two ways of working with numbers and expressions. When using either method, you need to remember that the times sign × must be used to indicate a product, and you must press the α key before typing any letter, even X. Now, press CALCC to enter your calculus directory.

Levels 1-4 of the *stack* are on your home screen. Like lines on a piece of paper, the stack is a sequence of temporary storage locations for numbers and the other kinds of objects used by the calculator.	4: 3: 2: 1:

Use the stack to combine numbers and expressions. The idea is this -- put inputs on the stack and then execute commands that use the inputs.

Evaluate $\frac{1}{4 * 15 + \frac{895}{7}}$. The result 5.32319391635E⁻3 means $5.32319391635*10^{-3}$, the scientific notation expression for 0.00532319391635.	Type 4 and press ENTER. Type 15 and press ×. Type 895 and press ENTER. Type 7 and press ÷. Press + and 1/x to see 5.32319391635E⁻3.
Evaluate $\frac{(^-3)^4 - 5}{8 + 1.456}$. (Use +/- for the negative symbol and − for the subtraction sign.)	Type 3; press +/- ENTER. Type 4 and press y^x. Type 5 and press − Type 8 and press ENTER. Type 1.456 and press + ÷ to see 8.0372250423.

- To recapture the stack after you perform an operation, press ↱ EVAL (UNDO).
- To change object positions in the bottom two levels of the stack, press ▷ (SWAP).
- You can build complicated expressions using stack operations. Just remember that whatever operation key you press will take as its inputs what is in level 1 and level 2 of the stack.
- Any time you want to erase or clear the entire stack, press ↰ DEL (CLEAR).

- Pressing ◀ drops what is in level 1 of the stack.

Another method of working with numbers or expressions on the HP is to use algebraic entry form. When you enclose an expression inside of the ' ' symbols, it becomes an algebraic object and is not evaluated until you press EVAL.

Evaluate $e^3*0.027$ and $e^{3*0.027}$. (After keying in the 3 in the first expression, use ▶ to move outside the right parenthesis before continuing to type. The calculator will assume you mean the first expression unless you use parentheses around the two values in the exponent. (It is not necessary to type in the 0 *before* the decimal point.)	4: 3: 2: ' EXP(3)*.027' 1: ' EXP(3*.027)'
Press EVAL ▶ to evaluate $e^3*0.027$ and place its value in level 2 of the stack. Press EVAL to evaluate $e^{3*0.027}$. Press ▶ to swap the values back to their original positions.	4: 3: 2: .542309496926 1: 1.08437089657

- You can type in lengthy expressions using this format; just make sure that you use parentheses when you are not sure of the calculator's order of operations. As a general rule, numerators and denominators of fractions and powers consisting of more than one term should be enclosed in parentheses.

1.1.3 Answer Display:
The HP-48 can provide the calculated answer as a fraction. The calculator often uses scientific display as the answer format.

The "to a fraction" key is obtained by pressing ← 9 (SYMBOLIC) NXT →Q . Find the sum $\frac{2}{5}+\frac{1}{3}$ and convert to a fraction. Convert 0.3875 to a fraction.	4: 3: 2: '11/15' 1: '31/80'
The calculator's symbol for "times 10^{12}" is **E**12. Thus, 7.945**E**12 means 7,945,000,000,000. Type in 5,600,000,000,000, press ENTER, type 2,345,000,000,000 and press + .	4: 3: 2: 1: 7.945E12

1.1.4 Storing Values: Sometimes it is beneficial to store numbers or expressions for later recall. To store a number or expression, type it on the display, press $\boxed{'}$, enter the name in which you wish to store the variable, and press $\boxed{\text{STO}}$.

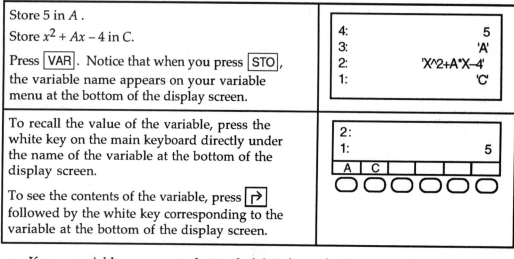

Store 5 in A. Store $x^2 + Ax - 4$ in C. Press $\boxed{\text{VAR}}$. Notice that when you press $\boxed{\text{STO}}$, the variable name appears on your variable menu at the bottom of the display screen.	4: 5 3: 'A' 2: 'X^2+A*X−4' 1: 'C'
To recall the value of the variable, press the white key on the main keyboard directly under the name of the variable at the bottom of the display screen. To see the contents of the variable, press $\boxed{\rightarrow}$ followed by the white key corresponding to the variable at the bottom of the display screen.	2: 1: 5 [A][C][ ][ ][ ][ ] ◯ ◯ ◯ ◯ ◯ ◯

• If your variable menu gets cluttered, delete (purge) all unwanted variables by first pressing $\boxed{'}$, press the white key corresponding to the unwanted variable on the menu at the bottom of the display screen, and then press $\boxed{\leftarrow}$ $\boxed{\text{EEX}}$ (PURGE). Be *very careful* that you only purge unwanted variables and not a built-in routine or a program you wish to keep. Things that are purged may not be able to be recovered.

1.1.5 Error Messages: When your input is incorrect, an error message is displayed. Pressing $\boxed{\text{ON}}$ or $\boxed{\text{ENTER}}$ should return the calculator to its normal operation mode. If things are not going well on the command line (where you enter expressions), remember that the $\boxed{\blacktriangleleft}$ key will backspace and delete. If you get an **invalid syntax** message, the cursor will appear at the location of the error. In that case, use $\boxed{\blacktriangleleft}$ or $\boxed{\blacktriangleright}$ to move the cursor, delete any incorrect symbol or insert a needed symbol, and press $\boxed{\text{ENTER}}$.

1.1.6 Entering an Equation to be Graphed: You can use either the screen interface or the stack interface to enter an equation to be graphed.

SCREEN INTERFACE METHOD: Press $\boxed{\leftarrow}$ $\boxed{8}$ (PLOT). If the Ptype is not FUNCTION, press $\boxed{\text{PTYPE}}$ and $\boxed{\text{FUNC}}$. Press $\boxed{'}$ and enter your *expression* in level 1 of the stack. Press $\boxed{\leftarrow}$ $\boxed{\text{EQ}}$ to store $y = expression$ as the current equation.

STACK INTERFACE METHOD: Press ⟦→⟧ ⟦8⟧ (PLOT). If the TYPE is not Function, press ⟦▲⟧ ⟦CHOOS⟧ and select Function with ⟦OK⟧. Press ⟦▼⟧, enter the expression, and press ⟦OK⟧. You can use any letter you wish for the input variable. However, you must tell your HP-48 the name of the input variable in the INDEP location by first moving to that location, entering the name of the variable, and then pressing ⟦OK⟧. ⟦OK⟧ exits.

Choose the method you prefer, and enter $A = 1000(1 + 0.05x)$ as your current EQ. (The expression to the right is entered as it appears in either the screen or stack interface method.)	4: 3: 2: 1: '1000*(1+.05*X)'

1.1.7 Drawing a Graph: Follow the basic procedures shown next to draw a graph with your calculator. Always begin by storing the *expression* part of $y = expression$ in EQ. Let us draw the graph of $1000(1 + 0.05x)$.

Press ⟦→⟧ ⟦8⟧ (PLOT). EQ should contain the equation entered in 1.1.6 of this *Guide*. Use ⟦▼⟧ and ⟦▶⟧ to move to the H-VIEW values. Press ⟦NXT⟧ ⟦RESET⟧. Use ⟦▼⟧ to move to the Reset plot option and press ⟦OK⟧.	The horizontal view is set to: ⁻6.5 6.5 The vertical view is set to: ⁻3.1 3.2
Press ⟦NXT⟧ ⟦ERASE⟧ ⟦DRAW⟧. Notice that the graphics screen is blank. Press ⟦ON⟧ to return to the PLOT menu.	

- The settings of the left and right edges of the viewing screen are the values in H-VIEW, and the settings for the lower and upper edges of the viewing screen are the values in V-VIEW. If you want to set the spacing between the tick marks on the x- and y-axes, press ⟦OPTS⟧ on the PLOT menu and choose appropriate settings for H-TICK and V-TICK.

- Remember that whenever you want to change a setting on the PLOT screen, you must first use the cursor keys to move to the position containing the setting you want to change. That position should then be darkened and ready for changes.

1.1.8 Changing the View of the Graph: If your view of the graph is not good or if you do not see the graph, change the view with one of the ZOOM options, autoscale the graph, or manually set the view.   (We later discuss the ZOOM options.)

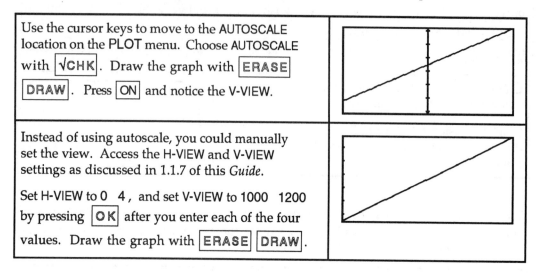

| Use the cursor keys to move to the AUTOSCALE location on the PLOT menu. Choose AUTOSCALE with √CHK . Draw the graph with ERASE DRAW . Press ON and notice the V-VIEW. | |
| Instead of using autoscale, you could manually set the view. Access the H-VIEW and V-VIEW settings as discussed in 1.1.7 of this *Guide*.

Set H-VIEW to 0   4 , and set V-VIEW to 1000   1200 by pressing OK after you enter each of the four values. Draw the graph with ERASE DRAW . | |

1.1.9 Tracing: You can display the coordinates of certain points on the graph by *tracing* the graph. The *x*-values shown when you trace are dependent on the horizontal view that is set for the graph, and the *y*-values are calculated by substituting the *x*-values into the equation that is being graphed.

| Press TRACE , and use ▶ to move the trace cursor to the right and ◀ to move the trace cursor to the left. | (x,y) removes the menu from the display screen and shows the coordinates as you trace. |

1.1.10 Estimating Outputs: You can estimate outputs from the graph of an equation in the graphing list using TRACE. It is important to realize that such outputs are *never* exact values unless the displayed *x*-value is *identically* the same as the value of the input variable.

| Estimate the value of *A* where $A = 1000(1 + 0.05x)$ when x = 5, x = 7, and x = 10.

If you do not have the settings shown to the right on your PLOT menu, reset those values. | H-VIEW: 0   4

V-VIEW   1000   1200 |

Draw the graph, and press $\boxed{\text{ZOOM}}$ $\boxed{\text{ZOUT}}$.	Press $\boxed{\text{ON}}$ and observe the values now defining the graphics screen.
Press $\boxed{\text{O K}}$ and use $\blacktriangleleft$ to return the graph to the screen. Press $\boxed{\text{TRACE}}$ $\boxed{\text{(x,y)}}$ and press and hold $\blacktriangleright$ to move as close as you can to $x = 5$.	An *estimate* for A when $x = 5$ is $1.25\text{E}3 = 1250$. (You may not obtain this same value, but yours should be close.)
Continue pressing $\blacktriangleright$ to obtain an *estimate* for A when $x = 7$.	An *estimate* for A when $x = 7$ is $1.35\text{E}3 = 1350$.

- If your H-VIEW has an upper value of 10, you should obtain from tracing the *exact* value $A = 1500$ when $x = 10$ because 10, not a value "close to" 10, is the displayed x-value.

- If you want "nice, friendly" values displayed for x when tracing, set the H-VIEW so that the difference in the upper and lower values is a multiple of 13, the width of the RESET viewing screen. For instance, if you set the H-VIEW: 0 13 in the example above, the *exact* values when $x = 5$, $x = 7$, and $x = 10$ are displayed when you trace. Another view that gives friendly values is H-VIEW: ⁻5 21 since $26 = 2(13)$. Try it!

1.1.11 Evaluating Outputs: The HP-48 evaluates outputs from an expression entered in EQ using either the screen interface or the stack interface. We illustrate the stack interface below. Explore the screen interface and choose the method you prefer.

Press $\boxed{\leftarrow}$ $\boxed{7}$ (SOLVE) $\boxed{\text{ROOT}}$. Press $\boxed{\text{E Q}}$. If '1000*(1+.05*X)' is not returned to the stack, store it as EQ.	If necessary, enter ' 1000*(1+.05*X) ' and press $\boxed{\leftarrow}$ $\boxed{\text{E Q}}$.
Press $\boxed{\text{SOLVR}}$. Type the input at which you want the expression evaluated and press $\boxed{\text{X}}$. Press $\boxed{\text{EXPR=}}$ and the output is returned to the stack. Evaluate EQ at $x = 5, 7,$ and 10.	4: 3: Expr: 1250 2: Expr: 1350 1: Expr: 1500

- The values obtained by this evaluation process are *actual* output values of the equation, not *estimated* values such as those generally obtained by tracing.

SECTION 1.2 FUNCTIONS AND GRAPHS

1.2.1 Evaluating Functions: Function outputs can be determined using the SOLVE application as discussed in 1.1.11 of this *Guide*. You can also evaluate functions from your VAR menu or automate the process using program F.val found in the HP-48 Appendix.

Press $\boxed{\text{VAR}}$ to return to your variables menu. Press $\boxed{\text{E Q}}$. If '1000*(1+.05*X)' is not returned to the stack, store it as EQ. Store an input value, say 5, in X with $\boxed{\leftharpoonup}$ $\boxed{\text{X}}$.	If there is no X on your variables menu, store the first value with 5 $\boxed{\text{ENTER}}$ $\boxed{\text{'}}$ $\boxed{\alpha}$ X $\boxed{\text{STO}}$.
Press $\boxed{\text{E Q}}$ $\boxed{\text{EVAL}}$. (Repeat this process for other input values.)	1250, the output for an input of 5, is returned to the stack.
To automate this process, run program F.val. Locate the program on your VAR menu. *Before executing the program, enter the input value, say 7, on the stack.* Execute the program by pressing $\boxed{\text{F.VAL}}$.	4: 3: 2: 1: 1350

1.2.2 Solving for Input Values: Your calculator solves for input values of an equation that you enter in the SOLVR application. You can use any letter you wish for the input variable when using SOLVR. You can even enter an equation consisting of several variables!

Suppose we want to solve $A = 1000(1 + 0.05x)$ for x when $A = 1800$.

Press $\boxed{\leftharpoonup}$ $\boxed{7}$ (SOLVE) $\boxed{\text{ROOT}}$ $\boxed{\text{E Q}}$. Press $\boxed{\leftharpoonup}$ $\boxed{+/-}$ (EDIT), press $\boxed{\blacktriangleright}$ to move inside the ' and type A $\boxed{\leftharpoonup}$ $\boxed{0}$ (=) so that you now have 'A=1000*(1+.05*X)' on the stack. Press $\boxed{\text{ENTER}}$. Store this as EQ with $\boxed{\leftharpoonup}$ $\boxed{\text{E Q}}$.	To solve for input values, you must have a "left-side" equal to a "right-side" in EQ. Either edit the current EQ to this form or enter a new equation.

Press $\boxed{\text{SOLVR}}$. What x gives $1800 = 1000(1 + 0.05x)$? Enter 1800 for **A** by entering 1800 and pressing $\boxed{\text{A}}$. Solve for x by pressing $\boxed{\text{←}}$ $\boxed{\text{X}}$.	4: 3: 2: 1: X: 16

Suppose you want to solve the equation $-2p^3 + 8p^2 + 4p - 4 = (p + 3)^2 - 8$ for p.

Press $\boxed{\text{←}}$ $\boxed{7}$ (SOLVE) $\boxed{\text{ROOT}}$. Enter the above equation on the stack. Store this as EQ with $\boxed{\text{←}}$ $\boxed{\text{EQ}}$.	3: 2: 1: '-2*P^3+8*P^2+4*P–4= (P+3)^2–8'
Press $\boxed{\text{SOLVR}}$. Solve for p by pressing $\boxed{\text{←}}$ $\boxed{\text{P}}$. (You may not get the same value as the one shown on the right.)	4: 3: 2: 1: P: 1.32716675345
There are several solutions to this equation. To see this, let us draw its graph. Access the **PLOT** application and notice that the equation is the current EQ. The variable is p, not x, so *enter P in the INDPT line.* Set a horizontal view of ⁻10 to 10 and choose autoscale. Draw the graph.	 The left and right-hand sides of EQ draw as two separate graphs.
Press $\boxed{\text{ON}}$, and reset the horizontal view to between ⁻2 and 4. This interval appears to contain all the points where the two curves intersect. Redraw the graph.	

You can now trace the graphs to determine approximately where they intersect. Record
the approximate p-location of each intersection point on paper. ($\approx$ ⁻0.7, 3, 1)

| To finish solving this equation using the SOLVR, press $\boxed{\text{ON}}$, enter your estimate of the p-value of the intersection in P by placing it on the stack and pressing $\boxed{\text{P}}$, and then solving for P with $\boxed{\Leftarrow}$ $\boxed{\text{P}}$.

Repeat with the other two estimates. | 4:
3: P: -.664015644747
2:    P: 2.8368488913
1:    P: 1.32716675345 |

It is also possible to solve this equation graphically. In fact, it is easier graphically.

| Press $\boxed{\blacktriangleleft}$ to return the last-drawn graph to the screen.

Press $\boxed{\text{FCN}}$ $\boxed{\text{ISECT}}$. One of the points of intersection is returned to the screen.

Find the other two points of intersection by using the cursor keys to move the cursor near the intersection point and pressing $\boxed{\text{ISECT}}$. | Return the FCN menu to the screen after each intersection point is found by pressing one of the white keys in the top row of keys directly under the display screen.

Press $\boxed{\text{ON}}$ and notice that the three points are on the stack. |

1.2.3 Graphically Finding Intercepts:
To find the y-intercept of a function $y = f(x)$, set $x=0$ and solve the resulting equation. To find the x-intercept of a function $y = f(x)$, set $y=0$ and solve the resulting equation. The solving process can be done graphically as well as by the methods indicated in 1.2.2 of this *Guide*.

Access the PLOT menu. Enter $4x - x^2 - 2$ in EQ. Choose x as the INDEP variable. Set H-VIEW to ⁻6.5 6.5 , and set V-VIEW to ⁻6 3.1. Draw the graph.	
Find the y-intercept of $y = 4x - x^2 - 2$ by letting x be 0 and using one of the methods of 2.1.1 to evaluate EQ.	The y-intercept is ⁻2.
To graphically find the x-intercepts, press $\boxed{\text{FCN}}$ $\boxed{\text{ROOT}}$. One of the intersection points is returned to the screen and put on the stack. Find the other point of intersection by moving the cursor near the point where the graph crosses the horizontal axis and press $\boxed{\text{ROOT}}$.	The graph shows there are two x-intercepts. The roots (x-intercepts) are 0.585786437628 and 3.41421356238.

1.2.4 Combining Functions: The HP-48 can easily draw the graph of the sum, difference, product, quotient, and composition of two functions. You can use any of the methods for evaluating functions to determine outputs for function combinations.

Enter $f(x) = x^2 - 1$ on the stack . Enter $g(x) = 0.3x + 5$ in on the stack. Press `←` `▲` (STACK) `NXT` `DUP2` to duplicate the two functions. Press `←` `+` ({}) `ENTER` `+` `+` to create a list containing the functions in levels 1 and 2.	3: 'X^2−1' 2: '.3*X +5' 1: { 'X^2 - 1' '.3*X +5 ' }

- You could also have entered this equation as 'X^2−1 = .3*X+5'. However, you can only graph two functions by joining them with the equal sign whereas using lists will allow you to graph any number of functions.

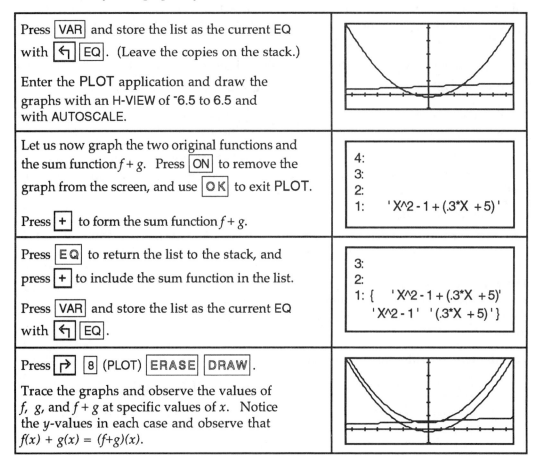

Press `VAR` and store the list as the current EQ with `←` `EQ`. (Leave the copies on the stack.) Enter the PLOT application and draw the graphs with an H-VIEW of ⁻6.5 to 6.5 and with AUTOSCALE.	
Let us now graph the two original functions and the sum function $f + g$. Press `ON` to remove the graph from the screen, and use `OK` to exit PLOT. Press `+` to form the sum function $f + g$.	4: 3: 2: 1: 'X^2 - 1 + (.3*X +5)'
Press `EQ` to return the list to the stack, and press `+` to include the sum function in the list. Press `VAR` and store the list as the current EQ with `←` `EQ`.	3: 2: 1: { 'X^2 - 1 + (.3*X +5)' 'X^2 - 1 ' '(.3*X +5)'}
Press `→` `8` (PLOT) `ERASE` `DRAW`. Trace the graphs and observe the values of f, g, and $f + g$ at specific values of x. Notice the y-values in each case and observe that $f(x) + g(x) = (f+g)(x)$.	

Repeat this procedure for the difference function $(f–g)(x)= f(x) – g(x)$ and the product function $(f^*g)(x)= f(x)\ g(x)$.	As you are tracing, remember that ▼ or ◄ lets you jump between the three graphs.
The HP-48 does not have a special notation for the composition of two functions. To have the calculator graph the composite function $f(g(x))$, you should enter the function on the right.	4: 3: 2: 1: '(.3*X +5)^2 – 1'

SECTION 1.3 LINEAR FUNCTIONS AND MODELS

1.3.1 Entering Data: Data you enter in the HP-48 is stored in the statistical matrix called ΣDAT. Different sets of data, each called ΣDAT, can be in different directories of your calculator. Therefore, it is important that you be in the directory you want to hold the data before entering any data.

- If you have changed directories, you should always recall ΣDAT to the stack by pressing |ΣDAT| to be sure you are working with the correct data.

- If you do not clear the old data before entering new data, the new data is appended to the end of the old data and you will obtain incorrect results.

There are several ways to input data in the HP-48. Two of these, entering data using the stack interface and using the screen interface, are discussed below. Try both methods, and then choose the one you prefer.

Enter the following data:

x	1984	1985	1987	1990	1992
y	37	35	29	20	14

The ΣDAT matrix contains a row for each data *point* and a column for each *variable*. The number of rows that are entered equals the number of data points. Thus, to enter the data above, you will use five rows with x in the first column and y in the second column.

To enter two-variable statistical data using screen interface:

- Press |↱| |5| (STAT)|OK| to choose Single-variable. If there already is data in ΣDAT (i.e., the highlighted space to the right of ΣDAT: is *not* empty), press |DEL| |OK|.

- Press |EDIT| to enter the MatrixWriter application.

- Key in the first x-data value (1984) press ENTER, key in the next x-data value (1985), press ENTER, etc. until you have entered all the x-data (i.e., the years) in the first column. Press ▶ to move to the top of the second column.

- Key in the y-data values in the same manner, remembering to press ENTER after typing each one.

- Press ENTER to temporarily store the data into the ΣDAT matrix and return to the **STAT** screen.

- Press OK to make the entered data the current ΣDAT matrix.

Press VAR ΣDAT.
 	
(On your calculator screen, the last row is hidden by the menu.)
	1: [[1984 37]
	     [1985 35]
	     [1987 29]
	     [1990 20]
	     [1992 14]]

To enter two-variable statistical data using screen interface:

- Press ◄┐ 5 (STAT) and DATA to bring up the statistics data entry menu.

- Press CLΣ *before* beginning data entry.

- Press ◄┐ X ([ ]) to let the HP-48 know you are entering two-variable data.

- Type in the first x-data value (1984), press SPC, and then type in the first y-data value (37). Press Σ+ to enter the first row of ΣDAT.

- After the first row is entered, do not use brackets. Key in the next data point (1985 35), separating the x- and y-values with SPC. Press Σ+. Continue in this manner until all 5 rows are entered.

- Press ΣDAT at any time during data entry to view the matrix.

Press VAR ΣDAT.
 	
(Your last row is hidden by the menu.)
 	
ΣDAT will be stored in the directory that is currently chosen in your **VAR** menu.
	1: [[1984 37]
	     [1985 35]
	     [1987 29]
	     [1990 20]
	     [1992 14]]

1.3.2 Editing Data: If you incorrectly type a data value before you enter it, use ◀
to delete the unwanted character(s) and type the correct value.

To check your data entry, press |ΣDAT| and ▼. The data appears in the **Matrix
Writer** and you can move around and view the values with ◀, ▶, ▲, and/or ▼.
If a value needs to be corrected, move the cursor to darken that value. Type the correct
value and press |ENTER|. Press |ENTER| to return to the stack. *You must now press* |↰|
|ΣDAT| *to store the edited matrix as ΣDAT -- otherwise, your corrections are not saved.*

1.3.3 Deleting Old Data: Whenever you enter new data in your calculator, you
should first delete any previously-entered data from your current **VAR** menu by pressing
|'| |ΣDAT| |↰| |EEX| |ENTER| (PURGE) **or** |↰| |5| (STAT) |DATA| |CLΣ|.

1.3.4 Aligning Data: Suppose you want the first column of ΣDAT to contain the
number of years since a certain year (here, 1984) instead of actual years. That is, you
want to *align* the x-data. Use program **ALIGN** (found in the HP Appendix) to align the
x-data.

Before running the program,

> *have ΣDAT on level 2 of the stack;*
> *have the number you want to subtract from each x-data value on level 1.*

Press |ΣDAT| and then type 1 9 8 4 |ENTER|.	1: [[0 37]
Press |ALIGN| and view the aligned data.	[1 35]
	[3 29]
Press |ΣDAT| and notice that the program	[6 20]
has stored the aligned data as the new ΣDAT.	[8 14]]
(Press ▼ to see all five data points.)	

1.3.5 Plotting Data: The HP-48 has a built-in scatterplot command accessed with
|↰| |5| (STAT) |PLOT| |SCATR|. Try it if you like, but you will find it more convenient
to use program **STPLT** to draw a scatterplot with large dots and to automatically
choose the horizontal and vertical views.

Let us draw a scatterplot of the aligned data given in 1.3.4 of this *Guide*.

Before running program STPLT,

> *have ΣDAT on level 1 of the stack.*

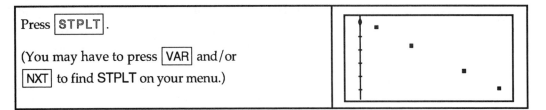

- Because the dots the calculator uses to plot data are sometimes difficult to see when overdrawing the model of best fit, the program places a small box around each data point. The boxes may appear a slightly different size in different views.

- Even though the HP-48 generally allows you to *store* data to any name you want, *you must have the data entered in ΣDAT when using any program given in this Guide or when using any of the statistics functions in your calculator.*

- It is not possible to trace a scatterplot drawn on the HP-48.

1.3.6 Finding First Differences: When the input values are evenly spaced, use program DIFF to compute first differences in the output values. If the data is perfectly linear (i.e., every data point falls on the linear model), the first differences in the output values are constant. If the first differences are "close" to constant, this is an indication that a linear model *may* be appropriate. (Program DIFF is given in the HP-48 Appendix.)

So that your VAR menu does not get too cluttered, create a new directory, NDIF, in the CALCC directory to hold program DIFF and the information it presents. (See "Setup" at the beginning of Part C and the HP Calculator Appendix for instructions.)

Before running program DIFF,

have ΣDAT on level 1 of the stack.

Press NDIF followed by DIFF. When the 'DONE' message appears, the first differences in the output values have been computed and placed in the list obtained by pressing FDIF. Press UP to return to the CALCC directory.	4: 3: 2: 1: { -2 -6 -9 -6 }

- Notice the results of program DIFF are **not valid** for the data in the above example because the *x*-values in this example are *not* evenly spaced. The first differences give no information about a possible linear fit to these data.

- Don't be concerned with the results appearing in SDIF and %CHG -- they are used in later sections.

1.3.7 Finding a Linear Model: Use your calculator to obtain the linear model that best fits two-variable data. Even though the HP-48 has a built-in routine for fitting a linear model, you will find it easier to use the general polynomial model-fitting program PFIT. The model used by this program is of the form

$$y = a_n x^n + a_{n-1} x^{n-1} + \ldots + a_2 x^2 + a_1 x + a_0.$$

Thus, the linear model (n=1) found by PFIT is of the standard form $y = ax + b$.

Before running program PFIT,

    have ΣDAT on level 2 of the stack and the value of n on level 1 of the stack.

Press ΣDAT and check that the data is as shown on the right. (Remember, to see all the data, press ▼ when ΣDAT is on the stack.)
 	
Press FIT to enter the FIT directory.
Store ΣDAT in the FIT directory.
	1: [[0 37]
	         [1 35]
	         [3 29]
	         [6 20]
	         [8 14]]

Press ΣDAT to place the data on the stack. Enter 1 to tell the program you want to fit a linear model.	4: 3: 2: [[1 5.4] [2 9.... 1: 1
Press PFIT. A scatterplot of the data first appears on the screen. Press ON and the program overdraws the graph of the linear model on the scatterplot.	
You are automatically returned to the stack after the graph is drawn. The absolute value of the correlation coefficient, r, is in level 2 and the "$ax + b$" portion of the equation of the linear model is in level 1.	3: 2: abs r: .9999363320... 1: ' - (2.9203539823*X)+ 37.5132743363'

1.3.8 Pasting a Model into the Function List: Program PFIT automatically stores the model in the function location EQ.

Press $\boxed{\text{E Q}}$ after executing program PFIT. (You may need to press $\boxed{\text{NXT}}$ first.) The equation remains in until EQ you run another model fitting program or until you manually store another equation in that location.	3: abs r: .9999363320... 2: ' - (2.9203539823*X)... 1: ' - (2.9203539823*X)+ 37.5132743363'

1.3.9 Graphing a Model: Program PFIT automatically draws the graph of the model on the scatterplot of the data. You can recall this graph at any time until you draw another graph.

Press $\boxed{\blacktriangleleft}$ after executing program PFIT. The last-drawn graph returns to the screen. All of the menu options at the bottom of the screen are available.	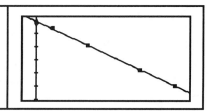

1.3.10 Predictions Using a Model: Use one of the methods described in 1.1.11 or 1.2.1 of this *Guide* to evaluate the linear model at the desired input value. If you prefer, use the HP's built-in prediction keys illustrated below. Remember, if you have aligned your data, the input value at which you evaluate the model may not be the value given in the question you are asked.

Press $\boxed{\text{←}}$ $\boxed{5}$ (STAT) $\boxed{\text{FIT}}$ after executing program PFIT. Predict the value of $y(x) = {}^-2.92036x + 37.513274$ in 1988 by entering the input, 4, on the stack and pressing $\boxed{\text{LR}}$ $\boxed{\text{PREDY}}$.	4: 3: 2: 1: 25.8318584071
Predict for which x-value $y(x)$ will be 17. We now wish to find an input value corresponding to the output value 17. Thus, enter 17 on the stack and press $\boxed{\text{PREDX}}$. (It is not necessary to press $\boxed{\text{LR}}$ again unless you change the data.)	4: 3: 2: 25.8318584071 1: 7.02424242425

1.3.11 Copying Graphs to Paper: Your instructor may ask you to copy what is on your graphics screen to paper. If so, refer to the horizontal and vertical views set by the calculator in order to help determine values to place on your input and output axes. Place a scale (tick marks) on each axis on your paper and plot the data values to construct the scatterplot. To help in drawing the model on paper, do the following:

Press ◀ to return the graph to the screen. Press TRACE to trace the graph. (Use a ruler to connect thelinear model points.)	Use ▶ and ◀ to locate several values that are as "nice" as possible and mark those points on your paper.

1.3.12 What Is "Best Fit"? Even though the HP-48 easily computes the values a and b for the best fitting linear model $y = ax + b$, it is important to understand the method of least-squares and the conditions necessary for its application if you intend to use this model. You can explore the process of finding the line of best fit with **program LSLNE.** (Program LSLNE is given in the HP-48 Appendix.) For your investigations of the least-squares process with this program, it is better to use data that is not perfectly linear and data for which you do *not* know the best-fitting line.

Before using LSLNE, enter your data in ΣDAT. Next, use program STPLT to draw a scatterplot and view the data. You may want to reset X-TIC and Y-TIC so that you can use the tick marks to help identify points on the graphics screen.

Run program LSLNE by pressing LSLN. The program first draws a scatterplot of your data. You should view the graph and estimate the slope and y-intercept of *some* line you think will go "through" the data. (You should not expect to guess the best fit line on your first try!) Press ON to continue the program. You are then asked for your *estimates* of the slope and y-intercept of the line of best fit. At the Input slope A prompt, type your guess for the slope of the line and press ENTER. At the Input y intercept B prompt, type your guess for where the line crosses the vertical axis and press ENTER. (The line the program fits to the data is of the form $y = A x + B$.)

You are next shown a graph of your line on the scatterplot with the errors displayed as vertical line segments on the graph. After you again press ON, your guesses for the slope and y-intercept and the sum of squares of errors, SSE, are displayed on the stack. Press ◀, view the graph and decide whether you want to move the y-intercept of the line or change its slope to improve the fit to the data.

Run the program again by pressing LSLN. After you enter another guess for the y-intercept and/or slope, the process of viewing your line, the errors, and display of SSE is repeated. If the new value of SSE is smaller than the SSE for your first guess, you have improved the fit. When you feel you have found an SSE value close to the minimum, you should press ← 5 (STAT) FIT LR. The y-intercept and slope of the best-fitting line for these data are displayed. Store these values on the stack in *A* (the slope) and *B* (the y-intercept). (Don't worry about the tags on the numbers.) Again execute program LSLNE (to find the minimum SSE). At the Input slope A prompt, type $\boxed{\alpha}$ A and press $\boxed{\text{ENTER}}$. At the Input y intercept B prompt, type $\boxed{\alpha}$ B and press $\boxed{\text{ENTER}}$. You now see the graph of the best-fitting line (and the errors for the best-fitting line) overdrawn on the scatterplot. $\boxed{\text{ON}}$ returns the y-intercept, slope, and minimum SSE to the stack.

- If the line that is drawn is horizontal, you probably have an X on some menu in your CALCC directory and the function has been evaluated at that X value. Press $\boxed{\text{UP}}$ and search for any X's and purge them. Rerun program LSLNE.

Use program LSLINE to explore finding the line of best fit.

1.3.13 Finding SSE for a Line:
The HP-48 lists are useful when finding the deviation (error) of *each* data point from a line entered in EQ and then computing SSE.

Enter, as a list, the output values 37, 35, 29, 20, and 14. Remember to press $\boxed{\leftarrow}$ $\boxed{+}$ ({ }) before entering the values and to separate the values with $\boxed{\text{SPC}}$.	4: 3: 2: 1: { 37 35 29 20 14 }
Press $\boxed{\text{EQ}}$. EQ should contain the linear model $-2.92036x + 37.513274$.	Enter on the stack each of the input values and determine the output calculated from the model in EQ by pressing F.val.
Put these five values in a list by entering 5 $\boxed{\text{PRG}}$ $\boxed{\text{TYPE}}$ $\boxed{\rightarrow\text{LIST}}$. (The last value is hidden by your menu.)	1: { 37.5132743363 34.592920354 28.7522123894 19.9911504425 14.1504424779
Find the deviation = error = $y_{data} - y_{line}$ with $\boxed{-}$. Find the squares of each of the errors with 2 $\boxed{y^x}$. Compute SSE, the sum of the squared errors with $\boxed{\text{MTH}}$ $\boxed{\text{LIST}}$ $\boxed{\Sigma\text{LIST}}$.	1: { .263450544304 .165713838187 6.13986999669E-2 7.83146679458E-5 2.26329391567E-2 } SSE = .513274336283

CHAPTER 2. THE INGREDIENTS OF CHANGE: NON-LINEAR MODELS

SECTION 2.1: EXPONENTIAL FUNCTIONS AND MODELS

2.1.1 Finding Percentage Change: When the input values are evenly spaced, use program DIFF to compute percentage change in the output values. If the data is perfectly exponential (i.e., every data point falls on the model of best fit), the percentage change in the output values is constant. If the percentage change is "close" to constant, this is an indication that an exponential model *may* be appropriate.

Clear any old data, and enter the following in ΣDAT:

x	0	1	2	3	4	5	6	7
y	23	38.4	64	107	179	299	499	833

Run program DIFF. Remember that ΣDAT must be on level 1 of the stack before pressing DIFF. Observe the percentage change after pressing %CHG. See the last value by pressing ▼. ENTER returns to the stack. An exponential model may be a good fit.	1: { 66.9565217391 66.6666666667 67.1875 67.2897196262 67.0391061453 The percentage change is very close to constant.

- You should always construct a scatterplot of the data either before or after using program DIFF. For the data in this example, the scatterplot confirms that an exponential model certainly seems appropriate!

2.1.2 Finding an Exponential Model: Use your calculator to obtain the best-fitting exponential model. The exponential model found by the HP-48's built-in routine in the statistics mode uses a base of e. In this text, the model used is of the form $y = ab^x$. Program EXPFT fits an exponential model with base b and is found in the HP-48 Appendix.

> *Before running program EXPFT,*
> > *have ΣDAT on level 1 of the stack.*

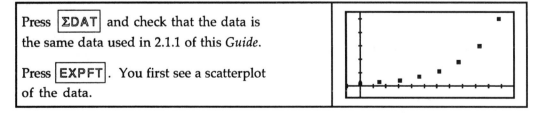

Press ΣDAT and check that the data is the same data used in 2.1.1 of this *Guide*.

Press EXPFT. You first see a scatterplot of the data.

Press ⬜ON and the best-fitting exponential model is overdrawn on the scatterplot.	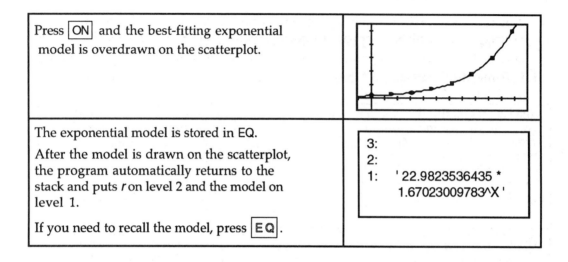
The exponential model is stored in EQ. After the model is drawn on the scatterplot, the program automatically returns to the stack and puts *r* on level 2 and the model on level 1. If you need to recall the model, press ⬜EQ.	3: 2: 1: '22.9823536435 * 1.67023009783^X '

2.1.3 Finding a Logistics Model:
Use your HP to obtain the logistics model with limiting value L that best fits data. Use program **LOGISTIC** to fit the logistic model $y = \dfrac{L}{1 + Ae^{-Bx}}$. (Program **LOGISTIC** is given in the HP-48 Appendix.)

Clear any old data, and enter the following data in ΣDAT:

x	0	1	2	3	4	5
y	1	2	4	6	8	9

Before running program LOGISTIC,

have ΣDAT on level 1 of the stack.

Construct a scatterplot of the data. A logistics model may be appropriate. Run program LOGISTIC by pressing ⬜LOGIS.	*(scatterplot)*
You are next given the information shown on the right. SSY is the *total variation* of the output variable. SSY gives the maximum value for SSE, the sum of squared errors. SSE changes with different limiting values *L*, but SSY remains constant for a particular data set.	HALT 3: SSY: 52 2: L: 9.77528089887 1: SSE: 5.39914560927E-2

- Notice the word HALT printed at the top of your display screen. Whenever you see HALT, it means that the program has stopped for you to read information on the stack. Whenever the program pauses <u>and</u> you see HALT, press ⟨←⟩ ⟨ON⟩ (CONT) to continue the program.

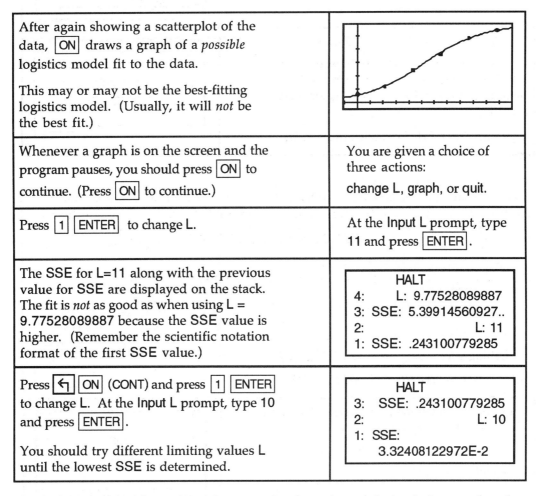

After again showing a scatterplot of the data, ⟨ON⟩ draws a graph of a *possible* logistics model fit to the data. This may or may not be the best-fitting logistics model. (Usually, it will *not* be the best fit.)	
Whenever a graph is on the screen and the program pauses, you should press ⟨ON⟩ to continue. (Press ⟨ON⟩ to continue.)	You are given a choice of three actions: change L, graph, or quit.
Press ⟨1⟩ ⟨ENTER⟩ to change L.	At the Input L prompt, type 11 and press ⟨ENTER⟩.
The SSE for L=11 along with the previous value for SSE are displayed on the stack. The fit is *not* as good as when using L = 9.77528089887 because the SSE value is higher. (Remember the scientific notation format of the first SSE value.)	HALT 4: L: 9.77528089887 3: SSE: 5.39914560927.. 2: L: 11 1: SSE: .243100779285
Press ⟨←⟩ ⟨ON⟩ (CONT) and press ⟨1⟩ ⟨ENTER⟩ to change L. At the Input L prompt, type 10 and press ⟨ENTER⟩. You should try different limiting values L until the lowest SSE is determined.	HALT 3: SSE: .243100779285 2: L: 10 1: SSE: 3.32408122972E-2

- If you would rather view values to a fixed number of decimal places rather than keep up with the scientific notation format, press ⟨→⟩ ⟨CST⟩ (MODES). Press ⟨CHOOSE⟩ from the NUMBER FORMAT location. Press ⟨▼⟩ to choose Fixed and press ⟨OK⟩. Press ⟨▶⟩, type the number of decimal places you want shown, say 5, and press ⟨OK⟩. Press ⟨OK⟩. You must wait until the program finishes to do this, however.

Press ⬅ |ON| (CONT) and press |1| |ENTER| to change L. At the **Input L** prompt, type 10 and press |ENTER|. You should try different limiting values L until the lowest **SSE** is determined.	HALT 3: SSE: .243100779285 2: L: 10 1: SSE: 3.32408122972E-2
Continue the program with ⬅ |ON| (CONT). To visually verify the fit for a particular value of L, press |2| |ENTER| to choose the **graph** option. After the scatterplot finishes drawing, press |ON| to see the graph of the model (with the current value of L). (If you want to view the graph each time you change L, always choose option 2 instead of option 1.)	
Press |ON|, and if you feel you have the best value for L, press |3| |ENTER| to **quit**.	The stack gives you a record of your L choices and the resulting SSE values.
The logistics model is stored in EQ. Press |E Q|. If you need to recall the values of **A**, **B** and/or L for the logistics model, press |A|, |B|, and/or |L|. (You may need to press |NXT| first.)	4: ' L / (1+A*EXP(-B*X)) ' 3: 9.22111412675 2: .888598347325 1: 10

If you prefer to see the model with the values of L, **A**, and B substituted in the general form, press |E Q| to put the model on level 1 of the stack and press |EVAL|.	1: ' 10 / (1+
	      9.22111412675*EXP(-
	         (.888598347325*X)))
	      '

- Program DIFF might be helpful when you are trying to determine if a logistics model is appropriate for certain data. If the first differences (in list FDIF after running program DIFF) *begin small, peak in the middle,* and *end small,* this is an indication that a logistics model *may* provide a good fit to the data. (For this particular example, there is not enough data for DIFF to be helpful.)

2.1.4 Random Numbers: Imagine all the real numbers between 0 and 1, including the 0 but not the 1, written on identical slips of paper and placed in a hat. Close your eyes and draw one slip of paper from the hat. You have just chosen a number "at random". Your calculator doesn't offer you a choice of all real numbers between 0 and 1, but it allows you to choose, *with an equal chance of obtaining each one*, any of 10^{12} different numbers between 0 and 1 with its random number generator called RAND.

First, "seed" the random number generator. (This is like mixing up all the slips of paper in the hat.) Pick some whole number and enter it on the stack as the "seed". (Everyone needs to have a different seed, or the choice will not be random.)	With your seed in level 1 of the stack, press MTH NXT PROB RDZ .
On the menu, directly to the left of RDZ, is the random number generator RAND. Press RAND several times. Your list of random numbers should be different from the one on the right.	4: .621559316411 3: .539738315531 2: .36838677361 1: .247020068596
If you want to choose, at random, a whole number between 1 and *N*, IP(N *rand + 1) does the job. (IP is the integer portion of a number.) Follow the directions shown on the right to generate a random integer between 1 and 10. Repeat the process to generate another random number between 1 and 10.	Press RAND . Press 1 0 × . Press 1 + . Press and hold α . Type I P and press ENTER .

SECTION 2.2 EXPONENTIAL MODELS IN FINANCE

2.2.1 Replay of Previous Entries to Find Formula Outputs: The easiest way to replay previous formula entries on the HP-48 is to create a user-defined formula. This is actually a program that takes a value from level 1 of the stack, substitutes it in a formula, and evaluates the formula.

Formulas can be entered in any directory; just don't forget where you put them. This example places the formula in **CALCC**. Press ➡ ' (HOME) and CALCC .

Suppose you need to evaluate the amount formula $\left(1+\frac{1}{n}\right)^{n}$ for several different values of *n*. (Remember that to type a lower-case letter, you should press α ⬅ before the letter key.)

Enter << → n '(1 + INV(n)) ^ n' EVAL >>. (Watch, as you type, that you move outside the ')' with ▶ after typing the n in INV(n).) Enter, with ⌐', the name of this formula, say AMT. Press STO.	Press ⟵ − for << >>. Press → 0 for →. Insert spaces where needed with SPC. Press ⟵ ⁒ for ( ). Press 1/x for INV( ).
Once your formula is stored, simply enter a value of n on the stack and press AMT. Repeat the procedure for different values of n. The screen to the right shows the results for $n = 1, 2,$ and 3.	4: 3: 2 2: 2.25 1: 2.37037037035

- You could have achieved the same results as illustrated above by storing the formula '(1 + INV(n)) ^ n' in EQ and finding the outputs using program F.val.

- You could also use the SOLVR application to find outputs. This method is especially useful when there is more than one input variable. To illustrate, consider the simple interest formula -- one that contains several input variables.

The formula for the amount in an account paying $r\%$ simple interest on an initial deposit of $\$P$ over a period of t years is $A = P(1 + rt)$. The value obtained depends on the values stored in P, R, and T.

Press ⟵ 7 (SOLVE) ROOT to enter the solve application. Press SOLVR and notice the variables appear at the bottom of the menu.	Type ' A = P*(1 + R*T) ' ENTER ⟵ EQ to store the formula as the current equation.
Determine the accumulated amount if $100 is invested at 5% interest for 1 year by pressing 100 P .05 R 1 T ⟵ A. Determine the accumulated amount if $500 is invested at 5% interest for 3 years.	4: 3: 2: A: 105 1: A: 575

- Use either a user-defined function or the solve application as described above to find future value.

2.2.2 Finding Present Value: The present value of an investment is easily found with the calculator's solve application. For instance, suppose you want to solve the equation $9438.40 = P\left(1 + \frac{0.075}{12}\right)^{60}$ for the present value P.

Refer to 1.2.2 and 2.2.1 of this *Guide* for instructions on using the HP-48's **SOLVR**. Enter the equation on the right in EQ.	Type ' 9438.40 = P* (1 + .075 / 12) ^ 60 ' and press ENTER ⟵ EQ .
Solve for P with ⟵ P to obtain the present value $6494.49. (Refer to 1.2.3 of this *Guide* for more detailed instructions on finding x-intercepts.)	If you prefer, you could find the *x*-intercept of ' 9438.4 – X*(1+.075/12)^60 ' to find the present value.

- If your **VAR** menu appears cluttered, recall that you can delete variables that are no longer used (such as A, P, R, and T from the above example) by entering them on level 1 of the stack inside { } and pressing ⟵ EEX (PURGE).

SECTION 2.3 POLYNOMIAL FUNCTIONS AND MODELS

2.3.1 Finding Second Differences: When the input values are evenly spaced, use program DIFF to compute second differences in the output values. If the data is perfectly quadratic (i.e., every data point falls on the quadratic model), the second differences in the output values are constant. If the second differences are "close" to constant, this is an indication that a quadratic model *may* be appropriate.

Clear any old data, and enter the following data in ΣDAT:

x	0	1	2	3	4	5
y	12	14	22	35	54	80

Run program DIFF and observe the second differences in list SDIF. The second differences are close to constant, so a quadratic model may be a good fit. Construct a scatterplot of the data. A quadratic model seems appropriate!	4: 3: 2: 'DONE' 1: { 6 5 6 7 }

2.3.2 Finding a Quadratic Model: Use your calculator to obtain the quadratic model that best fits the data. The HP-48 quadratic model is found using program PFIT with $n = 2$ and is of the form $y = ax^2 + bx + c$.

Before running program PFIT,

have ΣDAT on level 2 of the stack and the value of n on level 1 of the stack.

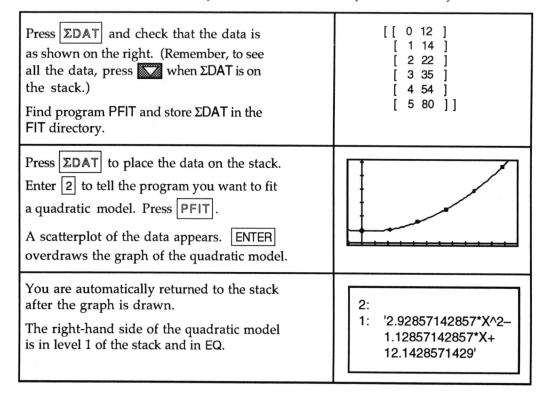

Press $\boxed{\Sigma DAT}$ and check that the data is as shown on the right. (Remember, to see all the data, press ▼ when ΣDAT is on the stack.) Find program PFIT and store ΣDAT in the FIT directory.	[[0 12] [1 14] [2 22] [3 35] [4 54] [5 80]]

Press $\boxed{\Sigma DAT}$ to place the data on the stack. Enter $\boxed{2}$ to tell the program you want to fit a quadratic model. Press $\boxed{PFIT}$.

A scatterplot of the data appears. $\boxed{ENTER}$ overdraws the graph of the quadratic model.

You are automatically returned to the stack after the graph is drawn.

The right-hand side of the quadratic model is in level 1 of the stack and in EQ.

```
2:
1:  '2.92857142857*X^2–
    1.12857142857*X+
    12.1428571429'
```

2.3.3 Finding a Cubic Model: Whenever a scatterplot of the data shows a single change in concavity, a cubic or logistic model is appropriate. If a limiting value is apparent, use the logistic model. Otherwise, a cubic model should be considered. When appropriate, use your calculator to obtain the cubic model that best fits data. Program PFIT with $n = 3$ finds the cubic model of the form $y = ax^3 + bx^2 + cx + d$ that best fits the data.

Clear any old data, and enter the following in ΣDAT:

Year	'80	'81	'82	'83	'84	'85	'86	'87	'88	'89	'90
Price	3.68	4.29	5.17	6.06	6.12	6.12	5.83	5.54	5.47	5.64	5.77

First, use program **ALIGN** to align the data so that *x* represents the number of years since 1980. Draw a scatterplot of these data with **STPLT**.	[[0 3.68] [1 4.29] [2 5.17] [3 6.06] [4 6.12] [5 6.12] [6 5.83] [7 5.54] [8 5.47] [9 5.64] [10 5.77]]
Notice that a concavity change is evident, but there do not appear to be any limiting values. Thus, a cubic model may fit the data.	As before, remember to have ΣDAT on level 2 of the stack and the value of *n* on level 1 before using program **PFIT**.
Press $\boxed{\text{ΣDAT}}$ $\boxed{3}$ $\boxed{\text{PFIT}}$. Press $\boxed{\text{ON}}$ after viewing the scatterplot to see the plot of the model.	
You are automatically returned to the stack after the graph is drawn. The right-hand side of the cubic model is in level 1 of the stack and in EQ.	2: 1: '1.24358974359E-2*X ^3−.242086247086*X^ 2+1.40699300699*X+ 3.44454545455'

CHAPTER 3.   DESCRIBING CHANGE: RATES

SECTION 3.1: AVERAGE RATES OF CHANGE

3.1.1 Finding Average Rates of Change: Finding the average rate of change using a model is just a matter of evaluating the model at two different values of the input variable and dividing by the difference in those input values. Let us consider the example where the April temperature is given by *temperature* = $^-0.8t^2 + 2t + 79$ $^\circ$F where $t = 0$ at noon and we wish to calculate the average rate of change between 11 a.m. and 6 p.m.

Store ' -.8* X^2 + 2*X + 79 ' in EQ in the directory containing program F.val. (X must be the name of the input variable whenever using program F.val.) Use program F.val to find the temperature at -1 (11 a.m.) and at 6 (6 p.m.).	4: 3: 2:　　　　　　　62.2 1:　　　　　　　76.2
Press ⊟ to find the difference in the temperatures. Next, enter 6, then ⁻1, and press ⊟. Press ⊡ to find the average rate of change.	4: 3: 2: 1:　　　　　　　-2

SECTION 3.4: DERIVATIVES

3.4.1 Magnifying a Portion of a Graph: The ZOOM menu of the HP-48 allows you to magnify any portion of the graph of a function. Suppose we are investigating the graph of $y = {}^-x^2 + 40x + 50$ and the tangent line, $y = 20x + 150$, to the graph of this function at $x = 10$.

Access the PLOT mode, change the type to FUNCTION and enter in EQ the list 　{ ' -X^2 +40*X +50 '　' 20*X+150 ' }. Using a H-VIEW of 0 to 20 and a V-VIEW of ⁻50 to 600, draw the graphs of the function and the line tangent to it at X = 10.	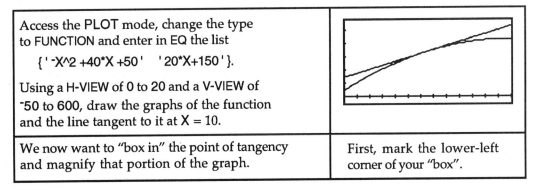
We now want to "box in" the point of tangency and magnify that portion of the graph.	First, mark the lower-left corner of your "box".

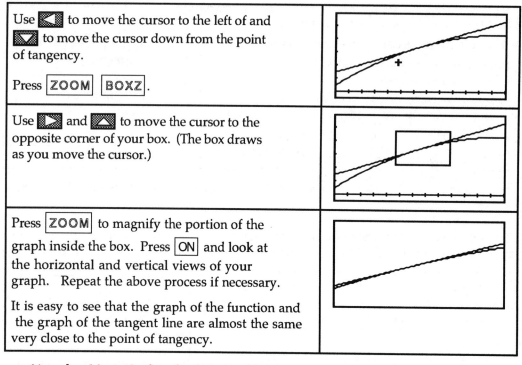

Use ◄ to move the cursor to the left of and ▼ to move the cursor down from the point of tangency. Press ZOOM BOXZ .	
Use ► and ▲ to move the cursor to the opposite corner of your box. (The box draws as you move the cursor.)	
Press ZOOM to magnify the portion of the graph inside the box. Press ON and look at the horizontal and vertical views of your graph. Repeat the above process if necessary. It is easy to see that the graph of the function and the graph of the tangent line are almost the same very close to the point of tangency.	

- You should verify that the function and its tangent have close output values near the point of tangency by tracing the graphs near the point of tangency. Recall that you jump from one function to the other with ▲ or ▼ as you trace.

SECTION 3.5: PERCENTAGE CHANGE AND PERCENTAGE RATES OF CHANGE

3.5.1 Percentage Change and Percentage Rates of Change: Recall that program DIFF stores percentage change in data in %CHG. Consider the following data giving quarterly earnings for a business:

Quarter ending	Mar '93	June '93	Sept '93	Dec '93	Mar '94	June '94
Earnings (in millions)	27.3	28.9	24.6	32.1	29.4	27.7

| Align the input data so that x is the number of quarters since March, 1993, and input x in the first column of ΣDAT and earnings (in millions) in the second column of ΣDAT. | 1:   [[0 27.3]
            [1 28.9]
            [2 24.6]
            [3 32.1]
            [4 29.4]
            [5 27.7]] |

Run program DIFF and view the percentage change with %CHG . (Remember to store these new data as the current ΣDAT if you have changed directories!)
 	
 Notice that the percentage change from the end of Sept '93 through Dec '93 is approximately 30.5%. Also, from the end of March '94 through June '94, the percentage change is approximately ‾5.8%.
	1: { 5.86080586081
	         -14.8788927336
	          30.487804878
	          -8.41121495327
	          -5.78231292517 }

- You may find it easier to use the stack to calculate percentage change than to have the program do it for you.

To evaluate percentage rate of change at a point, suppose you are told or otherwise find that the rate of change at the end of the June, 1993 is 1.8 million dollars per quarter.

Divide the rate of change at the end of June, 1993 by the earnings, in millions, at the end of June, 1993 and multiply by 100 to obtain the percentage rate of change at that point.	The percentage rate of change in earnings at the end of June, 1993 is approximately 6.2% per quarter.

CHAPTER 4.   DETERMINING CHANGE: DERIVATIVES

SECTION 4.1: NUMERICALLY FINDING SLOPES

4.1.1 Numerically Investigating Slopes: Finding slopes of secant lines joining the point at which the tangent line is drawn to increasingly "close" points on a function to the left and right of the point of tangency is easily done using your calculator. Suppose we want to find the slope of the tangent line at $t = 8$ to the graph of the function $y = \dfrac{44000}{1 + 484e^{-0.7698\,t}}$.

Enter the directory containing program F.val. Using X as the input variable, store the right-hand side of the above equation in EQ. We now evaluate the slopes joining nearby points to the *left* of $x = 8$.	Enter 7.9 on the stack. Press F.val . Enter 8 on the stack. Press F.val . Press − .
Enter the two input values, *in the same order as you entered them in the previous step*, on the stack.	4: 3: -845.8580519 2: 7.9 1: 8
Compute the slope of the secant line joining the points where $x = 7.9$ and $x = 8$ by pressing − ÷ .	4: 3: 2: 1: 8458.580518
Continue in this manner, letting x be 7.99, 7.999, 7.9999, etc. recording each result on paper, until you can determine the value the slopes from the left are approaching.	4: 8458.580518 3: 8466.184863 2: 8466.573547 1: 8466.60869
We now evaluate the slopes joining nearby points to the *right* of $x = 8$. To illustrate another method for determining the slopes, we use the solve application.	Clear the screen with ← DEL (CLEAR). Press EQ . Press ← 7 (SOLVE) ROOT and ← EQ to store the equation.

Press $\boxed{\text{SOLVR}}$ and be sure the correct equation appears at the top of the screen.	Type 8.1 and press $\boxed{\text{X}}$. Press $\boxed{\text{EVAL}}$. Type 8 and press $\boxed{\text{X}}$. Press $\boxed{\text{EVAL}}$. Press $\boxed{-}$.
Enter the two input values, *in the same order as you entered them in the previous step*, on the stack. Compute the slope of the secant line joining the points where $x = 7.9$ and $x = 8$ by pressing $\boxed{-}$ $\boxed{\div}$.	4: 3: 2: 1: 8466.290978
Continue in this manner, letting x be 8.01, 8.001, 8/0001, etc. recording each result on paper, until you can determine the value the slopes from the right are approaching. When the slopes from the left and the slopes from the right get closer to the same value, that value is the slope of the tangent line at $x = 8$.	4: 8466.290978 3: 8466.956663 2: 8466.650728 1: 8466.61641

SECTION 4.3: SLOPE FORMULAS

4.3.1 Discovering Slope Formulas: You can often see a pattern in a table of values for the slopes of a function at indicated values of the input variable and discover a formula for the slope (derivative). The process of calculating the slopes uses the calculator's symbol for finding slopes, ∂.

Suppose we want to calculate $\frac{dy}{dx}$ for $y = x^2$ evaluated at $x = 2$.

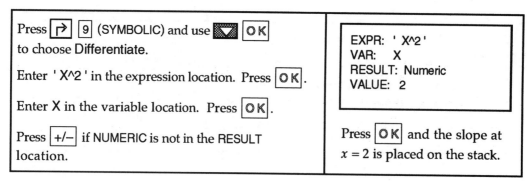

Press $\boxed{\nearrow}$ $\boxed{9}$ (SYMBOLIC) and use $\boxed{\blacktriangledown}$ $\boxed{\text{OK}}$ to choose Differentiate. Enter ' X^2 ' in the expression location. Press $\boxed{\text{OK}}$. Enter X in the variable location. Press $\boxed{\text{OK}}$. Press $\boxed{+/-}$ if NUMERIC is not in the RESULT location.	EXPR: ' X^2 ' VAR: X RESULT: Numeric VALUE: 2 Press $\boxed{\text{OK}}$ and the slope at $x = 2$ is placed on the stack.

Suppose you are asked to construct a table of values for $y = x^2$ evaluated at different values of x. You could find the slope as just illustrated, changing VALUE each time. However, you probably will find the following method takes less time.

Press ⟨← ⟩ ⟨ENTER⟩ (EQUATION) to enter the EQUATIONWRITER. Press ⟨→ ⟩ ⟨ENTER⟩ (∂) to enter the calculator's slope symbol. Type the input variable in the box that appears. Press ⟨▶⟩ and enter the function. (Press ⟨▶⟩ to move out of the power.) Press ⟨▶⟩ when you have finished typing the function.	$\dfrac{\partial}{\partial X}(X^2)\square$ Press ⟨ENTER⟩ and $'\partial X(X^2)'$ is placed on the stack. (Note: You could enter the formula directly on the stack.)
Change to the directory containing program F.val. Press ⟨← ⟩ ⟨O K⟩ to store this expression as the current equation.	Place the value of X on the stack and press ⟨F.val⟩. Press ⟨EVAL⟩ to find the slope formula value.
Evaluate the calculator's slope formula at $x = {}^-3, {}^-2, {}^-1, 0, 1, 2,$ and 3. Record these values as they are displayed and try to determine a relationship (pattern) between the calculated slopes and the values of x.	4: 0 3: 2 2: 4 1: 6

- If you have difficulty determining a pattern, enter the x-values at which you are evaluating the slope in the first column of ΣDAT and the evaluated values of $'\partial X(f(x))'$ in the second column of ΣDAT. Use program STPLT to draw a scatterplot of the x-values and the calculated slope formula values. The shape of the scatterplot should give you a clue as to the equation of the slope formula. If not, try drawing another scatterplot where the first column of ΣDAT contains the values of $f(x)$ and the second column contains the calculated slope formula values. Note that this method might help only if you consider a variety of values for x.

- The HP-48 finds numeric and symbolic slopes. Using your calculator to find the symbolic derivative (i. e., the formula form) is discussed in a later section.

SECTION 4.4: THE SUM RULE

4.4.1 Numerically Checking Slope Formulas:
When you use a formula to find the derivative of a function, it is possible to check your answer using the calculator's numerical derivative. The basic idea of the checking process is that if you evaluate your derivative and the calculator's derivative at several randomly chosen values of the input variable and the output values are the same, your derivative is *probably* correct.

Let $g(t) = 0.775t^2 - 140.460t + 6868.818$. Applying the sum, power, and constant multiplier rules for derivatives, suppose you determine $g'(t) = 1.55t - 140.460$. Now, let us numerically check this answer.

Store the calculator's derivative in C and your derivative formula, $\frac{dg}{dt} = g'(t)$, in some other name, say D.	C = ' ∂T(.775*T^2– 140.46*T+6868.818) ' D = '1.55*T–140.46'
Enter 'C=D' on the stack. Go to the solve application and store C=D as the current equation.	Press ROOT and notice the variable T on the menu along with EXPR=.
Since the $g(t)$ model represents average fuel consumption per car where $t = 80$ in 1980, it makes sense to check using only positive values of t .	Check to see that C and D are the same at least three different values of x.
Enter a value of T, say 80, with T . Press EXPR= . The left side, C, and right side, D, are displayed but not evaluated.	3: 2: Left: '∂ T(.775*T^2... 1: Right: ' 1.55*T - 140.46'
Press ← EVAL (→NUM) ▶ (SWAP) ← EVAL (→NUM) to evaluate C and D. Repeat the procedure for two other values of T, say 86 and 89. Verify that the two outputs are the same.	4: 3: 2: -16.46 1: -16.46

• If you obtain a number when you enter an expression containing ∂ *before* you use EVAL or →NUM, the variable you are using appears on your current menu or is in a menu one or more levels above the current menu. Find the variable and purge it.

4.4.2 Graphically Checking Slope Formulas: Another method of checking your answer for a slope formula (derivative) is to draw the calculator's graph of the derivative and draw the graph of your derivative.   If the graphs appear identical *in the same viewing window*, your derivative is probably correct.

Again use $g(t) = 0.775t^2 - 140.460t + 6868.818$ and $g'(t) = 1.55t - 140.460$.

Enter a list containing the function you are taking the derivative of and your derivative formula. *Be sure you put the function first.* Go to the PLOT application and store this list as the current equation.	EQ = { '.775*T^2140.46*T+ 6868.818) ' '1.55*T−140.46' } (Remember to enter T as the independent variable.)
Set an appropriate horizontal view (such as between 80 and 90) and vertical view (between ⁻25 and 25). Draw the graph of the function and your derivative. Do not be concerned that the view does not include the function. We are only interested in the graph of the derivative.	
Press FCN NXT F' to have the HP plot the derivative of the *first* function in the list, the function, and your derivative. Since you see only one graph, your derivative formula is *probably* correct.	

- When you are trying to determine an appropriate viewing window, use the range of the input data for x. If you do not have data, but an equation, use your knowledge of the general shape of the function to find appropriate values for the horizontal view. Recall that you can trace on the graph to see some of the output values to help you determine values for the vertical view.

The HP-48 offers another way of checking your slope formulas - it will find some of them for you!   However, your calculator can only find the formula form of certain derivatives, not all of them. Thus, it is still very important that you learn the slope (derivative) formulas!

The symbolic mode of the HP-48 also offers you an opportunity to experience how the sum, difference, and product formulas as well as the chain rule, power rule, etc. apply to certain functions. We illustrate these ideas by having the calculator show the process of finding the formula form of the derivative of $f(x) = 5x^3 - x^2 + 3$.

First, press [←] [CST] (MODES) [MISC] and check to see that the symbolic mode is active. If it is, [SYM→] should have a small white box after the "M". If not, press [SYM] and the box will appear. Press [VAR].

To use the symbolic mode of the HP-48, the input variable cannot appear on the menu in your directory or any directory above your directory. Thus, if you are using X as the input variable, you must purge X in the CALCC directory and any directory you must pass through to get to your current directory.

Press [→] [9] (SYMBOLIC) and use [▼] [OK] to choose Differentiate. Enter ' 5*X^3–X^2+3 ' in the expression location. Press [OK].	Enter X in the variable location. Press [OK]. Press [+/−] if SYMBOLIC is not in the RESULT location.
Press [STEP]. You are lead through a series of steps showing how the formulas for taking the derivative of a constant, the sum rule, and the power rule apply to obtain the derivative of this function. Carefully examine each step that you see to understand the process.	Press [EVAL] after viewing each expression. Remember that the HP's notation for $\frac{dy}{dx}$ is ∂X(y).
If you only wish to view the symbolic form to check your use of the derivative formulas, press [OK] after you have entered the function and chosen SYMBOLIC in the SYMBOLIC menu.	4: 3: 2: 1: ' 5*(3*X^2)–2*X '
The expression that appears is the derivative, but it has not been simplified. Press [←] [9] (SYMBOLIC) [COLCT]. (For more complicated expressions, keep pressing [COLCT] until there are no more changes.)	4: 3: 2: 1: ' 15*X^2–2*X '

CHAPTER 5. ANALYZING CHANGE: EXTREMA AND POINTS OF INFLECTION

SECTION 5.1: OPTIMIZATION

5.1.1 Finding Local Maxima and/or Minima:

Finding where a function has a high point or a low point is an easy task for the HP-48.

Consider, for example, the model for the average price (per 1000 ft^3) of natural gas for residential use from 1980 to 1991:

$$price = p(x) = 0.012436x^3 - 0.242086x^2 + 1.406993x + 3.444545 \text{ dollars}$$

where x is the number of years since 1980.

Enter the PLOT application. Enter the price model as the current EQ. (Be sure FUNCTION is selected as TYPE and X is entered as INDPT.) Graph the model in an appropriate view, say x between 0 and 11 and *price* between 3 and 7.	
Prepare to find the local (relative) maximum by pressing ◄ (and maybe ▲ and/or ▼) to move the cursor to your *estimate* of the high point. Press $\boxed{\text{FCN}}$ $\boxed{\text{EXTR}}$ and the coordinates of the maximum are displayed at the bottom of the graph and are also copied to the stack.	EXTRM: (4.39307634743, 6.00788120804) Thus, a maximum price was \$6.01 per 1000 ft^3 and the price peaked in May, 1984 (4.393 months after January 1, 1980).

- Note that this maximum is a local or relative maximum, but it is not *the* highest average price of natural gas from 1980 to 1991. Look at the graph and see that the price in January of 1991 ($x = 11$) is the highest price at \$6.18 per 1000 ft^3 .

Next, use the cursor keys to move the cursor to the approximate location of the low point. (Press any of the white keys at the bottom of the graphics screen to bring back the menu.) Press $\boxed{\text{FCN}}$ $\boxed{\text{EXTR}}$ and the coordinates of the local minimum are displayed at the bottom of the graph and are also copied to the stack.	EXTRM: (8.58462280551, 5.54997812235) Thus, a minimum price was \$5.55 per 1000 ft^3 and the price declined to this low point in August, 1988 (8.585 months after Jan. 1, 1980).

- Note that this minimum is a local or relative minimum, but it is not *the* lowest average price of natural gas from 1980 to 1991. View the graph and see that the price in January of 1980 ($x = 0$) is the lowest price at \$3.44 per 1000 ft^3 .

5.1.2 Finding x-Intercepts of Slope Graphs:
Where the graph of a function has a local maximum or minimum, the slope graph has a horizontal tangent. Where the tangent is horizontal, the derivative is zero. Thus, finding where the slope graph crosses the x-axis is the same as finding the location of the local maxima and minima.

We emphasize this fact by finding the x-intercepts of the derivative (where the slope graph crosses the x-axis) and showing those intercepts occur at the local maximum and minimum of the graph of $p(x) = 0.012436x^3 - 0.242086x^2 + 1.406993x + 3.444545$.

Enter the PLOT application. Have $p(x)$, the price model, as the current EQ. Graph the model in an appropriate view, say x between 0 and 11 and *price* between 3 and 7.	
Press [FCN] [NXT] [F'] to have the HP graph the model and its derivative. Evidently the view is not good for the slope graph, so return to the plot application with [ON] and check AUTOSCALE. Redraw the graphs with [ERASE] [DRAW].	
Find the x-intercepts of the slope graph using [FCN] [ROOT]. Before pressing [ROOT], move the cursor to your estimate of the location of the x-intercept.	The x-intercept (root) is displayed and copied to the stack. ROOT: 4.39307634743
Repeat the process to find the other x-intercept. Compare the values of the x-intercepts with the x-values of the locations of the local maximum and local minimum found in 5.1.1 of this *Guide*. They are the same!	Use [▶] to move the cursor near the location of the other x-intercept and press [ROOT]. ROOT: 8.58462280551
It is often difficult to find one view that allows a good look at both a function and its derivative. However, look at the graph of $p(x)$ and $p'(x)$ in the view that has x between 0 and 11 and y between ⁻1 and 6.5.	

- Carefully look at the graph at the bottom of the preceding page. Notice the relationship between the locations of the local maximum of $p(x)$, the local minimum of $p(x)$, and the x-intercepts of $p'(x)$.

SECTION 5.2: INFLECTION POINTS

5.2.1 Finding Inflection Points: The HP-48 offers a graphical method of finding an inflection point of a function. To illustrate, consider a model for the percentage of students graduating from high school in South Carolina from 1982 to 1990 who enter post-secondary institutions:

$$f(x) = {}^-0.105724x^3 + 1.355375x^2 - 3.672379x + 50.791919 \text{ percent}$$

where $x = 0$ in 1982.

Enter $' \partial X(f(x))'$, substituting in the above model for $f(x)$, as the current EQ in the plot application. Instead of $' \partial X(f(x))'$, you could enter your derivative. (Hopefully, you have checked that your derivative and the calculator's derivative are the same!)	If you prefer, you could have the calculator draw the derivative graph from the FCN menu with $\boxed{\text{F'}}$ as illustrated in 5.1.2 of this *Guide*.
Graph $f'(x)$ in an appropriate view , say x between 0 and 8 and $f(x)$ between ‾4 and 4.	
Use the methods illustrated in 5.1.1 of this *Guide* to find the maximum of the slope graph. The x-value of the maximum of the slope graph $f'(x)$ is the x-value of the inflection point of the function $f(x)$.	The function $f(x)$ has an inflection point at $x =$ 4.2733122722.
If you are asked to give the inflection <u>point</u> of $f(x)$, you should give both an x-value and an $f(x)$ value. Find the y-value by substituting this x-value in the function $f(x)$.	$x = 4.2733122722$ $f(x) = 51.5992118947$

Even though it is difficult to find a view that shows a good graph of both the function and its derivative in *this* case, you can often see that the location of the inflection point is at the maximum or minimum of the function.	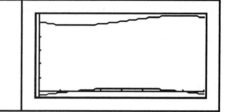

Another method you can use to find the x-value of an inflection point is to find the x-intercept (root) of the second derivative of the function. We again use the model

$$f(x) = -0.105724x^3 + 1.355375x^2 - 3.672379x + 50.791919.$$

Have ' $\partial X(f(x))$ ', substituting in the above model for $f(x)$, as the current EQ in the plot application. Graph $f'(x)$ in an appropriate view, say x between 0 and 8 and $f(x)$ between ⁻4 and 4.	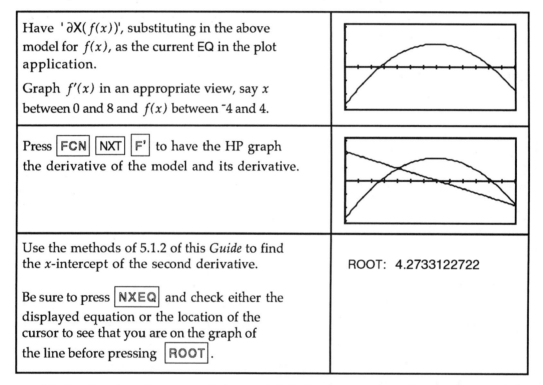
Press FCN NXT F' to have the HP graph the derivative of the model and its derivative.	
Use the methods of 5.1.2 of this *Guide* to find the x-intercept of the second derivative. Be sure to press NXEQ and check either the displayed equation or the location of the cursor to see that you are on the graph of the line before pressing ROOT .	ROOT: 4.2733122722

- Notice that the x-intercept of the second derivative occurs at the maximum of the graph of $f'(x)$. Isn't the second derivative the derivative of the first derivative?

CHAPTER 6. ACCUMULATING CHANGE: LIMITS OF SUMS

SECTION 6.1: RESULTS OF CHANGE

6.1.1 Using a Model to Determine Change:

The HP-48 can be used to perform the required calculations to approximate, using left rectangles, the area between the horizontal axis, a (non-negative) rate of change function, and two specific input values. The general procedure for approximating the change in the function $y = f(x)$ between $x = a$ and $x = b$ begins with using the given number, n, of subintervals or determining a suitable value for n. Then, find the equal width of each subinterval, Δx, by using $\Delta x = \frac{b-a}{n}$. Next, when you enter the x-data values in the first column of ΣDAT, remember that the x-data values should differ by Δx. Program MDVAL simplifies computations by evaluating the model at the x-data values and storing the evaluated values as the second column of ΣDAT.

Consider, for example, the model for the number of customers per minute who came to a Saturday sale from 9 AM to 9 PM at a large department store:

$$c(m) = (4.589036*10^{-8})m^3 - (7.781267*10^{-5})m^2 + 0.033033\,m + 0.887630$$

customers per minute where m is the number of minutes after 9 AM.

Enter the right-hand side of this model in EQ. (Remember that "10 to a power" is denoted by **E** on the calculator. Access **E** with $\boxed{\text{EEX}}$.)	Use x as the input variable since we use a program that calls upon program F.val.
Suppose we want to estimate the total number of customers who came to the sale between $m = x = 0$ and $m = x = 660$ (9 AM to 9 PM) with 12 rectangles such that $\Delta x = 60$. Enter these x-values in column 1 of ΣDAT. Do <u>not</u> enter any values in column 2 of ΣDAT.	[[0] [60] [120] [180] [240] [300] [360] [420] [480] [540] [600] [660]]

Use program MVAL (found in the HP-48 Appendix) to calculate the $c(m)$ model values. The program also puts these values as the second column of ΣDAT.

- MVAL (model values)

  Model must be stored in EQ before running program MVAL.

  Input: one-column ΣDAT matrix of x-data values in level 1 of stack

  Output: two-column ΣDAT matrix containing x-data values in column 1 and y-values calculated from the model in column 2

  (Program F.val must be in the same directory as program MVAL.)

Enter the directory containing program **MVAL**. Be certain that the correct ΣDAT and EQ are stored in *this* directory.	With ΣDAT on level 1 of the stack, press ⬛MVAL⬛.
Column 2 of ΣDAT now contains the *heights* of the 12 rectangles.	1: [[0 .88763] [60 2.5993967057...] [120 3.810386094..] [180 4.580072071..]

We now need to use the heights of the rectangles that are in the second column of ΣDAT. Program MVTL will extract a column of ΣDAT and convert it to a list.

- MVTL (multivariable matrix to list)

   Input: two or more column ΣDAT on level 2 of the stack

              number of column to be extracted on level 1 of the stack

   Output: extracted column in the form of a list

ΣDAT should be in level 1 of the stack. If not, press ⬛ΣDAT⬛. Since we want to get the heights in column 2, press ⬛2⬛ ⬛ENTER⬛. Press ⬛MVTL⬛.	1: { .88763 2.59939370576 3.81038609408 4.58007207152...
Since the *width* of each rectangle is 60, the area of each rectangle is 60*height. Find the *areas* of the 12 rectangles by entering 6 0 on the stack and pressing ⬛×⬛.	1: { 53.2578 155.963802346 228.623165645 274.804324291...
Find the sum of the areas of the rectangles with ⬛MTH⬛ ⬛LIST⬛ ⬛ΣLIST⬛. (Remember, if you make a mistake, you may be able to recover your last stack with ⬛↱⬛ ⬛EVAL⬛ (UNDO).)	2573.80418944 We estimate, with 12 rectangles, that 2,574 customers came to the Saturday sale.

6.1.2 Using Count Data to Determine Change:
This method is very similar to that using a model to determine change. The main difference is that you enter the data values into ΣDAT instead of using the model and program MVAL to generate the values in the second column of ΣDAT.

Consider the following data showing the number of aluminum cans that were recycled each year from 1978 to 1988:

year	'78	'79	'80	'81	'82	'83	'84	'85	'86	'87	'88
cans (in billions)	8.0	8.5	14.8	24.9	28.3	29.4	31.9	33.1	33.3	36.6	42.0

Enter the number of years since 1978 in the first column of ΣDAT or enter the year in the first column of ΣDAT and use program ALIGN to align the data.
 	
Enter the cans recycled each year (in billions) in the second column of ΣDAT.
	1: [[0 8]
	      [1 8.5
	      [2 14.8
	      [3 24.9..

Suppose we want to estimate the number of cans recycled during the ten year period 1978-1988. Since $\Delta x = 1$ and the heights of the rectangles are in the second column of ΣDAT, the areas of the 11 rectangles spanning the years 1978 *through* 1988 are the values in the second column of ΣDAT.	Since we want to get the areas in column 2, press ⌷2⌷ ⌷ENTER⌷. Press ⌷MVTL⌷. Find the sum of the areas of the rectangles with ⌷MTH⌷ ⌷LIST⌷ ⌷ΣLIST⌷ to be 290.8.
If you needed an estimate of the number of cans recycled during the 3 year period 1982-1984, press ⌷←⌷ ⌷+/−⌷ (EDIT). Delete all but the three values for those years. The estimate is 89.6 billion cans.	The sum of list { 28.3 29.4 31.9 } is 89.6.

- Read each question carefully, especially when the data involves years. If you are considering data from one year *to* another, the data for the last year should not be included. If you are considering data from one year *through* another, the data for the last year is included.

SECTION 6.2: APPROXIMATING AREA

6.2.1 Left-Rectangle Approximation: The HP-48 lists are used to perform the required calculations to find area using left rectangles when given data or a model defining a function $y = f(x)$. For the examples in this section, we consider the function $f(x) = x^3 - 2x^2 + 3x + 1$. Enter this function in EQ.

To approximate the area, from 0 to 3, of the region beneath the graph of $f(x)$ and the horizontal axis using *left* rectangles with $n = 4$ subintervals, determine $\Delta x = 0.75$ and the first column of ΣDAT as shown on the right.
 	
Use program MVAL to generate the second column of ΣDAT.
	1: [[0 1]
	     [.75 2.546875]
	     [1.5 4.375]
	     [2.25 9.015625]
	     [3 19]]

Choose column 2 of ΣDAT, the y-values, and convert it to a list with MVTL. The list on the stack contains the heights of the rectangles. Notice that when using left rectangles, the value of the function at the rightmost endpoint b of the interval (in this case, 19) is not the height of a rectangle. Thus, delete the *last* value in the list.	Press ▽ ▽ and use ▷ until you reach the 1 in 19. Press DEL→ ENTER. 3: 2: 1: {1 2.546875 4.375 9.015625}
Remember, the rectangle width is Δx (here, 0.75) and the rectangle heights are in the list on the stack. Thus, entering .75 and pressing ✕ gives the areas of the rectangles.	3: 2: 1: {.75 1.91015625 3.28125 6.76171875}
Use ΣLIST to find the sum of the areas of the four left rectangles.	The left-rectangle approximation is 12.703125.

- It is always a good idea to draw the graph of the function and sketch the approximating rectangles. By doing so, you should notice that the last y-data value on the right is not the height of a left rectangle and should not be included when determining area *up to* that value.

6.2.2 Right-Rectangle Approximation: The HP-48 lists are used to perform the required calculations to find area using right rectangles when given data or a model defining a function $y = f(x)$. Enter $f(x) = x^3 - 2x^2 + 3x + 1$ in EQ.

To approximate the area, from 0 to 3, of the region beneath the graph of $f(x)$ and the horizontal axis using *right* rectangles with $n = 4$ subintervals, determine $\Delta x = 0.75$ and the first column of ΣDAT as shown on the right.
 	
Use program MVAL to generate the second column of ΣDAT.
	1: [[0 1]
	      [.75 2.546875]
	      [1.5 4.375]
	      [2.25 9.015625]
	      [3 19]]

Choose column 2 of ΣDAT, the y-values, and convert it to a list with MVTL. The list on the stack contains the heights of the rectangles. Notice that when using right rectangles, the value of the function at the leftmost endpoint a (in this case, 1) is not the height of a rectangle. Thus, delete the *first* value in the list.	Press ▼ and use ▶ until you reach the 1 . Press DEL→ ENTER . 3: 2: 1: { 2.546875 4.375 9.015625 }
Remember, the rectangle width is Δx (here, 0.75) and the rectangle heights are in the list on the stack. Thus, entering .75 and pressing ☒ gives the areas of the rectangles.	3: 2: 1: { 1.91015625 3.28125 6.76171875 14.25 }
Use ΣLIST to find the sum of the areas of the four right rectangles.	The right-rectangle approximation is 26.203125.

6.2.3 Trapezoid Approximation: The HP-48 lists are used to perform the required calculations to find area using trapezoids when given data or a model defining a function $y = f(x)$. Enter $f(x) = x^3 - 2x^2 + 3x + 1$ in EQ.

Determine ΣDAT.	See 6.2.1 and 6.2.2 of this *Guide*.

To approximate the area, from 0 to 3, of the region beneath the graph of $f(x)$ and the horizontal axis using $n = 4$ *trapezoids* , note that the second column of ΣDAT contains the heights of the sides of the trapezoids.	Choose column 2 of ΣDAT, the function values, and convert it to a list with MVTL.
Notice that when using trapezoids, all heights occur twice except for the leftmost and rightmost endpoints a and b. Thus, enter a list with first and last values of 1 and all other values 2.	3: 2: { 1 2.546875 4.375.. 1: { 1 2 2 2 1 }
Determine the "function values portion" of the trapezoid area formula T_n. (Suppose this list is called L.)	Press $\boxed{\times}$.
Find the area of the trapezoids using the formula $T_n = (\Delta x\,/\,2)$ sum L. $T_4 = (0.75/2)$ sum L $= 19.453125$	Key in $\boxed{\Sigma\text{LIST}}$ .75 2 $\boxed{\div}$ $\boxed{\times}$ to find 19.453125.

6.2.4 Midpoint-Rectangle Approximation:
The HP-48 lists can be used to perform the required calculations to find area using midpoint rectangles when given a model defining a function $y = f(x)$. Enter $f(x) = x^3 - 2x^2 + 3x + 1$ in EQ.

- If you are using the data points and *not* a model for function values and there are no data points given at the midpoint x-values, this method should not be used.

To approximate the area, from 0 to 3, of the region beneath the graph of $f(x)$ and the horizontal axis using $n = 4$ *midpoint* rectangles, determine $\Delta x = 0.75$.
 	
Replace each pair of original x-values with their average found by adding the values together and dividing by 2. The midpoints of each interval become the new values that are entered in the first column of ΣDAT.
	1: [[.375]
	        [1.125]
	        [1.875]
	        [2.625]]

Use program MDVAL to generate and store in the second column of ΣDAT the function values evaluated at the midpoints .	The second column of ΣDAT now contains the heights of the midpoint rectangles.

Choose column 2 of ΣDAT and convert it to a list with $\boxed{2}$ $\boxed{\text{MVTL}}$. The list on the stack contains the heights of the midpoint rectangles.	1: { 1.896484375
	        3.267575125
	        6.185546875
	        13.181640625 }

Since the width of each rectangle is $\Delta x = 0.75$, keying in .75 $\boxed{\times}$ gives a list containing the area of each midpoint rectangle.	1: { 1.42236328125
	        2.45068359375
	        4.63916015625
	        9.88623046875 }

Find the sum of the areas of the four midpoint rectangles.	$\boxed{\Sigma\text{LIST}}$ gives 18.3984375.

6.2.5 Simpson's Rule:
The HP-48 lists are used to perform the required calculations to find area approximations using Simpson's Rule when given data or a model defining a function $y = f(x)$. Enter $f(x) = x^3 - 2x^2 + 3x + 1$ in EQ.

- The number, n, of subintervals must be an *even* number in order to use the method presented below.

- If the number, n, of subintervals is *odd*, use this form of Simpson's Rule:
$$S = \frac{2}{3} (\text{Midpoint Area}) + \frac{1}{3} (\text{Trapezoid Area})$$

Determine ΣDAT.	See 6.2.1 and 6.2.2 of this *Guide*.
Choose column 2 of ΣDAT, the function values, and convert it to a list with MVTL. Notice that when using Simpson's Rule, the coefficients of the function-values in the formula for S_n alternate in a 1-4-2-4-2 ⋯ 2-4-1 pattern. Enter a list containing these coefficients.	3: 2: { 1 2.546875 4.375.. 1: { 1 4 2 4 1 } The list in level 1 must have the same number of elements as the one currently on the stack.

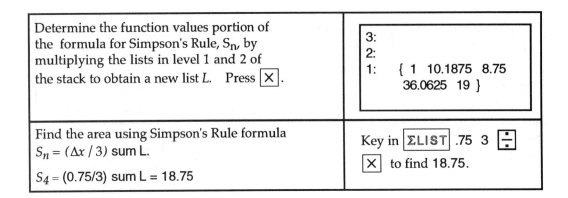

Determine the function values portion of the formula for Simpson's Rule, S_n, by multiplying the lists in level 1 and 2 of the stack to obtain a new list L. Press $\boxed{\times}$.	3: 2: 1: { 1 10.1875 8.75 36.0625 19 }
Find the area using Simpson's Rule formula $S_n = (\Delta x / 3)$ sum L. $S_4 = (0.75/3)$ sum L = 18.75	Key in $\boxed{\Sigma\text{LIST}}$ .75 3 $\boxed{\div}$ $\boxed{\times}$ to find 18.75.

SECTION 6.3: LIMITS OF SUMS

6.3.1 Simplifying Area Calculations: When the number of subintervals, n, is large, it is impractical to calculate areas using the methods previously given. In such a case, the programs GRECT, LRECT, RRECT, MID, TRAP, and SIMP in the HP-48 Appendix are used to calculate the corresponding areas and draw the graphs of the approximating rectangles or trapezoids. (The other programs that are indicated to go in the directory containing these programs are needed as subroutines and must also be entered in your calculator.)

Before using any of these programs, store the model, the endpoints of the interval, and the number of approximating rectangles by placing on the stack, in this order:

- the model, using x as the input variable

- a, the left endpoint of the interval

- b, the right endpoint of the interval

    Press $\boxed{\text{FABSTO}}$.

- n, the number of subintervals

    Press $\boxed{\text{NSTO}}$.

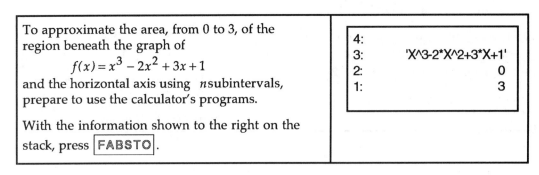

To approximate the area, from 0 to 3, of the region beneath the graph of $$f(x) = x^3 - 2x^2 + 3x + 1$$ and the horizontal axis using n subintervals, prepare to use the calculator's programs. With the information shown to the right on the stack, press $\boxed{\text{FABSTO}}$.	4: 3: 'X^3-2*X^2+3*X+1' 2: 0 1: 3

Let us first use $n = 4$ subintervals to illustrate the programs. Compare the values obtained with those from 6.2.1 through 6.2.5 of this *Guide*.	Place 4 on level 1 of the stack and press NSTO. (You may need to press NXT to find the program names.)

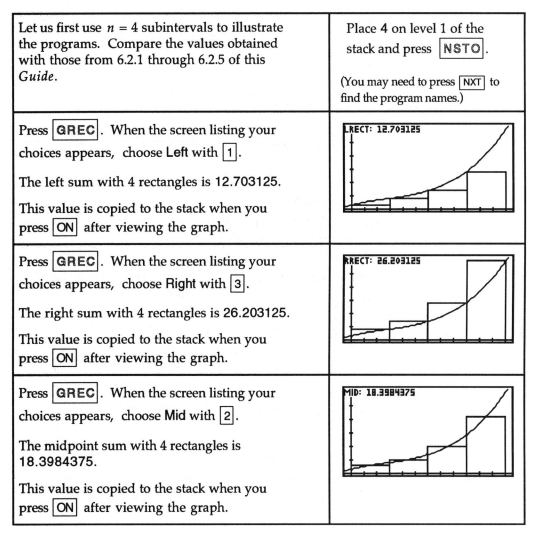

Press GREC. When the screen listing your choices appears, choose **Left** with 1. The left sum with 4 rectangles is 12.703125. This value is copied to the stack when you press ON after viewing the graph.	LRECT: 12.703125
Press GREC. When the screen listing your choices appears, choose **Right** with 3. The right sum with 4 rectangles is 26.203125. This value is copied to the stack when you press ON after viewing the graph.	RRECT: 26.203125
Press GREC. When the screen listing your choices appears, choose **Mid** with 2. The midpoint sum with 4 rectangles is 18.3984375. This value is copied to the stack when you press ON after viewing the graph.	MID: 18.3984375

- Notice that program GREC draws an autoscaled graph of the model. You need not do this before running the program.

For the trapezoidal approximation using 4 subintervals, press TRAP. For the Simpson's Rule approximation using 4 subintervals, press SIMP.	4: 3: 2: trap: 19.453125 1: simp: 18.75

- The programs do not draw a graph of the approximating trapezoids, and the programs do not draw a picture for Simpson's Rule.

- When n, the number of subintervals, is large, it is not advisable to draw pictures. For area approximations only (without pictures), press $\boxed{\text{LREC}}$, $\boxed{\text{RREC}}$, and $\boxed{\text{MID}}$ instead of $\boxed{\text{GREC}}$.

- To change the number of subintervals, n, place the new value for n on the stack and press $\boxed{\text{NSTO}}$.

- These area approximation programs cannot be used with data unless you use a model you fit to the data.

6.3.2 Limits of Sums:
When finding the trend in the midpoint approximations to the area between a non-negative function and the horizontal axis between two values of the input variable, program MID is extremely helpful!

To construct a chart of midpoint approximations for the area between $f(x) = x^3 - 2x^2 + 3x + 1$ and the x-axis between $x=0$ and $x=3$, first follow the instructions in 6.3.1 of this *Guide* to store the function and the two values of x with $\boxed{\text{FABSTO}}$.	Next, input some number of subintervals, say $n = 4$. Place 4 on level 1 of the stack and press $\boxed{\text{NSTO}}$.
Press $\boxed{\text{MID}}$ and record the midpoint approximation **18.3984375**.	Double the number of subintervals. Place 8 on level 1 of the stack and press $\boxed{\text{NSTO}}$.
Press $\boxed{\text{MID}}$ and record the midpoint approximation **18.662109375**.	Double the number of subintervals. Place 16 on level 1 of the stack and press $\boxed{\text{NSTO}}$.
Press $\boxed{\text{MID}}$ and record the midpoint approximation **18.7280273438**. (Finding a trend means that you can tell what specific number the values are getting closer and closer to without having to run the program ad infinitum!)	Continue on in this manner, each time using $\boxed{\text{NSTO}}$ to increase the number of subintervals until a trend is evident.

SECTION 6.4: INDEFINITE INTEGRALS

6.4.1 Finding Integral Formulas: The HP-48 performs the required calculations to help you find integral formulas. You can create a table of values for the definite integral and look for a pattern in those values to help determine an indefinite integral formula. The process of calculating the definite integral uses the calculator's notation for finding the integral, ∫.

Suppose we are investigating $\int_{0}^{x} t\,dt$ for various values of x, namely $x = 0, 1, 2, 3,$ 4, and 5 in order to find a formula for this indefinite integral.

Press ↱ 9 (SYMBOLIC) and press OK to choose Integrate. Enter T in the expression location, enter T in the variable location, enter 0 in the "low" location, and enter X in the "high" location. Press OK after each entry.	EXPR: T VAR: T LO: 0 HI: X RESULT: Symbolic Press +/− if SYMBOLIC is not in the RESULT location.
Press OK and the HP-48 notation for the indefinite integral is returned to the stack.	3: 2: 1: ' T^2/2 I (T=X) – T^2/2 I (T=0)'
Press ↰ 7 (SOLVE) ROOT ↰ EQ to store the above expression as the current equation. Press SOLVR and you see a menu containing T and X. *Ignore the T.*	If X does not appear on your solver menu, it means you have an X on the menu in your directory or some directory containing your directory. Find X, purge it, and reenter the solver application.
Enter the first x-value, 0, and press X. Next press EXPR= to see Expr: 0. Enter the next x-value, 1, and press X. Next press EXPR= to see Expr: .5. Continue on in this manner until you have evaluated the expression for all the x-values.	4: Expr: 2 3: Expr: 4.5 2: Expr: 8 1: Expr: 12.5

Seeing the fractional form of these values may help in determining the pattern. The "to a fraction" key is found with ⟨←⟩ ⟨9⟩ (SOLVE) ⟨NXT⟩ ⟨→Q⟩.	The fractional form of the integral values is 0 1/2 2 9/2 8 25/2.

Finding the EXPR values might take a short time since the calculator is determining definite integral values. Now, to determine an integral formula, all you need do is find the pattern in these values.

- If you have difficulty determining a pattern, draw a scatterplot of the x-values and the calculated definite integral values. The shape of the scatterplot should give you a clue as to the equation of the indefinite integral formula. Note that this method might help only if you consider a variety of values for x.

- The HP-48 finds the values of definite integrals and the symbolic (formula) form of some indefinite integrals. Using your calculator to find the indefinite integral formula is discussed in a later section.

To create a list of values for the indefinite integral $\int_{a}^{x} f(t)\, dt$ for varying values of a, use basically the same procedure as illustrated above. Suppose we want to compare, for various values of a, $\int_{a}^{x} t\, dt$ to $\int_{0}^{x} t\, dt$.

Press ⟨→⟩ ⟨9⟩ (SYMBOLIC) and press ⟨OK⟩ to choose **Integrate**. Enter **T** in the expression location, enter **T** in the variable location, enter **A** in the "low" location, and enter **X** in the "high" location. Press ⟨OK⟩ after each entry and ⟨OK⟩ when finished.	EXPR: T VAR: T LO: A HI: X RESULT: Symbolic Press ⟨+/−⟩ if SYMBOLIC is not in the RESULT location.
Press ⟨←⟩ ⟨7⟩ (SOLVE) ⟨ROOT⟩ ⟨←⟩ ⟨EQ⟩ to store the symbolic expression as the current equation.	3: 2: 1: ' T^2/2 I (T=X) – T^2/2 I (T=A)'
Press ⟨SOLVR⟩ and you see a menu containing **T**, **X**, and **A**.	*Ignore the T.*

Type 1 and press $\boxed{A}$. Follow the instructions in 6.4.1 of this Guide to evaluate $\int_{1}^{x} t\, dt$ for $x =$ 0, 1, 2, 3, 4, and 5 and convert these values to fractional form. Compare these values to the output for $\int_{0}^{x} t\, dt$. Repeat for $A = 2$.	For X = 0 1 2 3 4 5, A = 1 gives EXPR= $^{-}$.5 0 1.5 4 7.5 12 A = 2 gives EXPR= $^{-}$2 -1.5 0 2.5 6 10.5 Repeat, if necessary, for other values of A.

SECTION 6.5: THE FUNDAMENTAL THEOREM

6.5.1 The Fundamental Theorem of Calculus: This theorem tells us that the derivative of an antiderivative of a function is the function itself. Let us consider this theorem numerically. We also illustrate the FTC using the Hewlett-Packard's unique capability of determining the symbolic form of certain derivatives and integrals.

Recall that when using the stack, the HP-48's derivative entry form for $\dfrac{d(f(x))}{dx}$ is '$\partial X(f(x))$'. The stack entry form for the integral $\int_{a}^{x} f(t)\, dt$ is '$\int (A, X, f(T), T)$ '.

Consider $F'(x) = \dfrac{d}{dx}\left(\displaystyle\int_{1}^{x} 3t^2 + 2t - 5\, dt \right)$. The FTC tells us $F'(x)$ should equal $f(x) = 3x^2 + 2x - 5$. Enter $F'(x)$ as shown to the right.	3: 2: 1: ' $\partial X(\int (1,X,3*T^2+2*T -5, T))$ '
Store this expression in EQ.	$F'(x)$ is now in EQ.
Since $F'(x)$ is a function of X, use program **F.val** to evaluate it at several different values of X. (Remember to enter the value of X before pressing $\boxed{\text{F.val}}$ and to press $\boxed{\leftarrow}\,\boxed{\text{EVAL}}$ (→NUM) after pressing $\boxed{\text{F.val}}$.)	X: $^{-}$2 0 3.5 10 EQ: 3 -5 38.75 315

Now, store $f(x) = 3x^2 + 2x - 5$ in EQ. Evaluate this function at the same values of x. Compare them to the values obtained for $F'(x)$.	X: ‾2 0 3.5 10 EQ: 3 -5 38.75 315 Compare these to the $F'(x)$ values above.

Let us now consider the symbolic representation and see the FTC in action!

Enter $\displaystyle\int_a^x f(t)\,dt$ on the stack as indicated on the right. Store the integral in EQ.	3: 2: 1: '∫ (1, X, 3*T^2+2*T–5, T)'
Enter $F'(x) = \dfrac{d}{dx}\left(\displaystyle\int_1^x 3t^2 + 2t - 5\,dt\right)$ on the stack as indicated on the right. *(Purge all X from your menus!)*	4: 3: 2: 1: '∂ X(EQ)'
Press EVAL repeatedly until the HP has finished applying the derivative formulas and simplified the "answer" to the expression on the right. Repeat this exploration for other functions and different lower limits. Are you convinced?	4: 3: 2: 1: '3*X^2+2*X–5'

CHAPTER 7.   MEASURING THE EFFECTS OF CHANGE: THE DEFINITE INTEGRAL

SECTION 7.2: THE DEFINITE INTEGRAL

7.2.1 Antiderivatives: All antiderivatives of a specific function differ only by a constant. We explore this idea using the function $f(x) = 3x^2 - 1$ and its antiderivative $F(x) = x^3 - x + C$ for various values of C.

Enter $f(x)$ on the stack. To simplify entry of the remaining functions, store $f(x) = 3x^2 - 1$ in some variable, say A. Store 'X^3 − X' in another variable, say B. Enter the functions, as they appear to the right, on the stack.	1: 'A' 2: '∫ (0, X, A, X)' 3: 'B+0' 4: 'B−2' 5: 'B−1' 6: 'B+2' 7: 'B−3'
Form a list of the seven functions on the stack by entering 7 and pressing $\boxed{\text{PRG}}$ $\boxed{\text{LIST}}$ $\boxed{\rightarrow\text{LIST}}$.	Store the list as the current EQ in the PLOT application.
Find a suitable view and graph all the functions. (Try x between ⁻3 and 3 and y between ⁻5 and 10.) It seems that the only difference in the graphs (other than the graph of A) is that the y-intercept is different. But, isn't C the y-intercept of the antiderivative?	

- Trace the graphs and then jump between them with $\boxed{\blacktriangledown}$. It appears that the graph of $F(x)$ with $C = 0$ and $\displaystyle\int_0^x (3t^2 - 1)\, dt$ are the same. If it becomes difficult to tell on which graph you are tracing, have TRACE activated, press $\boxed{\text{FCN}}$ $\boxed{\text{NXT}}$ and $\boxed{\text{VIEW}}$. The equation of the graph the trace cursor is on is displayed on the screen.

- What if you changed the function in level 2 of the stack to '∫ (2, X, A, X)'? Would find the graphs of ∫ (2, X, A, X) and $x^3 - x + 2$, or maybe ∫ (2, X, A, X) and $x^3 - x - 2$, the same? Can you justify your answer with antiderivative formulas? Explore!

7.2.2 Evaluating a Definite Integral on the Home Screen: The HP-48 finds

a numerical approximation for the definite integral $\int_a^b f(x)\, dx$. Since the HP-48 "home

screen" is the stack, all you have to do is type $\int (a, b, f(x), X)$ for a specific function

$f(x)$ and specific values of a and b, and press ENTER ⬅ EVAL →NUM. The
function can be stored in another variable such as A, EQ, etc., or it can be entered directly
into the integral form.

- If you evaluate a definite integral using antiderivative formulas and check you
  answer using the calculator, you may sometimes find a slight difference in the
  trailing decimal places. Remember, the HP-48 is sometimes evaluating the
  definite integral using approximation techniques.

Find $\displaystyle\int_1^5 (2^x - x)\, dx$. Notice that as long as you specify the variable you are using in the position after the function, you can use any letter to represent the variable.	4: 3: 2: $\int$ (1, 5, 2^T–T, T)' 1: $'\int$ (1, 5, 2^X–X, X)'
Type ⬅ EVAL →NUM.	The value of the definite integral is **31.2808512266**.

7.2.3 Rates into Amounts: The integral, between two input values, say a and b,

of a rate of change is the change in amount of the antiderivative from a to b. Suppose
you have modeled marginal cost data to find the rate of change in the marginal cost of
ovens to be $C'(x) = {}^-1.12744 + 6137.6892\, x^{-1}$ dollars per oven where x is the number of
ovens produced per day. What is the change in cost if production is increased from 300
to 500 ovens per day?

Enter the expression on the right and press ⬅ EVAL →NUM. The change in amount is $2909.80.	2: 1: $\int$ (300, 500, -1.12744 +6137.6892*INV(X),X)'

You have just used the stack interface to evaluate the integral. You may find it easier
to use the screen interface. Investigate this method as illustrated below, and choose
the one you prefer for the remainder of this chapter.

Press ⇨ 9 SYMBOLIC and press OK to choose INTEGRATE. DEL the current EXPR and type ‾1.12744 + 6137.6892*INV(X). Choose the other settings shown on the right. Press OK to get 2909.80091407.	EXPR: '-1.12744+6137.... VAR: X LO: 300 HI: 500 RESULT: Numeric NUMBER FORMAT: Fix 5 (See the note below.)

Note: When you choose a numeric result, a NUMBER FORMAT field appears. Press CHOOS and use ▼ to select **Fixed**. Press OK ▶ and enter 5 (or the number of decimal places required by your instructor). Press OK. If you use Std as the number format, the HP may take quite a while to calculate the result to twelve-digit precision.

You now have the knowledge to understand the notation the calculator used in an earlier section. Recall from 6.4.1 of this *Guide* that you observed the HP-48 symbolic notation for $\int_0^x t \, dt$ to be ' T^2/2 | (T=X) − T^2/2 | (T+0) '. What is the HP-48 doing here? Isn't ' T^2/2 | (T=X) − T^2/2 | (T+0) ' what you do when you write

$$\int_0^x t \, dt = \left.\frac{t^2}{2}\right|_0^x = \frac{t^2}{2} \text{ (let } t = x) - \frac{t^2}{2} \text{ (let } t = 0)?$$

Of course, we use this procedure for a specific value of x, but so does the HP when you press EVAL with an X on the menu or when you press →NUM! Do you now understand why you need to purge the x's from your menu when you want a symbolic result?

Let us now have the HP-48 find the amount function $C(t)$ and illustrate that

$$\int_{300}^{500} C'(t)dt = C(500) - C(300).$$

Press ⇨ 9 SYMBOLIC and press OK to choose INTEGRATE. Edit the current EXPR to ‾1.12744 + 6137.6892*INV(T). Choose the other settings shown on the right. Press OK.	EXPR: '-1.12744+6137.... VAR: T LO: 300 HI: X RESULT: Symbolic

*Purge all **X** from your menus!*
 	
Press [ENTER] to evaluate the expression that is returned to the stack.
 	
Store the evaluated integral in EQ.
	2:
	1: ' 6137.6892*LN(X)–
	           1.12744*X–
	           34669.8120939 '

Use [F.val] to evaluate at 500. (Remember, we used a lower limit of 300 to obtain the expression in EQ.)	The result is 2909.800914.

7.2.4 Integrals and Area:

Finding the area between two functions utilizes the ideas presented in preceding sections. Suppose we want to find the area between the functions $f(x) = 2 - x$ and $g(x) = -x^3 + 2x + 2$.

First, we must find where the two functions intersect.	Enter { '2–X' '-X^3+2*X+2' } as the expression in the PLOT application.
Graph both functions in an appropriate viewing window, say x between ⁻6.5 and 6.5 and y between ⁻5 and 5.	
Next, find the three points of intersection. (The x-values of these intersection points will be the limits on the integrals we use to find the area.) Use the procedure on the right to find each point of intersection. The HP displays the intersection point on the screen and copies it to the stack.	Press [FCN]. Use [◄], [►], [▲], [▼] to move the cursor close to the intersection point. Press [ISECT]. Press any white key to return the menu to the screen.
Store the x-values of the intersection points in A, B, and C. (See note below.)	-1.73205080757 'A' [STO] 0 'B' [STO] 1.73205080757 'C' [STO]

Note: You can either retype these values or use [PRG] [TYPE] [OBJ→] to disassemble the points, [DROP] what you do not need, and hold the x-values on the stack.

The area between the two curves is given by $$\int_A^B (f-g)\, dx + \int_B^C (g-f)\, dx = 2.25 + 2.25 = 4.5.$$ (For better accuracy, use the letters A, B, and C when typing in the integral limits.)	Be certain that you use parentheses properly: $f - g = $ ' 2–X – (-X^3+2*X+2) ' $g - f = $ ' -X^3+2*X+2 – (2–X) '

7.2.5 Evaluating a Definite Integral from the Graphics Screen:

You can graphically find the value of the definite integral $\int_a^b f(x)\, dx$ provided that a and b are possible x-values displayed when move the cursor on the graphics screen.

- For "nice" numbers, you can often find the exact x-value you need if you graph in the RESET screen or set the viewing window so that the horizontal view is a multiple of 13.

Find $\displaystyle\int_1^5 (2^x - x)\, dx$. Choose the PLOT application settings shown on the right.	TYPE: Function EQ: '2^X–X' INDEP: X H-VIEW: 0 6.5 V-VIEW: -10 40
Graph the function.	
Either use ◀ or TRACE to move the cursor to where X=1. (The y-value is not important.) Press X to mark the location.	Next, use ▶ to move the cursor to where X=5. Press + or one of the white keys to return the menu to the screen.
Press FCN and then AREA. The area appears on screen and on level 1 of the stack.	AREA: 31.2808512266

Bring back the menu, and press $\boxed{\text{SHADE}}$ to shade the area the definite integral represents. The value of the integral equals the area since this function is not negative from 1 to 5.	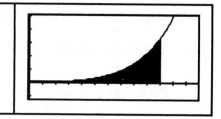

SECTION 7.3: AVERAGES

7.3.1 Average Value of a Function: Use the HP-48 to find the numerical value of and aid in your geometric interpretation of the average value of a function. Consider a model for the average daytime temperature between 7 AM and 7 PM:

$$f(t) = {}^-0.65684t^2 + 9.38212t + 45.54945 \text{ degrees } t \text{ hours after 7 AM.}$$

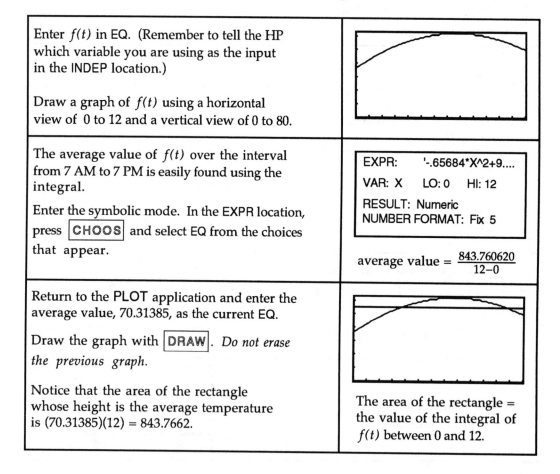

Enter $f(t)$ in EQ. (Remember to tell the HP which variable you are using as the input in the INDEP location.)

Draw a graph of $f(t)$ using a horizontal view of 0 to 12 and a vertical view of 0 to 80.

The average value of $f(t)$ over the interval from 7 AM to 7 PM is easily found using the integral.

Enter the symbolic mode. In the EXPR location, press $\boxed{\text{CHOOS}}$ and select EQ from the choices that appear.

EXPR: '-.65684*X^2+9....

VAR: X   LO: 0   HI: 12

RESULT: Numeric
NUMBER FORMAT: Fix 5

average value $= \dfrac{843.760620}{12-0}$

Return to the PLOT application and enter the average value, 70.31385, as the current EQ.

Draw the graph with $\boxed{\text{DRAW}}$. *Do not erase the previous graph.*

Notice that the area of the rectangle whose height is the average temperature is (70.31385)(12) = 843.7662.

The area of the rectangle = the value of the integral of $f(t)$ between 0 and 12.

SECTION 7.4: INCOME STREAMS

7.4.1 Future and Present Value of an Income Stream: Since future and present value of an income stream are defined by definite integrals, finding these values is easily done with your calculator.

Suppose we want to find the present and future values of an investment of $3.3 million each year that earns continuously compounded interest at a rate of 19.4% annually for a period of 10 years.

The *future value* of the investment is the amount to which the $3.3 million invested each year and the interest it earns would accumulate to at the end of 10 years. (We assume the $3.3 million is flowing in continuously.)

Future value = $e^{0.194(10)} \int\limits_{0}^{10} 3.3 e^{-0.194t} \, dt$ which equals $101.360 million.	Use, in SYMBOLIC, EXPR: '3.3*EXP(-.194*T)' VAR: T LO: 0 HI: 10 RESULT: NUMERIC On the stack, multiply this result by EXP(.194*10).

The *present value* of the investment is the amount that would have to be deposited <u>now</u> and remain untouched (except for accumulating interest) to equal the amount to which the $3.3 million invested each year and the interest it earns would accumulate at the end of 10 years. (We assume the investment is flowing in continuously.)

Present value = $\int\limits_{0}^{10} 3.3 e^{-0.194t} \, dt$ which equals $14.566 million.	Evaluate the integral as indicated above or press $\boxed{\rhd}$ $\boxed{\text{EVAL}}$ (UNDO) to find, in level 2, the value you already calculated.

7.4.2 Present Value in Perpetuity: Your calculator provides numerical values for definite integrals, not an integral whose upper limit approaches infinity. You can try to use your HP to find an antiderivative in symbolic form. If the integral sign, $\int$, appears in your answer, the HP can not show you the symbolic form. You can, however, evaluate, using integral formulas, the present value in perpetuity integral for a fixed T and consider what happens numerically and graphically as T gets larger and larger.

Suppose we want to evaluate $\int\limits_{0}^{\infty} 10000 e^{-0.135t} \, dt = \lim\limits_{T \to \infty} \int\limits_{0}^{T} 10000 e^{-0.135t} \, dt =$

$\lim\limits_{T \to \infty} 74074.07(1 - e^{-0.135T})$. We find $\lim\limits_{T \to \infty} (1 - e^{-0.135T})$ and multiply by 74074.07.

To investigate this limit *numerically*, first enter 'EXP(-.135*X)' in EQ. Now, evaluate EQ at increasingly larger values of x. (You may want to begin at $x = 0$ and let x increase by 10 each time.)	You can evaluate EQ using program F.val, using the SOLVE application, or using program MVAL. (We use program F.val below.)
Enter the values of X on the stack, pressing ⌐F.val⌐ after each entry. (See note below.) It appears that $1 - e^{-.135x}$ is getting closer and closer to 1 as x gets larger and larger.	1: .999696460862 2: .999921310435 3: .999979600497 4: .999994711627

Note: If you chose **FIX 5** when you evaluated integrals numerically, you need to reset your calculator to standard format in order to determine the limit. To do this, press ⌐↱⌐ ⌐CST⌐ (MODES) ⌐CHOOS⌐, select Standard, and press ⌐OK⌐ ⌐OK⌐.

To investigate this limit *graphically*, go to the PLOT application and have 'EXP(-.135*X)' in EQ. Set a suitable view, such as a horizontal view of 0 to 100 and vertical view of 0 to 2.	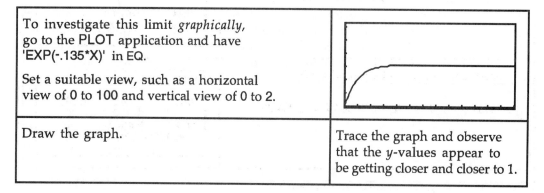
Draw the graph.	Trace the graph and observe that the y-values appear to be getting closer and closer to 1.

Thus, $\lim\limits_{T \to \infty} 74074.07(1 - e^{-0.135T}) = 74074.07 \lim\limits_{T \to \infty} (1 - e^{-0.135T}) = 74074.07 * 1 = 74074.07.$

SECTION 7.5: INTEGRALS IN ECONOMICS

7.5.1 Consumers' and Producers' Surplus: Consumers' and producers' surplus, being defined by definite integrals, are easy to do using the calculator. You should always draw a graph of the demand and supply functions to better understand the activity. Suppose the demand curve is $D(q) = -0.06q + 71.863$ and the supply curve is $S(q) = 16.977(1.001117)^q$ where q is the number of units of the product. We want to find the social gain at the equilibrium price.

Enter a list containing $D(q) = ^-0.06q + 71.863$ and $S(q) = 16.977(1.001117)^q$ in EQ.	{ '-0.06*X+71.863' '16.977 *1.001117^X' }
Graph EQ in a suitable view, say H-VIEW: 0 1000 and V-VIEW: 0 80. Use the methods of 7.2.4 of this *Guide* to find the intersection of the demand and supply functions. $q = 628$ and $D(q) = S(q) \approx 34.21$ is the equilibrium point. (Note that since $x = q$ is the number of units of a product, it should be a whole number.)	 ISECT X=627.57660514 _y=34.208403692 _
The consumers' surplus at equilibrium is $$\int_0^{628} -0.06x + 71.863 \, dx - 628(34.21) = 11{,}814.56$$	EXPR: '-.06*X+71.863' VAR: X LO: 0 HI: 628 RESULT: Numeric NUMBER FORMAT: Fix 5
The producers' surplus at equilibrium is $$\int_0^{628} 16.977(1.001117)^x \, dx - 628(34.21) = 6{,}034.28$$	EXPR: '16.977*1.001117^X' VAR: X LO: 0 HI: 628 RESULT: Numeric NUMBER FORMAT: Fix 5
Thus, the social gain is 11,814.56 + 6,034.28 = 17,848.84.	Note that you could have calculated the social gain as the area between the demand and supply curves.

HP-48G Series Calculator Appendix

Programs listed below are referenced in *Part C* of this *Guide*. They appear in the order in which they are discussed in the *Guide*. Programs should be typed in your calculator, transferred to you via infrared transmission using the I/O mode of HP-48, or transferred to your calculator using Kermit™ for a PC or Macintosh computer or the HP F1201A Serial Interface Kit (PC) and a disk containing these programs. Refer to your owner's manual for instructions on typing in the programs or transferring them via infrared transmission from another calculator.

Any program called by another program must be included in the same directory as the 'calling' program. Some of the programs listed below function only as subroutines of other programs. The subroutines must be included in the same directory as the program using them. All programs should execute properly if you use the directory structure listed below. (Any other items in your directory should go at the end of each menu.)

CALCC

F.val	EQ	ΣDAT	STPLT	ALIGN	FIT
NDIF	NUINT	APLY			

The **FIT** directory should contain the following programs:

FIT

ΣDAT	STPLT	PFIT	EXPFT	LOGIS	EQ
L	A	B	LSLN	DATA	UP
LSUB1	LSUB2	LSUB3	LSUB4	LGPH	

The **NDIF** directory should contain the following programs:

NDIF

ΣDAT	DIFF	FDIF	SDIF	%CHG	UP

The **NUINT** directory should contain the following programs:

NUINT

ΣDAT	FABST	NSTO	MVAL	GREC	UP
LREC	RREC	MID	TRAP	SIMP	MVTL
LTSV	SUM	F.val	X		

PROGRAMMING NOTES:

- Hewlett-Packard calculators distinguish between upper- and lower-case letters. If you are typing in the programs that follow, be certain to match the case shown in the program. Lower-case letters are obtained by pressing $\boxed{\alpha}$ $\boxed{\leftarrow}$ followed by the letter key. Spaces between symbols are also important for correct execution.

- If you cannot find a particular command in a menu, consult the appendix in your owner's manual. Also, you can type any command on the HP-48 using the keyboard keys and it will be recognized by the calculator.

```
F.val              • Program        ALIGN                • Program
<< 'X' STO EQ EVAL                  << → f
>>                                    << 1 COL-
                                      << f -
                                      >> APLY
                                   >> 1 COL+ DUP
                                  'ΣDAT' STO >>
```

Program **APLY** is already in the **EXAM** directory of your HP-48G. To place a copy of it in your **CALCC** directory, do the following:

- Press $\boxed{\nearrow}$ $\boxed{\prime}$ (HOME) to enter your home directory. Press $\boxed{\text{EXAM}}$ $\boxed{\text{PRGS}}$ to find APLY on the menu (use NXT if necessary). If the **EXAM** directory is not on your **HOME** menu, type TEACH and press $\boxed{\text{ENTER}}$ to place it there.

- Press $\boxed{\nearrow}$ $\boxed{\text{APLY}}$ to place a copy of the program on the stack.

- Press $\boxed{\prime}$ $\boxed{\text{APLY}}$ to place the name of the program on the stack.

- Press $\boxed{\nearrow}$ $\boxed{\prime}$ (HOME) to enter your home directory and $\boxed{\text{CALCC}}$ to enter your CALCC directory.

- Press $\boxed{\text{STO}}$. You should see $\boxed{\text{APLY}}$ on the menu in your CALCC directory.

```
APLY              • Program        STPLT            • Program
<< → a P                          << 'ΣDAT' STO MAXΣ
  << a DUP SIZE DUP               MINΣ DUP2 - DUP .1
SIZE IF 1 ==                      * DUP 3 ROLL .2 *
     THEN 1 SF 1 +                V→ SWAP DROP SWAP
SWAP OBJ→ OBJ→ DROP               V→ DROP SWAP →V2
1 + ROLL                         SWAP 4 ROLL + 3
     ELSE DROP2 a OBJ→            ROLLD - V→ 3 ROLL
   END DUP OBJ→                   V→ 3 ROLL SWAP 4
DROP * SWAP OVER 2                DUPN YRNG XRNG
+ ROLLD →LIST 1 P                 SCATTER ERASE DRAX
DOSUBS OBJ→ 1 +                   DRAW - 63 / NEG 3
ROLL IFERR IF 1 FS?C             ROLLD - 130 / NEG
THEN OBJ→ DROP                    NΣ → h w n
 →LIST END →ARRY                    << 1 n
   THEN OBJ→                          FOR j 'ΣDAT(j,1)'
       IF 1 FC?C                  EVAL DUP w -
       THEN DROP                  SWAP w + 'ΣDAT(j,2)'
       END → n m                  EVAL DUP h + SWAP
     << 1 n                       h - 4 ROLL SWAP R→C
        FOR i m                   3 ROLLD R→C BOX
→LIST 'm*(n-i)+i'                     NEXT
EVAL ROLLD NEXT n                  >> PICTURE
→LIST >>                          >>
   END
  >>
>>
```

You will find it helpful to organize the menus in your directories, placing the most frequently used keys at the beginning of the menu. We illustrate by organizing the **CALCC** directory:

- Press $\boxed{\text{VAR}}$ and enter the **CALCC** directory if you are not already there.

- Next, create directories for the remainder of the programs in this Appendix. You will need the directories FIT, NDIF, and NUINT. Refer to your owners manual or *Setup* on page *B1* of this *Guide* for instructions on creating directories.

- From the **CALCC** directory, press $\boxed{\text{←}}$ $\boxed{+}$ ({ }) and press the menu keys, in the order in which you want the programs to appear, from left to right, on your menu. We suggest { F.val EQ ΣDAT STPLT ALIGN FIT NDIF NUINT APLY }. Press $\boxed{\text{ENTER}}$.

- Press $\boxed{\text{←}}$ $\boxed{\text{VAR}}$ (MEMORY) $\boxed{\text{DIR}}$ $\boxed{\text{ORDER}}$.

- Press $\boxed{\text{VAR}}$ to see your ordered **CALCC** directory. You can reorder any directory at any time you want a different arrangement of programs and/or stored variables.

Program STPLT needs to be in several of your directories. (Reference the organizational chart at the beginning of this Appendix.) After creating those directories, copy STPLT to them using the methods illustrated on the previous page for copying program APLY. Be certain you are in the directory in which you want the program to appear before pressing [STO].

```
DIFF               • Program
<< DUP 'ΣDAT' STO 2
COL- SWAP DROP OBJ→
OBJ→ DROP →LIST DUP
ΔLIST DUP DUP
'FDIF' STO ΔLIST
'SDIF' STO SWAP
OBJ→ 1 - SWAP DROP
→LIST / 100 *
'%CHG' STO 'DONE'
>>
```

```
UP                 • Program
<< UPDIR
>>
```

```
PFIT               • Program[1]
<< DUP 'R' STO SWAP
'ΣDAT' STO 'ΣPAR(1)'
→NUM 'ΣPAR(2)'
→NUM → N XCOL YCOL
  << ΣDAT XCOL COL-
SWAP DROP DUP SIZE
1 GET → XS CS
  << 1 CS
    FOR J 'XS(J)'
EVAL → X
  << N 0
    FOR I X I ^ -1
    STEP
      >>
    NEXT CS N 1 +
2 →LIST →ARRY ΣDAT
```

```
(Program PFIT continued)
YCOL COL- SWAP DROP
DUP2 SWAP LSQ → XX
YY BB
  << 'ABS(XX*BB)
/ ABS(YY)' EVAL
"abs r" →TAG
    IF R 2 ≥
    THEN DROP
    END 'Σ(K=0,
N,BB(K+1)*QUOTE(X)^
(N-K))' EVAL DUP
    → ΣDAT 'R'
PURGE STPLT STEQ
FUNCTION 'X' INDEP
DRAW
>>  >>  >>
```

```
LSLNE              • Program

<< ΣDAT STPLT
"Input slope A" ""
INPUT OBJ→ 'A' STO
A 'slope' →TAG
"Input y intercept B"
"" INPUT OBJ→ 'B'
STO B 'yint' →TAG
FUNCTION 'X' PURGE
'A*X+B' STEQ DRAW 0
'S' STO ΣDAT SIZE 1
GET → n
  << 0 1 n
     FOR j 'ΣDAT(j,2
)' EVAL DUP 'ΣDAT(j
,1)' EVAL 'X' STO
'A*X+B' EVAL DUP 3
ROLL X SWAP R→C
SWAP X SWAP R→C
LINE - SQ S + 'S'
STO
     NEXT
  >> PICTURE 2 MENU
DROP S 'SSE' →TAG
{ X S B A } PURGE
>>


EXPFT              • Program

<< 'ΣDAT' STO EXPFIT
LR EXP 'B' STO 'A'
STO CORR "r" →TAG
'A*B^QUOTE(X)' EVAL
DUP DUP 'EQ' STO
{ A B } PURGE ΣDAT
STPLT STEQ FUNCTION
DRAW
>>


LOGISTIC           • Program

<< LSUB1 LSUB2 LSUB3
>>
```

The subroutines of LOGISTIC follow. They must be placed in the same directory as program LOGISTIC .

```
LSUB2              • Program
<< NΣ 2 -  → n
  << { n 2 } 1 CON
'F' STO 1 n
    FOR j ΣDAT j 1
+ 2 2 →LIST GET F {
j 1 } 3 ROLL PUT
'F' STO
    NEXT
  >> NΣ 2 -  → m
  << 0 1 m
    FOR i ΣDAT DUP
DUP i 2 + 2 2 →LIST
GET SWAP { i 2 }
GET - SWAP i 2 + 1
2 →LIST GET ΣDAT
DUP { i 1 } GET 3
ROLL - NEG SWAP i 1
+ 2 2 →LIST GET * /
F { i 2 } 3 ROLL
PUT 'F' STO
    NEXT
  >> F 'ΣDAT' STO
LINFIT LR / NEG
'U' STO DATA
'ΣDAT' STO MAXΣ
OBJ→ DROP .0001 +
'L' STO
    IF U L >
    THEN U 'L' STO
    END
ΣDAT MEAN OBJ→
DROP 'M' STO 0 'W'
STO NΣ  → n
  << 0 1 n
    FOR j W M 'ΣDAT
(j,2)' EVAL - SQ +
'W' STO
    NEXT
  >> CLEAR W 'SSY'
→TAG L 'L' →TAG
{ W M U F } PURGE
>>
```

```
LSUB3              • Program
<< IF MAXΣ OBJ→ DROP
L ≥
  THEN
"BAD VALUE...Increase L"
6 DISP 2 WAIT LSUB4
  END DROP ΣDAT DUP
2 COL- OBJ→ OBJ→
DROP →LIST
  << INV L * 1 - LN
  >> EVAL OBJ→ →ARRY
2 COL+ 'ΣDAT' STO
LINFIT LR NEG 'B'
STO EXP 'A' STO
'ΣDAT' STO NΣ  → n
  << 0 1 n
    FOR j 'ΣDAT(j,1
)' EVAL B NEG * EXP
A * 1 + INV L * '
ΣDAT(j,2)' EVAL -
SQ +
    NEXT
  >> 'SSE' →TAG HALT
  IF G 1 ==
  THEN LGPH
  ELSE LSUB4
  END
>>
```

```
LSUB1              • Program
<< DUP 'ΣDAT' STO
'DATA' STO 'L/(1+A*
EXP(-B*X))' STEQ 1
'G' STO
  >>
```

```
LGPH                    • Program

<< ΣDAT STPLT 'EQ'
EVAL STEQ FUNCTION
'X' INDEP DRAW
PICTURE LSUB4
>>


LSUB4                   • Program

<<
"Enter 1 to change L
Enter 2 to graph
Enter 3 to quit "
"" INPUT OBJ→ 'Z'
STO
  IF Z 1 ==
  THEN " Input L" ""
INPUT OBJ→ 'L' STO
L 'L' →TAG 2 'G'
STO LSUB3
  ELSE
    IF Z 2 ==
    THEN 1 'G' STO
LGPH
    ELSE { Z G }
PURGE 1 FREEZE
    END
  END
>>
```

The remainder of the programs listed in this Appendix should be placed in the NUINT directory.

```
LTSUM                • Program
<< CLΣ REVLIST OBJ→
→ n
  << 1 n
    FOR k Σ+
    NEXT
  >> ΣDAT
>>
```

```
MUTL                 • Program
<< COL- OBJ→ OBJ→
DROP →LIST
>>
```

```
FABST                • Program
<< →NUM 'B' STO →NUM
'A' STO STEQ B A -
N / 'H' STO
>>
```

```
NSTO                 • Program
<< 'N' STO B A - N /
'H' STO
>>
```

```
SUM                  • Program
<< → X
  << 0 1 N
    START X F.val +
X H + 'X' STO
    NEXT H *
  >> 'X' PURGE
>>
```

```
MVAL                 • Program
<< DUP DUP 'ΣDAT'
STO SIZE 1 GET → n
  << 1 n
    FOR j 'ΣDAT(j,1)'
    EVAL F.val
    NEXT n →ARRY 2
COL+ 'ΣDAT' STO
  >> ΣDAT
>>
```

```
LRECT                • Program
<< A SUM "lrect"
→TAG
>>
```

```
RRECT                • Program
<< A H + SUM "rrect"
→TAG
>>
```

```
MID                  • Program
<< A H 2 / + SUM
"mid" →TAG
>>
```

```
TRAP                 • Program
<< A SUM B F.val A
F.val - 2 / H * +
'X' PURGE "trap"
→TAG
>>
```

```
SIMP                 • Program
<< MID 2 * TRAP + 3
/ "simp" →TAG
>>
```

GRECT[2]   • Program

```
<< N 120 MIN 1 MAX
DUP B A - SWAP / →
n h
  << CLLCD
"Select rectangle type

1 for Left
2 for Mid
3 for Right"
1 DISP 7 FREEZE
    IFERR 0 WAIT
    THEN DROP
    ELSE → c
      <<
        CASE c 82.1
==
        THEN
'LRECT' A
        END c
83.1 ==
        THEN
'MID' A h 2 / +
        END c
84.1 ==
        THEN
'RRECT' A h +
        END KILL
        END
      >> 0 0 10
    FOR z A B A -
10 / z * + 'X' STO
EQ EVAL
    NEXT 12 DUPN
```

(Program GRECT continued)

```
1 11
    START MAX
    NEXT 13 ROLLD
1 11
    START MIN
    NEXT DUP2
DUP2 - 2 60 / * 5
ROLLD - 1 60 / * -
3 ROLLD + YRNG B A
- 5 120 / * DUP NEG
A + SWAP B + XRNG
# 131d # 64d PDIM
{ # 0d # 0d } PVIEW
DRAX DRAW 'X' STO
    IFERR A 1 n
        START DUP 0
R→C C→PX SWAP h +
DUP 3 ROLLD EQ EVAL
R→C C→PX BOX 'X' h
STO+
        NEXT DROP
PICT { # 0d # 0d }
3 ROLL EVAL DUP 4
ROLLD 1 →GROB REPL
7 FREEZE
    THEN
    END 'X' PURGE
  END
  >>
>>
```

---

[1]Program PFIT is provided by Dr. Charles M. Patton of Hewlett-Packard's Calculator Research and Development team and is reproduced with permission.

[2]Program GRECT was written by Robert E. Simms of Clemson University and is reproduced with permission.